# DEEP DISTRESSES

# DEEP DISTRESSES

William Wordsworth
John Wordsworth
Sir George Beaumont
1800–1808

Richard E. Matlak

DELAWARE

Newark: University of Delaware Press
London: Associated University Presses

Associated University Presses
2010 Eastpark Boulevard
Cranbury, NJ 08512

Associated University Presses
Unit 304
The Chandlery
50 Westminster Bridge Road
London SE1 7QY, England

Associated University Presses
P.O. Box 338, Port Credit
Mississauga, Ontario
Canada L5G 4L8

The paper used in this publication meets the requirements of the American National Standard for Permanence of Paper for Printed Library Materials Z39.48-1984.

Library of Congress Cataloging-in-Publication Data

Matlak, Richard E., 1944–
    Deep distresses : William Wordsworth, John Wordsworth, Sir George
Beaumont : 1800–1808 / Richard E. Matlak.
        p.   cm.
    Includes bibliographical references and index.
    ISBN 0-87413-815-9 (alk. paper)
    1. Wordsworth, William, 1770–1850—Family.   2. Poets, English—19th
century—Family relationships.   3. Wordsworth, William, 1770–1850.
Elegiac stanzas.   4. Wordsworth, John, 1772–1805—Death and burial   5.
Elegiac poetry, English—History and criticism.   6. Beaumont, George
Howland, Sir, 1753–1827.   7. Poets, English—19th century—Biography.
8. Brothers—Great Britain—Biography.   9. Sailors—Great
Britain—Biography.   10. Death in literature.   I. Title.
PR5883 .M337   2003
821'.7—dc21                                                        2003001167

PRINTED IN THE UNITED STATES OF AMERICA

*For my brother*

# Contents

# Illustrations

# Preface

THE FIRST DRAFT OF THIS BOOK WAS WRITTEN AT A TIME OF REAL JOY IN my life. Begun during a few sabbatical months in Oxford and London in 1996–97, it proceeded quickly and rewardingly as the specialty libraries of the United Kingdom revealed the relevance of their collections to my questions. I admit beginning naively, wanting only to understand the principal problem of "Elegiac Stanzas": Wordsworth's declarations of his youthful naïveté transformed into wisdom, yet undermined by awkward syntax and biographical contradiction. The poem's inspiration was apparently a painting by Sir George Beaumont, which prompted an epiphanic reinterpretation of his poetic vision, but I wondered why Beaumont painted the oil in the first place. And what of the precipitating biographical event, the poet's brother dying at sea as a captain of an East Indiaman? What did it mean to be a captain of a merchant vessel? Why did the poet's desperately needed money get involved in John's risk-filled ventures? What were the facts of the sinking that caused a controversy? What did Beaumont's oils on *Peel Castle in a Storm* have to do with all of this?

My personal history as well as my love for "Elegiac Stanzas" drew me to an embedded story of military and commercial misadventure, lurid lives in exotic lands, innocence betrayed, love suppressed, and suicidal despair. I have had a long part-time experience with both military and commercial ocean operations and felt an interest in understanding the story of the *Abergavenny* from a military point of view. Having some awareness of what soldiers and civilian laborers would expect at a time of crisis and what they would be inclined to do out of self-interest—should leadership be wanting—I hoped that my background might help me to interpret the reports on the shortcomings charged against John Wordsworth with more insight and possibly more interest than past investigators.

The libraries of Oxford University—the Bodleian, the Indian Institute, and the English Faculty libraries; the print and drawing collections of the National Maritime Museum in Greenwich, England;

11

the collection of the Leicester Museum and Art Gallery in England; the Indian and Oriental Collections of the British Library; the magnificent mine of unpublished materials of the Wordsworth library at Dove Cottage; the Houghton Library at Harvard University; the unique holdings of the American Antiquarian Society; the Boston College and Holy Cross libraries: all of these opened their collections to me in answering questions generated by this project. To all of these and especially to their reference librarians, I here express my gratitude. My hope is that I have constructed a narrative not unworthy of their collections. In particular, I would like to thank Jeff Cowton, the curator at Dove Cottage, for keeping the library opened on Easter Saturday, 1997, so that I might make the most of my short stay. Finally, I would like to thank Thomas Parsons and Sharon Matys of the Graphic Arts department at Holy Cross for their assistance in scanning illustrations to disk.

I would be remiss to ignore the relationships, both professional and personal, that matter in my understanding of literature and biography, a connection that has obsessed me since graduate school at Indiana University. As always, I owe to Kenneth R. Johnston appreciation for his influence upon my early development in biographical thinking, close reading, understanding of the early nineteenth century, and for his influence, through his splendid scholarly works, on my scholarship and style. I have been steadily and increasingly influenced by the originality, importance, and learning of Nicholas Roe's work. Duncan Wu's seminal books on Wordsworth's reading have been delightful to learn from. To my mind, Thomas McFarland has never written anything without importance. Jonathan Wordsworth is a reader whose opinion one seeks and I have done so. Associated with Professor Wordsworth and the important Wordsworth Summer Conference are devotees and scholars whose opinions I highly respect: Frederick Burwick, Christoph Bode, Molly LeFebure, Richard Gravil, Marilyn Gaull, and Pamela and Robert Woof. All of these have been of personal as well as remote importance through their publications and in their response to my reflections on this project. Leon Waldoff has also been a very keen observer of my work and has raised important questions about this study for my reconsideration. The great Swift scholar, Hermann J. Real of Münster University, Germany, has provided at all times a model of erudition and scholarly excellence to emulate, surpassed only by his friendship and generosity.

Those who have read this manuscript in its early stages have assured its improvement. Kenneth R. Johnston, Anne K. Mellor, Nicholas Roe, and Christopher Merrill read and commented thoughtfully on the strengths and weaknesses of the entire manuscript. My colleague at Holy Cross, Lee Oser, responded with spirit to Part I on "Michael," as did the English Department and a small group at the Center for Literary and Cultural Studies at Harvard on a snowy night in February, 1998 when several came out to discuss the substance of my argument on "Michael," including Sonja Hofkosh, John Mahoney, a few others I didn't know, and my daughter, Maura.

Finally, I would like to acknowledge less scholarly influences. Having done psychobiography for some years, I appreciate how unpredictably and imperceptively daily associations and personal relationships work their way into literary-biographical matters by awakening empathy and shaping perception. The friends I made on active duty in Viet Nam and during the course of a career in the Army Reserve, especially Dean Saluti and Bill Wood, assisted me in honing leadership skills and achieving some success that throws into relief the woeful story of John Wordsworth. This book is dedicated to my younger brother, Regis, who, like Wordsworth's brother, has traveled the world, repeatedly in harm's way, during a stunning career in the CIA. I have been lately influenced on a daily basis by my assistant in the Center for Interdisciplinary and Special Studies at Holy Cross, Maureen Consigli. While believing in this project, she has encouraged me to fantasize about more lucrative literary endeavors, e.g., romance novels, which has led to amusing speculations. I suspect her influence has evoked my understanding of Dorothy Wordsworth's unfulfilled hopes for prosperity through her brother's work. Finally, my wife, Jo; my daughters, Meegan, Mandy, and Maura; my sons-in-law, Dave and Brad; and my grandchildren, Madeline, Ryan, and Simon have provided me the loving familial context from which I view, as did William and Dorothy Wordsworth, John's sacrifice of domestic for material riches, made all the more poignant by his complete failure.

# DEEP DISTRESSES

# Introduction

İT MAY BE THAT EVEN THOSE WELL-VERSED IN WILLIAM WORDSWORTH'S biography will not recollect much of the detail of his brother John's death at sea. Most will be unaware of John's mundane life of sacrifice on behalf of William's poetic vocation. Yet we know that his death prompted William's dramatic renunciation of his youthful romanticism in the great lyrics of *Poems, in Two Volumes* (1807), "Elegiac Stanzas," "Stepping Westward," "The Solitary Reaper," and a few lesser poems, which suggests that understanding the magnitude of John's death may have aesthetic consequences.

Yet, the facts are simple: John's vessel, the *Earl of Abergavenny*, East Indiaman, went down two miles off the coast of the Bill of Portland, England, in a night storm. Later Sir George Beaumont made an oil of a vessel in distress that reminded the poet of his brother's demise. These details prepare the way for musing upon some startling admissions in "Elegiac Stanzas," the chiefest of which concern the poet's renunciation of his gladsome belief in Nature's benignity:

> I have submitted to a new controul:
> A power is gone, which nothing can restore;
> A deep distress hath humaniz'd my Soul.
>
> Not for a moment could I now behold
> A smiling sea and be what I have been:
> The feeling of my loss will ne'er be old;
> This, which I know, I speak with mind serene.[1]

The first three lines are generally conceded to be difficult, not least for mourning a transformation of self rather than the loss of John, but as well for their vague referentiality: What is the "new controul"? What is the "power [that] is gone"? One could go on: What was the point of Beaumont painting a vessel in distress? How does Beaumont figure in Wordsworth's new self-awareness, which his painting apparently inspired? Although John's business as a mariner

17

and the sinking of the *Abergavenny* is succinctly reviewed by Kenneth R. Johnston in his magisterial biography of Wordsworth's early years, *The Hidden Wordsworth: Poet Lover Rebel Spy*, the present study will show that the details of the life of John Wordsworth bear more importantly on his brother's poetry than Johnston and others have surmised.

Besides "Elegiac Stanzas," we find the influence of William Wordsworth's relationship with John figuring in "Michael," the Dream of the Arab in *Prelude*, Book V, "The Character of the Happy Warrior," "Stepping Westward," several powerful elegies, *Benjamin the Waggoner*, and the structure of the principal section of *Poems, in Two Volumes*. It is likewise arguable that Beaumont was responsible for Wordsworth's turn to history in *The Prelude*, that is, his sudden movement into his experience in the French Revolution a compositional moment before concluding the poem in five books.

I will attempt to show that John's life as a mariner and his dedication to William is in many ways comparable to the importance of Dorothy's commitment to their older brother. Furthermore, William's relationship with Sir George Beaumont transcends the influence of a single painting and figures prominently in an attempt to shape the public vocation and popularity that William Wordsworth desired,[2] which was threatened by John's infamous death. An overview of this tragical biographical narrative will locate more precisely its importance for the study of Wordsworth and the understanding of his middle years and verse.

To begin with some obvious observations, the drowning at sea of John Wordsworth and the sinking of the *Abergavenny* was a public as well as private disaster. The death of hundreds of passengers and crew and the loss of a richly laden vessel was a matter of national interest for being the worst British maritime accident on record.[3] Press coverage of survivors' accounts threatened embarrassment, and disgrace, to John's memory and significant culpability to his employer, the East India Company. It was the combined result of all these factors that became the catalyst of a profound transformation in Wordsworth's "vision and faculty divine."

Adding poignancy to the family's grief, John Wordsworth was at the point of salvaging a lucrative career as one of the youngest captains of one of the largest vessels in the merchant fleet of the East India Company. Even today the financial loss of several hundred thousand pounds sterling worth of cargo and a noble vessel worth about £70,000 seems significant; how much more so in 1805, when the *Abergavenny* sank only a few miles off Portland Bill. Immediately, however, rumors were afloat in seeking to place blame for excessive loss of life—some 246 died[4]—on the deceased captain, who was officially exonerated by his employers, but convicted in the press of at least a failure in judgment, to which were added imputations of negligence in not using the ship's boats to save lives. In our publicity-tormented age, we can readily sympathize with the consternation the Wordsworths suffered over an attack on their brother's reputation and behavior. "The Newspapers have given contradictory and unintelligible accounts of the dismal event—this was very harassing to us," Dorothy Wordsworth wrote to a friend:

> We knew that our Brother would do his duty, of this we were confident—that he would not lose his presence of mind, or blunder, or forget, but we wanted to have all cleared up, to know *how* it was. This as far as concerned ourselves—and then for the sake of the relatives of those poor three hundred who went down with him we were greatly distressed. It cut us to the heart to think that their sorrow should be aggravated by a thought that his errors or weakness, or any other misconduct should have occasioned or encreased the calamity. God be praised we are now satisfied in our knowledge—we know how it was, and I hope that many of those who have mourned for their friends may have received such information as may have settled their minds also.[5]

William Wordsworth's most important poem related to the experience, composed about a year later with "mind serene," is "Elegiac Stanzas." Implicitly about the loss of John, explicitly about an internal transformation, Wordsworth writes in lines almost too familiar to bear quoting—indeed, in lines that seem to explain themselves—of a "power [being] gone, which nothing can restore," of "A deep distress [that] hath humaniz'd [his] soul."[6] These consequences—human grief, financial loss, the provocations of a critical press, even a change of poetic heart—are not necessarily problematic, and untroubled readings of "Elegiac Stanzas" and somber but cloudless biographical narratives have resulted from human empathy.[7]

But I think this is insufficient to represent the difficulties in the record and Wordsworth's own response. He could not explain why, apart from normal grief, John's death wracked him so. No matter how confident we may be with our guesses/glosses on the "power . . . which nothing can restore," Wordsworth could not (or would not) name it and thus interpretation of the poem has reached an exasperating condition of arbitrary plausibility. To rephrase the issue in E. D. Hirsch's parlance, interpretations have been rich in "divinatory moments," but short on "the second, or critical, moment of interpretation."[8]

Karl Kroeber reasonably accounts for the lost power as follows: Wordsworth "is separated from his past. At this point his memory fails, not in the sense of being unable to recall but in the sense of being unable to restore."[9] Geoffrey H. Hartman summarizes in his wonderfully oracular fashion, "Wordsworth tells us quite precisely what is lost: this kind of potentiality, this capacity for generous error and noble illusion, which made life correspond to the heart's desire."[10] Ernest Bernhardt-Kabisch risks reductiveness in suggesting that the lost power is John Wordsworth himself.[11] Leon Waldoff offers a very fine psychological insight into the loss as being a compression of past losses:

> The loss represented in "Elegiac Stanzas" is . . . overdetermined, representing not only the death of John and the deaths of Wordsworth's parents but also, one could argue, the experience of being orphaned, the separation from Dorothy, the loss of Nature as a maternal substitute, and the loss of Nature, in Hartman's phrase, as a noble illusion corresponding to the heart's desire.[12]

Yet, we, like the disconsolate Gloucester of *King Lear*, find ourselves conceding "And that's true, too" to these and other interpretations as wise, eloquently expressed, and as partial as Edgar's half-truth that "ripeness is all."[13]

Not unexpectedly, the exception to these sympathetic interpretations belongs to Marjorie Levinson. Levinson says that "The power that is gone, 'that nothing can restore,' is the power of the Real—the experientially extrinsic, stable datum—to impress itself as such on the mind of the poet, a mind which, by its ceaseless digestion of the universe of things, has finally incapacitated itself."[14] In a critique of Levinson's far-ranging, intertextual reading, Thomas McFarland chastises her for forgetting that "Elegiac Stanzas" represents a "grief [that] reached into every fibre of Wordsworth's personal being" as his expert culling of statements from the *Letters* powerfully supports:

> Even through the protective armor of Wordsworth's stoicism we can, by accumulating his brief remarks to various correspondents after his brother's death, perhaps see—as in time-lapse photography—this depth

of feeling. Their amassed weight is overwhelming: ". . . a great affliction
. . . the set is now broken . . .;" "I can say nothing higher of my ever dear
Brother than that he was worthy of his Sister who is now weeping beside
me . . .;" ". . . oh my dear Friends! what have we not endured!"; "We
know what we have lost, and what we have to endure; our anguish is al-
layed, but pain and sadness have taken place of it; with fits of sorrow
which we endeavour to suppress but cannot"; ". . . Let me again mention my beloved Brother"; "I shall never forget him, never lose sight of
him"; "This affliction weighs so heavy on the hearts of all in this house,
that we have neither strength nor spirits for any thing. Our Brother was
the pride and delight of our hearts. . ."; . . . "he was innocent as
brave . . ."; "I never wrote a line without a thought of its giving him
pleasure . . ."; "We have lost so much hope and gladsome thought . . .";
"He loved every thing which we did, and every thing about us here incessantly reminds us of him and our irreparable loss. But I will not distress
you, for you can give us no relief"; "He did not know how I loved and
honored him, and how often he was in my thoughts . . ."[15]

McFarland identifies "stoic cheerfulness" as the replacement for the
"power" that is gone, suggesting that the "philosophy of joy" was, if
not the power, at least its source.[16]

In his own plain prose, Wordsworth does not provide a more specific gloss on his experience than to say, almost six weeks after learning of the tragedy: "For myself I feel that there is something cut out
of my life which cannot be restored" (*EY* 565). According to his
wife's report of approximately the same time, William spoke of suffering the "greatest loss" of anyone in the family, "because he says
it is only our pleasures and our joys that are broken in upon—but
[this] loss of John is deeply connected with his *business*." It is a comment entirely out of sympathy with the laments gathered by McFarland. Mary Wordsworth concedes, as if she understood what her
husband was talking about: "This is true—but is not *his* sorrow,
ours.—[?]"[17] The answer would seem to be, apparently not. Wordsworth's use of the word *business* carries a masculine connotation, as
if to say, I share with you, my beloved women, the affective and domestic distress of our brother's loss, but its connection with my
"business" as a poet is unique and incalculable. The reading of
"Elegiac Stanzas" in part III of this study will support Wordsworth's
frank admission of the material consequences of his loss.

But what can the "business" be that is "deeply connected" with
John's mortality? *Business* carries a worldly and oddly perfunctory
connotation to be "deeply connected" with anything as important

to the poet as a creative act or an act of creative seeing. It is also a fact that, except for a few months of intense bereavement following John's death in February 1805, Wordsworth's poetic facility did not wane, nor did the quality of his verse suffer. His immediate production was completing the final books of the 1805 *Prelude*, further work on *Home at Grasmere*, "Stepping Westward," "The Solitary Reaper," several gripping elegies on John's death, and, of course, "Elegiac Stanzas." He had also composed sometime between 1802–4 the great antimaterialist statement: "The world is too much with us; late and soon, / Getting and Spending, we lay waste our powers: / Little we see in nature that is ours; / We have given our hearts away, a sordid boon!"[18] And, of course, in our estimation, his greatest single collection, *Poems, in Two Volumes* (1807), was shortly forthcoming.

If not producing poetry, could the "business" affected be selling poetry? Wordsworth bore a permanent grudge toward Robert Southey for reviewing *Lyrical Ballads* (1798) harshly. In a remarkably candid letter, he admits to publisher Joseph Cottle:

> He knew that I published those poems for money and money alone. He knew that money was of importance to me. If he could not conscientiously have spoken differently of the volume, he ought to have declined the task of reviewing it. . . . I care little for the praise of any other professional critic, but as it may help me to pudding. (*EY* 267–68)

One would have to employ some curious intertextualizing to associate John's death with selling poetry in the sense intended here. Even if it were true that adverse publicity would now attach to their surname, it seems unthinkable that Wordsworth would argue that an unfortunate accident would carry some deep connection with his business.

If Wordsworth had commented to his wife that John's death was deeply connected with his *power*, this would align with the claim of "Elegiac Stanzas." By "power" we would at least understand the familiar Romantic discourse of power and poetry and its springs in soulful depths. Or, to put it another way, we would not be confronted with the oxymoronic association of *business* and *power* in a discussion of Romantic poetry, although in a more worldly context we would expect their relationship. One of the purposes of this study, then, is to unpack Wordsworth's prosaic comments about John's loss in order better to appreciate the complexity of his famous poetic comments from "Elegiac Stanzas" and to evaluate the influence of what he may have meant on his later verse.

This study will proceed by 1) reviewing the evidence relevant to the subtopics of grief, financial loss, and Wordsworth's defensive reaction to public accounts of the sinking of the *Abergavenny*; 2) then addressing the "something that was cut out of" the poet's life "deeply connected" with his "business"; and 3) reading "Elegiac Stanzas" as the end of the cultural and domestic doom foreseen in *Michael*. I will argue that Luke, the prodigal son of "Michael," is another name for John and that Luke's descent into "ignominy and shame" became uncannily prophetic of John's posthumous vilification. But while the press expressed abhorrence at John's apparent disregard for the welfare of his crew and passengers, representing him, as we will see in a cartoon on the sinking, as a stoic observer of human distress, William primarily addressed himself to reports that John displayed an utter disregard for his own life as the end came near; in other words, that his drowning was a passive act of suicide, perhaps not unlike the questionable demise of James of *The Brothers*. Wordsworth's obsession with the issue of suicide is an indication that he was conscious of the reasons John might have had for preferring to die.

Sir George Beaumont's two oils of *Peel Castle*,[19] the smaller, practice study, which Wordsworth seemed to prefer, and the larger canvas exhibited at the Royal Academy in April–May 1806, were intended as a consolation in representing a vessel's descent into the horizon of a meaningful setting sun. The smaller canvas also includes a well-aimed bolt of lightning striking the vessel, which might bear on the issue of suicide. It seems likely that Beaumont also painted with the public intention of visually rebutting the negative image of a self-absorbed captain, indifferent to his responsibility for the lives of his crew and passengers. "Elegiac Stanzas" will be read as a poem filtered through all of these pre-texts, including Wordsworth's relationship with Sir George Beaumont, in order to appreciate the weakness of the foundation underlying its structural solidity and its dubious declarations of certainty. Finally, Wordsworth's reference to John's loss being "deeply connected with his *business*" will be considered as an oxymoronic statement implicating the deep creation of poetry with the bond William shared with John, who had said to William, "I will work for you and you shall attempt to do something for the world" (*EY* 563).

# Part I

## Capt. John Wordsworth and the Prophecy of "Michael"

### 1. THE PURE

CARL H. KETCHAM'S SYMPATHETIC BIOGRAPHY OF JOHN WORDSWORTH justifies the extraordinary grief suffered by the Wordsworth circle upon his death.[1] Although Robert Southey was not a favorite of the family, he wrote to a friend that John's death had "disordered [him] from head to foot," and he was welcomed as a fellow mourner at Dove Cottage. From Malta, Coleridge wrote of an hysterical reaction to the news and confessed in the privacy of his Notebooks that he felt envious when he reflected on the moment of John's death:

> On being told abruptly by Lady Ball of John Wordsworth's fate I attempted to stagger out of the room (the great Saloon of the Palace with 50 people present) and before I could reach the door fell down on the ground in a convulsive hysteric Fit /—I was confined to my room for a fortnight after.[2]

Most likely, Mrs. Alexander Ball passed on to Coleridge the more problematic, sensational version of the sinking: not the sympathetic account of a dutiful captain going down with his ship, but the devastated entrepeneur, who, as one of the narratives of the accident memorably phrased it, "perished with his ship, disdaining to survive the loss of so valuable a cargo."[3] In the privacy of his Notebooks, Coleridge indulged in a fancy of suicide: "O dear John Wordsworth! Ah that I could but have died for you, and you have gone home, married Sara Hutchinson, and protected my poor little ones. O how very, very gladly would I have accepted the conditions."[4] The conditions were public gossip and family woe.

Mary Hutchinson Wordsworth's special grief for John derived from the time they spent together during her visit to Dove Cottage in February–April 1800, shortly after John's arrival in late January. Now desiring to leave Grasmere because of its morose associations, Mary writes to Catherine Clarkson that "there is nothing that does not bring his figure before us. . . . [John] loved everything about this dear spot, and John was the first who led me to every thing that I love in this neighbourhood."[5] Mary was also the recipient of John's most affectionate letters. Ketcham remarks that "John was not a man to scorch the paper with his passions,"[6] yet his fondness for Mary was openly acknowledged by all. After William married Mary, Moorman reasonably concludes that the family wished for John to marry Mary's sister, Sara.[7]

The fourth born of the Wordsworth children, John was nick-named Ibex by their father, the "shyest of beasts."[8] Dorothy recalls that John was considered a dunce for enjoying fishing more than his "[school]master's Tasks" (*MY* 136). Being a third son and without academic inclination, John took the path of many boys of his day in going to sea[9] at the age of sixteen. His first voyages were to the Barbados (1788), Jamaica (1788–89), and then to America (1789), where he must have been exposed to the slave trade, for he found Americans to be "a bad race—much worse than they are represented to be" (*LJW* 116–17).[10]

In 1789, their older cousin Capt. John Wordsworth, age thirty-eight, assumed command of the East Indiaman, *Earl of Abergavenny*, and offered John a berth as midshipman. John's rise in the Company began, graced by the patronage and financial support of relatives and powerful associates, especially members of the Clapham Sect—the "Saints in Politics"—who grew to favor John for his high moral standards. His shipboard moniker was "the philosopher," because he would read poetry instead of whoring and drinking in ports of call with his mates. John made several voyages of nearly two years each under his cousin's command (1790–91, 1793–94); another as fourth mate on the *Osterley*, East Indiaman (1795–96); and then one on the *Duke of Montross*, East Indiaman, on which he served as second mate, in his steady climb up the ladder of responsibility from midshipman to commodore.[11]

Between voyages and waiting to assume the captaincy of the *Abergavenny*, now that his like-named cousin, Capt. John Wordsworth, was retiring after immensely profitable years at sea, John decided to visit his siblings' domicile at Dove Cottage. He would remain for the nine-month period, January to September 1800. William and Dorothy had spent some time in London with brothers John and Richard in December 1789, but neither had seen John until he joined William, accompanied by Coleridge, in his search for a Lake District residence in November 1799. The search for a home must have been meaningful to John as well, for he offered to give William £40 to buy a lakeside plot in Grasmere (*EY* 272).

Yet John's shyness seemed to prevail when he finally made his visit to Dove Cottage. He walked up to the front door but could not bring himself to knock. Dorothy writes:

> We did not know on what day he would come, though we were expecting him every hour, therefore he had no reason to fear that he should surprize us suddenly; yet twice did he approach the door and lay his hand upon the latch, and stop, and turn away without the courage to enter (we had not met for several years) he then went to the Inn and sent us word that he was come.

"This will give you a notion of the depth of his affections, and the delicacy of his feelings," Dorothy continues in her letter to Lady Beaumont (*EY* 649).

The maritime scholar Basil Greenhill offers a different perspective on John's temerity. He says of those "who took to the sea," that over time they

> became more and more isolated, more cut off from the normal society of the land and of landward looking communities. The very intensity of their occupational specialisation emphasised the social isolation of their calling. And between them and the landsmen, as always, there was a kind of alienation. They even spoke a form of the language which was different from that of the landsman and they were hard to understand.[12]

Nevertheless, William and Dorothy accepted their brother, and together they walked, fished, bathed in the lake, gathered peas, and shared the beauties of the reclusive life of Grasmere. In *Home at Grasmere*, William speaks for Dorothy and himself when he writes of their "beautiful and quiet home, enriched / Already with a Stranger whom we love / Deeply, a Stranger of our Father's house, / A never-resting Pilgrim of the Sea, / Who finds at last an hour to his content / Beneath our roof."[13] Dorothy comments that John would pace "over this floor in pride before we had been six weeks in this house, exulting within his noble heart that his Father's Children had once again a home together" (*EY* 649). William gradually got to know the "Stranger," only to find that he was stranger when known.

In "The Brothers" William describes John's life at sea as a metaphor for a life in the Lake District. The long absent brother, Leonard, the poetic counterpart for John,

> had been rear'd
> Among the mountains, and he in his heart
> Was half a Shepherd on the stormy seas.
> Oft in the piping shrouds had Leonard heard
> The tones of waterfalls, and inland sounds
> Of caves and trees: and when the regular wind
> Between the tropics fill'd the steady sail
> And blew with the same breath through days and weeks,
> Lengthening invisibly its weary line
> Along the cloudless main, he, in those hours
> Of tiresome indolence would often hang
> Over the vessel's side, and gaze and gaze,
> And, while the broad green wave and sparkling foam
> Flash'd round him images and hues, that wrought
> In union with the employment of his heart,
> He, thus by feverish passion overcome,
> Even with the organs of his bodily eye,
> Below him, in the bosom of the deep,
> Saw mountains, saw the forms of sheep that graz'd
> On verdant hills, with dwellings among trees,
> And Shepherds clad in the same country grey
> Which he himself had worn.[14]

William undermines the authenticity of Leonard's salubrious fancies with a note on calenture being the cause of his visions: "This description of the Calenture is sketch'd from an imperfect recollection of an admirable one in prose, by Mr. Gilbert, author of the Hurricane" (*LB* 144, n. to line 62). *Calenture* is defined by the *OED* as "a disease incident to sailors within the tropics, characterized by delirium in which the patient, it is said, fancies the sea to be green fields, and desires to leap into it."

Wordsworth began "The Brothers" in late December 1799, or shortly after moving to Grasmere and before John's arrival. He completed the poem by early April 1800 (*LB* 24–25). William, John, and Coleridge first heard the tale of a shepherd who had sleepwalked to death during their recent walking tour of the Lake District. Never original in his narrative designs or characterization, William incorporated some basic facts of John's life, the gist of John's experience at sea, and the motivations of John's career into the poem: 1) Leonard was "A shepherd-lad who ere his thirteenth year / Had changed his calling, with the mariners / A fellow-mariner, and so had fared / Through twenty seasons" (*Brothers* 38–41). Wordsworth corrected the year of Leonard's departure for the seas to conform to John's departing "ere his sixteenth year" in the 1815 edition of the poem; 2) Wordsworth writes that when Leonard "had approach'd his home, his heart / Fail'd in him" (74–75) and he turns to the churchyard, which suggests John's comparable reaction at the door of Dove Cottage; 3) Wordsworth introduces the function of Capt. John Wordsworth as "an Uncle, he was at that time / A thriving man, and traffic'd on the seas: / And, but for this same Uncle, to this hour / Leonard had never handled rope or shroud. / For the Boy lov'd the life which we lead here" (288–92); 4) the misfortunes of the Wordsworth family after the death of their father are reflected in the fate of the brothers after the death of their surrogate father, Walter Ewbank: "when he died, / The estate and house were sold, and all their sheep, / . . . / Well—all was gone, and they were destitute" (296–300); 5) John's promise to William that he would work for him (*EY* 563) finds expression in the narrative when we learn that, "Leonard, chiefly for his Brother's sake, / Resolv'd to try his fortune on the seas" (301–2); and finally 6) the pastor-narrator reveals that Leonard promised him at parting that "If ever the day came when he was rich, / He would return, and on his Father's Land / He would grow old among us" (317–21), which speaks to John's final intentions in the subjunctive mode—"If ever," "He would," again "He would"—without considering further the need for becoming "rich." Thus Wordsworth constructs in relief the shape and motivations of John/Leonard's life, with an embedded warning that, as Leonard found, loved ones might well be dead and gone before a superfluity of wealth might be gained.

James's habitual sleepwalking, which commences with Leonard's departure, leads to his early death. The parson interprets James's longing:

> But, whether blithe or sad, 'tis my belief
> His absent Brother still was at his heart.
> And, when he liv'd beneath our roof, we found
> (A practice till this time unknown to him)
> That often, rising from his bed at night,
> He in his sleep would walk about, and sleeping
> He sought his Brother Leonard.
>
> (*Brothers*, 343–49)

The embedded stress in this moving pastoral becomes an irresolution of values, that is, between providing reasonably for loved ones or questing for superfluous riches at the risk of losing those very loved ones. John's relationship with Mary became a victim of this conflict in values.

From late February to early April, Mary Hutchinson visited Dove Cottage and was often in John's company. It must have seemed that they were courting. Dorothy later wrote of Mary's "tender love of John and an intimate knowledge of his virtues" and of their being "exceedingly attached to each other" (*EY* 560). William makes the remarkable concession that "Mary . . . loved John with her whole soul." It is worth quoting again Mary's comment: "John was the first who led me to every thing that I love in this neighbourhood." After departing Grasmere, John's letters to Mary were his most affectionate:

> write to me often and *long* letters. . . . I have a dozen letters to write in a day & this you may believe is no small task to one who dislikes that business as much as I do—I make this request because my dear mary there is nothing that thou canst write but what will give me pleasure & to be with *thee* I read thy letters over a *dozen* times in a day— (*LJW* 96)

Upon learning from Mary two years later of her imminent marriage to William, John responds with disappointment, as if he hoped that Mary would wait for him without his asking. A prophetic paraphrase from "Michael," his favorite poem from *Lyrical Ballads*, haunts his response:

> I have been reading your Letter over & over again My dearest Mary til tears have come into my eyes & I known not how to express myself thou ar't kind & dear creature But what ever fate Befal me I shall love to the last and bear thy memory with me to the grave. (*LJW* 125–26)

Yet, John's material values prevailed over romance and love. He planned to spend ten years at sea in making his fortune and knowingly risked a life with Mary. Ketcham is correct in stating that "[t]hough nothing in his letters proves that he had not dreamed of Mary as a possible wife, he was not in a position to form definite expectations or ask her to wait for him, and there is no indication of even a tacit understanding between them" (*LJW* 26). Nevertheless, by the time Mary accepted William's proposal in 1802 it would have been apparent that John's commitment to his quest for riches revealed values and priorities she did not share. There is a humorous anecdote that suggests how little Mary desired in the way of material goods. William comments facetiously on Mary's "*blasted expectations*" at not receiving "the *expected Silver Coffee Pot*" for a "*marriage present*" from her family, because she had married "a Vagabond." Mary concludes that "it is a fact that we did not receive a single *Wedding Present*,"[15] clearly indicating that it was the love and respect that she desired rather than a quantity of goods.

Another anecdote, this one from the Coleridge family, makes the point by contrast. Mary was not Maria Northcote, the young woman who pledged her troth to Coleridge's brother Frank, on the condition that he return from military service in India with £10,000. As Frank recounts the conditions of their romance to his sister Ann: "without ten thousand pound I was not to expect her hand, that was the bargain; so you see I am to marry her, and she marries my ten thousand pound."[16] Frank, like his older brother, Captain John Coleridge, committed suicide in India.[17]

William's next poem inspired by John's difference is "When to the attractions of the busy World," much of which was composed in late August 1800, a month before John's departure on 29 September.[18] William discovered a footworn path made by John's pacing in a fir grove near Dove Cottage. While finding the density of trees inhibiting for walking out his verse, William speculates that John found the restrictions of the grove ideal:

> With a sense
> Of lively joy did I behold this path
> Beneath the fir-trees, for at once I knew
> That by my Brother's steps it had been trac'd.
> My thoughts were pleas'd within me to perceive
> That hither he had brought a finer eye,
> A heart more wakeful: that more loth to part
> From place so lovely he had worn the track,
> One of his own deep paths! by pacing here
> With that habitual restlessness of foot
> Wherewith the Sailor measures o'er and o'er
> His short domain upon the Vessel's deck
> While she is travelling through the dreary seas.
>
> (*P2V*, 565, lines 62–74)

Although William reads John's path as a sign of his brother's superior sensitivity, he realistically accounts for John's attraction to the
spatial restrictions of the grove as a dumb habituation to the vessel's
deck. It is noteworthy that he does not speculate on John's meditations. Rather, he acknowledges that John's mind had been an unknown entity to him because of their disparate backgrounds—"Year
followed year my Brother! and we two / Conversing not knew little
in what mold / Each other's minds were fashioned, and at length /
When once again we met in Grasmere Vale / Between us there was
little other bond / Than common feelings of fraternal love" (78–
83). But now John's apparent affection for nature reveals that "thou
a School-boy to the Sea hadst carried / Undying recollections, Nature there / Was with thee, she who lov'd us both, she still / Was
with thee, and even so thou didst become / A silent Poet!" (84–88).
But while he ventures to speculate on John's thoughts at sea—that
he there daydreamed of the English countryside—he leaves unstated John's thoughts at home. There seems little doubt, however,
that John suffered from the inner turmoil of William's Wandering
Jew: "Night and day, I feel the trouble, / Of the Wanderer in my
soul."[19]

John's nine-month visit to Grasmere did find him delighted in the
household, in the mundane tasks of rural life, in the salubrious environment, in his love-like relationship with Mary Hutchinson, and in
his renewed intimacy with his sister and brother. Still, he was leaving,
he said for altruistic, economic reasons. William understood, but
later admitted to Sir George Beaumont that it was an unnecessary
sacrifice and proved to be especially so following the Lowther settlement:

> A thousand times has he said could I but see you in a green field of your
> own, and a Cow, and two or three other little comforts, I should be very
> happy! He went to sea as Commander with this hope; his voyage was very
> unsuccessful, [he] having lost by it considerably. When he came home
> we chanced to be in London and saw him. "Oh! said he, I have thought
> of you and nothing but you; if ever of myself and my bad success it was
> only on your account.["] He went again to sea a second time [as captain
> of the *Abergavenny*] and also was unsuccessful; still with the same hopes
> on our account, though then not so necessary, Lord Lowther having
> paid the money. Lastly came this lamentable voyage. (*EY* 547)

With his share of the family inheritance, John could have retired to
the Lake District, rather than insisting—as he did—that the whole

family risk their modest financial futures by investing their complete shares in his final "lamentable voyage." The tone of Dorothy's description of John's departure, not in retrospect, but in her journal entry for 29 September 1800, reveals in yet another way that something unspoken divided her and William from John: "On Monday 29th John left us. Wm & I parted with him in sight of Ulswater. It was a fine day, showery but with sunshine & fine clouds—poor fellow my heart was right sad."[20] Dorothy's epithet for John as a "poor fellow" who saddened her implies a judgment on her brother's life, and, at bottom, his values. As Henry David Thoreau was to say in *Walden*, "the cost of a thing is the amount of . . . life which is required to be exchanged for it."[21] John was leaving a loving environment and its "significant group," whose model is the family and whose extended family, as Wordsworth says in *The Prelude*, is the "noble living and the noble dead"[22] for "dreary seas" and the worst of companionship. "[A] more stupid place than a ship cannot well be imagined" (*LJW* 112), he wrote to Dorothy. He did not have to add that Dorothy would have had equal difficulty imagining places more debauched and dangerous than his ports of call.

For unless John attempted to deny his experience as a mariner for eleven formative years, William and Dorothy would have learned a great deal to trouble them about his way of life, regardless of their staunch belief in their brother's goodness. Indeed, we know that John must have described the moral hue of a mariner's life, for in one of William's memorial letters, he wrote to Sir George Beaumont that "my departed Brother . . . walked all his life pure among many impure" (*EY* 556), a comment that is echoed by Dorothy's claim that "among the impure he lived uncontaminated" (*EY* 559). Johnson's *Dictionary* (1755) reminds us that *impure* would then be defined as "unholy" and "unchaste." Thus, it is important to know something about the moral risks of a mariner's life and of the special temptations awaiting a mariner captain in the East India Company. Knowledge about the Company in the early nineteenth century is also pertinent, because the role of the captain or commodore for this great international corporation was as ambassador, literally, to the world. Important insiders hoped that John would become one of the East India Company's brightest stars.

## 2. *JEHAN KUMPANI*

The Indians referred to the Company *as Jehan Kumpani*, which translates as "World Company." Its English nickname became sound-related as "John Company," which carries the swagger commonly associated with the most important commercial organization in England from the seventeeth through the nineteenth centuries:

> the greatest and most beneficent trading organisation of any age or nation ... [which] more than any other material or moral influence within the United Kingdom, served to exalt the dominion, might, and majesty of the British Empire to the unparalleled pitch of glory and praise reached by it in the fateful reign of the Queen-Empress Victoria.[23]

Its personnel were looked upon as heroic. A reviewer for the *Times* (17 May 1926), praises H. B. Morse's *Chronicles of the East India Company Trading to China, 1635–1834*[24] for reminding the reader of the noble dead who traversed the globe in magnificent sailing ships:

> And what a perilous adventure it was, when one considers it. Danger from shipwreck, danger from pirates, danger from belligerent men-of-war, danger from Chinese mandarins. Scattered among the details of mere business are wonderful hints of adventures and escapes, of treachery and obstacles, of a dogged determination to win through, despite all hazards. They were giants in those days. Every page of these records is an illustration of their greatness.

The "Old India House" with adjacent localities occupied $1^1/_2$ acres of prime London real estate on Leadenhall Street. The Company then moved to Whitehall, London, to a one-acre facility off St. James Park. The tens of thousands of square feet of business offices were in addition to the Company's extensive docking facilities along the Thames. Among the hundreds who worked for the Company in London were the prominent literary figures Sir Charles Wilkins, Librarian (1801–36), who translated the *Bhagavadgita* (1785); James Mill, Examiner of India Correspondence (1830–36), who composed the *History of India* (1818) as well as the more familiar *Elements of Political Economy* (1821); Thomas Love Peacock, Examiner of India Correspondence (1837–56); John Stuart Mill (1806–73), Examiner of India (1856–58); and, of course, the humble clerk, Charles Lamb. Lamb's memorable description of his thirty inglorious years among the account books—"I had grown to my desk, as it were; and the wood had entered my soul"[25]—was not the advertised life of the adventurers, entrepeneurs, soldiers, and mariners employed in foreign operations.

The business of the East India Company was principally with Asia.

Its fleet of chartered merchant vessels was owned by private investors, the "Shipping Interest,"[26] who contracted that the vessels be built specifically for East India trade to accommodate its most important commodity of tea from China. The Company chartered one hundred ships per annum: thirty in the 1,200-ton class, which would include John Wordsworth's vessel, the *Earl of Abergavenny,* and most of the other vessels in the China trade; thirty in the 800-ton class; and forty in the 500-ton class—where tonnage, in long tons,[27] designates the actual weight of cargo the vessel is capable of stowing and safely transporting.[28] The Shipping Interest worked together with the Council of Shipping of the Company in making personnel appointments for the captains and crews.

A great romance flourished around the fleets of splendid sailing vessels and their exotic destinations—St. Helena, Wampoa, Malacca, Calcutta, Canton. Dreams of fortunes to be made from trade on the sea and in the employ of the Company in its vast presidencies of Bombay, Madras, and Bengal[29] produced a continuous invasion of youthful British adventurers and a transplantation of British culture to the Indian subcontinent. The Court of Directors of the Company estimated that besides the thousands of administrative personnel it employed in its three presidencies, more than twenty thousand British troops were serving in India in 1807[30] to protect British economic interests.

One might well wonder what tea from China had to do with the British colonization of India. The explanation is very simply economic. Believing British manufactured goods, especially textiles, to be inferior, the Chinese refused to import British commodities and England soon accrued a substantial imbalance of payments with a great loss of specie. From 1792 to 1807, the Company shipped £27,157,000 worth of tea to England but carried only £16,602,338 worth of British goods to Canton, China. During the period 1811–1828, the imbalance would have become ruinous, as exports exceeded imports by almost 550 percent,[31] had there not been a ready solution of supply and demand, in this case, providing the Chinese with the commodities they desired—Indian raw cotton, dyes, and, above all, opium.

Although officially outlawed by the Chinese government since 1799, opium soon became the king of the markets. Opium production in the Bengal presidency of India and drug running to China became *the* trade of opportunity. As Michael Greenberg, a leading historian of economic relations between England and China states:

"Opium was no hole-in-the-corner petty smuggling trade, but *proba-bly the largest commerce of the time in any single commodity*" (Greenberg's italics, 104). At the macroeconomic level, trade in opium brought bullion back to England via India because profits in the opium trade increased the demand for British goods in the vast Indian continent. All commerce in smuggling being conducted on a cash basis, millions of pounds were infused into the Indian economy and then back to England in payment for British goods. At the same time, the price of the fine opium from the Patna region, produced in the Bengal factories, rose from about $575 a chest in 1800 to as high as $1,400 a chest in 1804–5, a season during which there were more than three thousand chests sold to China at a profit of more than $1,000 a chest. Such profits had everyone, including John Words-worth, salivating. By 1820, high-grade Patna opium sold for $2,500 a chest. William Jardine, the leading British merchant of opium in China, advised his friends to invest in opium, "the safest and most gentlemanlike speculation" he was aware of (Greenberg, 104–19).

Being an entity of the British Crown, the Company could not dirty its hands in the direct sale of opium to China; rather, it assured the manufacture of high-quality opium in its Indian factories, auctioning off its high-value commodity at Calcutta to merchants called Country Traders, who ran either their own smaller vessels from India to China or who "leased" space on Company-chartered vessels. By 1832, the Company was making more than a million pounds profit per annum from its Indian factories[32] and Country Traders were becoming very rich.

England did not introduce opium to the Far East, but rather organized the industry into a "world problem," largely through the genius of Warren Hastings, who became governor-general of Bengal in 1793.[33] A brilliant administrator and cultivated man who was something of an orientalist and thus unusually respectful of Indian culture, Hastings was not especially proud of his success. He admitted that opium "is not a necessary of life, but a pernicious article of luxury, which ought not to be permitted but for purposes of foreign commerce only."[34] As far as foreign commerce was concerned, the general attitude about the trade was that it was a forgivable because necessary sin. The judgment of John William Kaye, one of the early historians of the East India Company, was common. Although he admits that the "surreptitious introduction of a compound into a large kingdom" was an unseemly business and that "a trade productive of nothing but demoralisation ought to be stopped," Kaye found room for equivocation:

> the truth is that, men who have been in China, while they describe in striking terms the fearful effects of the drug on the confirmed and habitual opium-eater, just as a man who had been in England might, from a few instances of delirium tremens, descant on the fearful effects of intemperance, allow that a moderate use of this stimulant is attended with beneficial effects.[35]

Parliament was sensitive to the impropriety of supporting an illicit trade but would not deny its necessary profitability. Despite conducting prolonged investigations into the conduct of Company business and often the unwise conduct of its governor-generals abroad, Parliament consistently found itself compromised.[36]

As David Spurr comments, "the colonizing imagination takes for granted that the land and its resources belong to those who are best able to exploit them according to the values of a Western commerical and industrial system."[37] Parliament sent some twenty thousand soldiers to the Indian continent to protect the commercial interests, that is, the opium factories, of the Honourable East India Company, largely because the interests of the Company were identical with the interests of British citizens. Indeed, so close was the association of business with government it proved difficult even for England's war heroes to distinguish between masters. The Court of Directors of the Company awarded Admiral Nelson £10,000 for winning the Battle of the Nile in 1799, because Nelson thereby thwarted Napoleon's designs on India Trade. Nelson himself was so conscious of the commercial significance of this victory to India and the Company that, as he lay wounded on the deck of his vessel, he thought to dictate an overland message for Bombay with news of his victory.

India was a recompense for the recent loss of America, and many families became dependent on the Company for careers for their children. The twenty-four directors of the Company were responsible for the selection of the 4,500 employees who served abroad. Fathers considered an Indian appointment "a liberal provision for their sons." The power of patronage became a bargaining chip for getting into Parliament, which meant that the influence flowed both ways. MPs had constituents needing Indian/Company appointments; directors had appointments to distribute and political ambitions of their own, certainly not unconnected with business.[38]

Fortunes were being made by many in investments, marine insurance, shipping ownership, smuggling, privateering, bribes, as well as in honest trade. The case of Charles Grant, twice director of the Company and later MP from Inverness, is the stuff of imperialistic legends and dreams. As a rising administrator in India, Grant made money so fast that he sent his books to Governor-General Cornwallis for audit to make sure he was not somehow making errors in his favor.[39] But even if a young appointee to the Company did not make his fortune in India, he was guaranteed a paddy for sowing wild rice.

## 3. The Many Impure

It used to be said that Englishmen abroad acted as though they had been "unbaptised" on the passage to India. Job Charnock, the "founder" of Calcutta, became a pagan and annually sacrificed a cock on the grave of his native wife. In 1802, English officials formed a procession to the temple of the goddess Kali, where they made an offering for the Company's success in India. To quell host country anxieties over cultural clash, Lord McCartney boasted before the court of China that the British settlements in Asia "have no priests or chaplains with them, as have other European nations."[40] There were a small minority of the Company in favor of missionaries and even a powerful few from the Clapham Sect who argued for Christianizing the Hindus. The India Bill of 1793 included "pious clauses" to this effect;[41] however, the Court of Directors of the Company "went so far as to 'Thank God' that the conversion of India was impracticable,"[42] for, what did religion have to do with business? and might not the "Good News" provoke unpredictable social change to affect business adversely? The Company believed that a mutiny in 1806 was most likely caused by a spread of Christianity among native soldiers in its employ. No matter that the sabbath in India had become a day off to celebrate in amusement and dissipation.[43]

The British settlements at Calcutta and other major cities and regions of India were youthful scenes of tens of thousands of young men, most of whom left India after achieving their financial dreams or not. In his 1783 "Speech on Fox's India Bill," Edmund Burke imagines the invasion from the Indian perspective:

> Animated with all the avarice of age, and all the impetuosity of youth, they roll in one after another; wave after wave; and there is nothing be-

fore the eyes of the natives but an endless, hopeless prospect of new flights of birds of prey and passage, with appetites continually renewing for a food that is continually wasting.[44]

The sweltering Indian continent, its putrid sanitary conditions,[45] and tropical diseases that preyed upon a nonindigenous population of pale Europeans, all stimulated an atmosphere of urgency in getting rich quick or getting out. However, days and nights were not wasted on the young. Hookah,[46] card playing, dinners, music, boating, exotic safaris, fireworks, balls, feasts celebrating battles and victories, six theater productions a season, horse racing, cricket, dueling, drinking, gaming, romancing, drug abuse, and suicide[47] were the components and results of a hedonistic culture abroad. Additionally, for the true soldier of fortune, privateering was always a way to get rich patriotically. An advertisement for crew members in 1780 Calcutta reads:

> To all gentlemen, seamen and lads of enterprize and true spirits, who are ambitious of making an honourable independence by the plunder of the enemies of their country, the *Death or Glory* privateer . . . mounting 22 pounders, twelve cohorns, and twenty swivels, and carrying a hundred and twenty men—will leave Calcutta in a few days on a five months' cruise against the Dutch, French, and Spaniards. The best treatment and encouragement will be given.[48]

Slavery was also rampant among the natives of Calcutta. Children were sold in open market, with girls headed for prostitution rings and venues of exotic dancing, and suttee—the de facto requirement for widows to die voluntarily upon the funeral pyres of their husbands—was practiced openly on city streets. The following missionary account bespeaks the moral climate of major Indian cities:

> A person informing us that a woman was about to be burnt with the corpse of her husband, near our house, I, with several of our brethren, hastened to the place: . . . It was a horrible sight. The most shocking indifference and levity appeared among those who were present. . . . A bamboo, perhaps twenty feet long, had been fastened at one end to a stake driven into the ground, and held down over the fire by men at the other. Such were the confusion, the levity, the bursts of brutal laughter, while the poor woman was burning alive before their eyes, that it seemed as if every spark of humanity was extinguished by this accursed superstition. That which added to the cruelty was the smallness of the fire. . . . I saw the legs of the poor creature hanging out of the fire. . . . Perceiving

the legs hanging out, they beat them with the bamboo for some time, in order to break the ligatures which fastened them at the knees. . . . She was the wife of a barber who . . . had died that morning, leaving [a] son . . . and a daughter of about eleven years of age.[49]

Wilberforce introduced this eyewitness account as an appendix to the East India Bill. Believing that "after the Slave Trade," England's delay in propagating the Gospel in India was her "greatest national sin,"[50] Wilberforce provided estimates of ten thousand women throughout India perishing annually in observance of the Hindu injunction that "it is proper for a woman, after her husband's death, to burn herself in the fire with his corpse."[51]

⛵

Adventurous British women received no administrative, maritime, or military appointments from the Company, but made their way to India as passengers on the Company's merchant ships, not for getting rich per se, but for finding a rich husband. Often success could be unpleasant, for the richest men were generally the oldest. As one new bride wrote to a friend back home: "True it is I am married; I have obtained that for which I came to India—a husband; but I have lost what I left behind me in my native country—happiness." Her husband, she says, treats her like a slave, so that she, like other young women married to older men in India, "are looking out with gratitude for the next mortality that may carry off their husbands. . . . They live a married life, an absolute misery, that they may enjoy a widowhood of affluence and independence." She concludes with, "this is no exaggeration, I assure you."[52] All told, out of approximately 31,000 British-born men and women in India in 1805, 22,000 were soldiers, 2,000 civil servants of the Company, about 500 were white women, and the remainder were seamen.[53]

The most sumptuous social events began when the East India fleets docked, with festivities focused on the parties thrown by the ships' officers. At the Captains' Balls in particular the "greater part of the ladies [were] disposed of," one participant explained; "it is really curious, but most melancholy, to see them ranged round the room, waiting with the utmost anxiety for offers, and looking with envy upon all who are more fortunate than themselves." The greatest catches were the military officers, "for being younger, healthier, and disposed to be romantic," in contrast with old and infirm "lechers," "leaning upon sticks and crutches."[54]

The situation was worse than melancholy for many of the fifty to sixty unmarried English women who ventured annually to India:

> the unmarried would fall into two distinct categories; those who were going to join friends in India, and those who were not. Those in the first category were often young women of good position but small fortune, sent to India on the invitation of some married relative or friend already resident there. On arrival, they would be met and welcomed into a respectable home. Convention then demanded that the hostess should at once give a series of parties, to which all interested bachelors might come. These gatherings were a recognised institution, and little attempt was made to conceal their function. The young women were deliberately displayed and frankly inspected, often receiving instantaneous offers of marriage. Those not very soon married would not be married at all, for their chief attraction lay in a complexion which the climate would ruin in a few months.

These, the women with awaiting friends, comprised the more fortunate of the two romantic categories; on the other hand,

> The fate of the women who had no friends to join was one of almost inconceivable barbarity. Those in this second category might be middle-aged women staking their all on a final attempt to get married. These at least knew what they were about. More often, however, they were young girls whose parents or guardians saw fit to dispose of them in this way. . . . Whatever might be the reason . . . for a girl being friendless, her fate was much the same. She had to accept the first offer of marriage she received.[55]

So serious was the requirement to entertain this displaced but very focussed measure of mankind that the Company provided their captains with a £500 and their first mates with a £300 entertainment allowance for shoreside entertainment, because it was expected that they would treat their customers well.[56] Especially if the fleet landed during the cool season, great profits could be made from the sale of ale, porter, wine, hams, spirits, and cheeses from England, in addition to the routine stores that the Company fleets brought to British citizens abroad.[57]

The captains of the Indiamen were thus personages. Onboard their vessels they were gods; when they landed with their retinue, they were greeted with thirteen-gun salutes. Sauntering about in their quasimilitary finery, including bejeweled swords,[58] they were the envy of males and objects of intense female desire. Even time at sea was described as an affair of the heart. As one woman described the protocol: "When [the ladies] appear on deck, [the captain] gives them his arm, and when they walk he walks with them. Everybody understands this."[59] A well-traveled male passenger corroborates exuberantly:

> I may as well remark that I know no situation in life which confers so many privileges on its possessor as are attached to the post of captain of an Indiaman—always provided that he be a *gentleman*, and a good-tempered, agreeable person. Talk of the power of an absolute sovereign! His Majesty of Prussia for instance! pshaw! compare a reign of fear with one of love? who can measure dominion over lives, with sway over hearts! It is nothing, a mere drop in the bucket, compared with the absolute dominion of an East India Captain. . . . There is one particular, and interesting class of his liege subjects who are more than any other under his protection and control. In plain terms, he usually has six, eight, or ten young ladies under his care . . . with each, and all of whom it is his especial duty to walk, dance, play at chess or back-gammon, read and take wine, not to say anything of the long tetes-a-tetes absolutely necessary for giving advice."[60]

It is more than a postscript to this titillating narrative of barbarians abroad that Charles Grant was to be appointed Director of the East India Company for the second time in 1805, the year John commenced his coveted but fatal Bombay-Canton voyage. John's letters reveal that he received an invitation to dine with Grant in 1800, or shortly before his first voyage as captain of the *Abergavenny* (*LJW*72); he came across Grant in the India Office in 1804, when he and William Dent went to see about a preferred voyage for John (*LJW*145); and John attracted both William Wilberforce and Grant to his cause later in 1804 when he was promised a Bombay-China voyage for his next run (*LJW*148). John must have impressed both men deeply for by the next month he had the voyage of his dreams (*LJW* 150). Grant had an improved vision for the Company and John was part of it.

Charles Grant (1746–1823) was a man to be reckoned with in his day. An evangelical, honest, philanthropic, self-made man; twice director of the Court of Directors (1792, 1805) of the East India Company, and thus one of the most powerful business leaders of Europe—indeed, it was said that Grant was "not a Director, but the Direction" of the Company;[61] one of the original members of the

Clapham Sect and staunch ally of William Wilberforce and Thomas Clarkson during their campaign against the slave trade that ended successfully in 1807; an early director of the Sierra Leone company, chartered in 1791 as a refuge for freed slaves; later Member of Parliament from Inverness; and, most importantly, and controversially, the force behind the "pious clauses" that successfully institutionalized the Christianizing of British India as part of the Company's renewed charter in 1813. Grant's position against Hindu culture was compromised by the behavior of the British in India and the unspoken half of his agenda was to reform his own Company.

The substantial document the Claphamites wielded against the antimissionary faction in the Company and Parliament was Grant's *Observations on the State of society among the Asiatic Subjects of Great Britain, particularly with respect to Morals; and on the means of improving it.— Written chiefly in the year 1792*,[62] prepared as a "paper of business" for the Court of Directors of the East India Company upon Grant's return from an eighteen-year career as a servant of the Company in India; delivered to a Select Committee of the House of Commons as early as 1797, and then widely circulated in Parliament. By 1813, when the charter of the Company again came up for its twenty-year renewal, Grant's *Observations* had reached the status of a definitive document on the depravity of Hindu culture and on the moral obligation of Christian England to save its millions of Hindu subjects rather than leave them in moral darkness. Contra the adulation paid to Hindu culture by eminent orientalists such as William Jones[63] or even the modest respect of Warren Hastings, who attempted to create as governor-general of India a system for "reconciling the people of England to the nature of Hindostan,"[64] Grant and the Claphamites found little worth saving in contemporary Hindu culture, except the souls of its inhabitants.

The campaign of the Claphamites and their evidence in hand against Hindu culture was hardly the subtle and insidious effects of culture brilliantly teased out of literary documents by Edward Said in *Orientalism* and *Culture and Imperialism*.[65] *Observations* was bluntly modeled upon Swift's *Gulliver's Travels*, IV, "A Voyage to the Land of the Houyhnhnms," as an attack by a nation of rationalists against a remotely human breed of Indian Yahoos.[66]

Grant's *Observations* became the ammunition for this latest crusade of the Clapham apostles—Grant, Wilberforce, Henry Thornton, and a few other eminent men of business and "Saints in Politics"—because none of the other Claphamites had experience of India. In Parliament as well, few knew firsthand of Indian life and culture. One recalls the striking admission of ignorance from Edmund Burke, the acknowledged parliamentary expert on Indian affairs, who admitted during the 1783 hearings on Fox's East India Bill, that

> we are in general . . . so little acquainted with Indian details, the instruments of oppression under which the people suffer are so hard to be understood, and even the very names of the sufferers are so uncouth and strange to our ears, that it is very difficult for our sympathy to fix upon these objects. (*Speeches* 403–4)

Indeed, few besides the Claphamites were interested in the matter at all, preferring to live and let live, as long as business could proceed as necessary. As the Governor-General-in-Council to the Court of Directors of the Company explained in 1787:

> We do not look upon the Eastern trade as a source from whence much specie can be drawn into this country, but the advantages to be expected from it for the Company are principally by its becoming more extensively than at present a mart for the barter of opium and the productions of Bengal for tin, pepper, and other commodities to be applied as funds in the Chinese markets for the purchase of tea, instead of the ruinous export of specie from this country as well as from Europe.[67]

Thus, in seeking to argue the case for Christianizing India, first before his peers at the Company and later in Parliament with Wilberforce, Grant had to overcome a moral inertia associated with a successful economic and political operation, somewhat comparable to the forces against the abolition of slavery. Having been successful against slavery, the Clapham Sect now sought a new moral battle to wage and focused on Indian culture as a moral abomination intolerable within the imperial domains of Christian England.

Grant's preference for John Wordsworth as one of his captains may seem a matter of micromanagement for the man at the helm of the world's greatest trading company and brother-in-arms with William Wilberforce against the institutionalized evils of the world. But the number of vessel captains was finite, and John and others like him could indeed have great impact in modeling—or enforcing—a moral life for mariners and thereby representing the Company abroad as Christians of pure hearts and sound minds, rather than the present cohort of avaricious immoralists who too often found their way through influence to the captaincies of the vessels chartered by the Company.

## 4. WHAT DOES IT PROFIT A MAN?

Great fortunes were made as readily as romantic liaisons for an average captain of an East Indiaman. An appointment as captain was treasured and appointments as well as specific voyages were sold for great sums in anticipation of even greater profits. John Wordsworth reports that another captain offered him £5000 for his final voyage, which was one of only four out of ninety to one hundred worldwide stops that called at Bombay as well as Canton. He also reports that his predecessor in command of the *Abergavenny*, cousin Captain John Wordsworth, probably made about £15,000 on his comparable final voyage, enabling him to retire after an entire adult life at sea. In his last nine years as a commodore, Capt. John Wordsworth had spent ninety out of 108 months at sea on four voyages, forty-five of those months being served on two voyages in the last forty-eight months of his career.[68]

In lieu of livable salaries, the captains and their subordinate officers were allotted space according to rank for carrying private cargo. The captain was allotted two pipes of madiera wine,[69] fifty-six tons of cargo space outward bound from England, and thirty-eight tons homeward bound from China, in addition to the dunnage, or the woods used to brace cargo so that it might travel securely in rough seas.[70] Since desired woods, such as rattan, cane, and bamboo could suffice as dunnage for a cargo as light as tea, there was also a handsome profit to be made from what might otherwise be, as it is now, a reusable resource of woods. Finally, the captain could use the vessel bottom up to a height of thirteen inches for whatever he deemed to be suitable "flooring," which usually turned out to be more woods. Besides the cargo space, which he could use for any and all kinds of cargo permitted by the Company, and besides the profit from dunnage, the captain also made a profit from passenger fees, which he himself was permitted to establish for each voyage. There are records of £350 being charged for a single cabin in 1805 and £1,000 for half a Great Cabin, which was exclusively the captain's property.[71] Passenger numbers were not great, usually less than forty, for the Indiamen were cargo vessels. Descriptions of deck parties hosted by captains could make for a pleasureable time at sea, however, if there were young women aboard. The captain's passengers ate all meals at his table and thus he was responsible for provisions and billeting, which meant that the deck would hold a menagerie of live-stock and poultry for consumption during the six- or seven-month journey to India. There the passengers—the soldiers, the husband-hunters, and administrative personnel of the Company and possibly their families—would disembark. His Majesty's soldiers were des-tined for an Indian mission of protection, or territorial expansion, as was the case between 1798 and 1805 under the governor-general-ship of Marquess Wellesley.[72]

As far as a captain's lucre was concerned, a £10,000 profit would not be uncommon for a single India–China voyage. The fly in the captain's ointment was raising money on credit to purchase the goods he would sell in India and then in China. For if he had no money to invest in trade, his opportunity, indeed, the opportunity of his and his family's lifetime would be squandered. Entire families, friends, acquaintances, the vessel's owners, anxious investors willing to lend at usurious rates, all became involved in the fortunes of the Company captain.

The Company officer did not make it to the rank of captain on merit alone. The eligibility requirements were surprisingly few—a prospective captain had to be at least twenty-five years of age and he needed experience as a second or chief mate on a single voyage in a regular ship—which means that at least three to four hundred of-ficers were probably eligible at all times. John provides evidence in his letters of how difficult it was even to remain employed in the Company. Mortified to inform Mary that he could not get her brother a position as even a fourth or fifth mate, he says:

> there are so many young men out of employment in our Service—yet belonging to the Service that I dare say there has been at least 50 applica-tions for the chief mates berth in the Abergavenny—& by men that have not the smallest chance of getting out this season—our Service is the very worst in the world without a young man has a certainty of getting a command— (*LJW* 76)

A captaincy could not be obtained until one of the present cap-tains retired, and, of all the captaincies on the one hundred or so vessels chartered by the Company on an annual basis, only thirty to forty were bound for the East India trade. Of these, only about four each season would make the India-China run, and only two the most

profitable Bombay-Canton voyage. So one indeed required influence and powerful allies to reach the top rung of the ladder at any
age, let alone at the relatively tender age of twenty-eight, as John had
when he was sworn in as captain.

John reached the top through hard work, through powerfully
placed relatives and friends, and through equally hard personal
campaigning. He also dealt in illicit commodities, suffered anxiety
in raising money to finance the private trade of his voyages, aggres-
sively insisted on his family's financial participation in his investment opportunities, avoided the social scene at familiar ports of call,
got entangled in a confrontation with enemy squadrons at sea, and
survived an act of God only days before going down with his vessel.

As a rising officer he brought a small amount of opium to England, which was a far more flourishing business for many.[73] Returning from a two-year's voyage in 1797, John had little to show for it
but a small profit from a consignment of opium. Brother Richard
Wordsworth, who handled all of John's accounts, records in a ledger
entry for 16 June 1797: "Received of Wm Smith for Opium Sold by
him for your Use £102. Allowed him for his trouble in selling same
£2 . . . Profit = 100." John's balance sheet as of March 1800 was
meager in the negative: "Owed RW—£416.14.5; Assets—383.9.6."[74]
John would also return with desired commodities for friends and
family—bamboo for fishing poles, wine, Chinese art, "Bang" or
marijuana, from Bengal, etc. (*LJW* 136). The bane of his existence
became raising funds for private investment, especially after he became a commodore and suffered a rare setback, or a setback rare
for a captain of a China vessel.

There was thus much of the above to consider, by William especially, to whom John must have described, perhaps in different detail, but with a comparable ominous thrust, the life of a mariner
hoping to remain good, though walking among the many impure.
William himself had "fallen" in Revolutionary France with far less
temptation. It could not have been difficult to imagine John succumbing to any of the resident demons of an Indiaman at sea for
eighteen months or those that awaited a doughty young officer in
ports of call. Innocence and naivete might even prove to be one's
undoing amid a sea and harbor life of drinking, drugs, gaming, carousing, dueling, womanizing, romantic entrapment, and smuggling. Then there were the routine instances of victimization by
naked and oiled thieves-in-the-night at Calcutta[75] and the unspeak-
ably brutal attacks of lurking pirates against the crews of merchant

vessels. Mutiny was not uncommon. There were also the ordinary dangers of a sailor's life, such as mortal illness, especially scurvy; hurricanes and other accidents brought on by incompetence, stupidity, and faulty instrumentation; and confrontations with enemy naval squadrons during these revolutionary war years. Lloyd's reports that from 1 January 1793 to 31 December 1799, 4,344 British ships were captured by the enemy, 2,385 ships were lost, and 652 driven onshore. These data did not include Navy ships, although only 62 Navy vessels were lost to the enemy and 152 to perils of the sea.[76]

Finally, there was the utterly unpredictable, such as the recent experience of their cousin Capt. John Wordsworth, who found himself implicated in an international incident with China over smuggling and the related wounding of a Chinese national. It occurred in 1799, the year of the Edict of Nanking forbidding the importation of opium. In what is referred to as the *Providence* Affair, the English schooner *Providence*, which was serving as a tender for HMS *Madras*, was being harrassed in Canton harbor by provocateurs in a sampan, who were attempting to cut its cable to set it adrift. The watch of the *Providence* fired on the Chinese, wounding one, and crew members in pursuit succeeded in removing the injured man to the nearest vessel for medical treatment, which happened to be the *Abergavenny*. Capt. John Wordsworth failed in an attempt to bribe the Chinese into silence over the incident and a messy exchange between the Company and the Chinese authorities ensued.[77]

In such an unpredictable world of the many impure it might be more difficult *not* to imagine an ambitious young man going adrift in his "wild dedication . . . / To unpath'd waters, undream'd shores."[78] Ignorance was most likely bliss prior to John's visit to Grasmere, but now fully aware of the dangers of a mariner's life, William had to be troubled when he contemplated his brother's voyages and the risk John was undertaking primarily out of commitment to his poetic vocation.

## 5. John/Luke and William/Michael

One of John Wordsworth's laments was the impoverishment of poets. He wrote that it was "a most melancholy thing to think that either [William or Coleridge] should want a reasonable share of money considering the times—that Wms health should be hurt by anxiety which I fear it is—that C. should be obliged to write for

Newspapers" (*LJW* 116). It was a high-minded reaction. John's personal mission was to get rich on his own behalf and to make enough money to improve materially the lives of his poet-brother and sister. Dorothy's financial state was his first concern, and to this end he promised to have the East India House send her £10 twice per annum (*LJW* 97) until he made his fortune. His promise to support William was vaguer, and after the Lonsdale debt was partially settled, perhaps practically unnecessary, but by then John was in debt and couldn't pull out, even if he had wanted to.

On Sunday 27 September 1800 the message reached Grasmere that the *Abergavenny* had returned from China. Two days later John parted from William and Dorothy at Grisedale Tarn. Dorothy later recalled that she and William "stood till we could see him no longer, watching him as he *hurried* down the stony mountain" (EY 598–99). He planned to be out of their lives for a considerable time. Writing several months later to Mary Hutchinson, John laid out his present situation and his future, both of which he considered to be "*as most most* fortunate*":

> I am sure you will be delighted to hear that in a few weeks time I am to be sworn into the command of the Abergavenny      Captn Wordsworth has made a very handsome fortune & is going to reside at W'haven—*and they* tell *me in 8 or ten* years I *am to* be a very *rich man* for in that time I am to make four voyages— (*LJW* 77)

John's fixation on becoming rich, his untested goodness and professional competence as he reached the pinnacle of power aboard a great vessel, the physically and morally dangerous worlds in which he would continue to dwell, and, finally, the unsettled feelings he aroused for leaving a contemplative pastoral life of love and domesticity for the "dreary seas"—all of these figure in the creation of "Michael." William had attempted to establish in the poems inspired by John's presence an innate similarity. John's happy participation in their quiet life corroborated the impression, although, as we have seen, both "When to the attractions of the busy world" and "The Brothers" contain deconstructive fault lines. On the day of his departure, John must have seemed a running contradiction, scurrying down the stony road to Patterdale.

A few days later, on 2 October 1800, Dorothy records in her journal that she, William, and the Lloyds "had a pleasant conversation about the manners of the rich—Avarice, inordinate desires, & the effeminacy unnaturalness & the unworthy objects of education." She closes the entry with a natural image that quietly justifies the riches of the life they have chosen: "The moonlight lay upon the hills like snow" (*DWJ* 23). As fortune would have it, the next day they met the beggar, later to be the leech gatherer of "Resolution and Independence," whom John believed to be a Jew when they crossed paths in Wythburn, for his dark eyes and long nose. The old man's story is familiar to Wordsworth scholars, but his fortitude and stark material values represent a sharp and meaningful contrast to John's excited ambition to become rich. On the face of it, the comparison is ridiculous: leeches sucking on a leg for pence or less, in comparison with thousands of pounds riding in profit for sailing and smuggling:

> He had had a wife "& a good woman & it pleased God to bless us with ten children"—all these were dead but one of whom he had not heard for many years, a Sailor—his trade was to gather leeches but now leeches are scarce & he had not strength for it—he lived by begging & was making his way to Carlisle where he should buy a few godly books to sell. He said leeches were very scarce partly owing to this dry season, but many years they have been scarce—he supposed it owing to their being much sought after, that they did not breed fast, & were of slow growth. (*DWJ* 23–24)

A week later William and Dorothy walked along Greenhead Ghyll in search of a sheepfold, passing on the way the field where their "house was to be built." Dorothy's description is one the most beautiful from the *Grasmere Journals*. The sheep at danger and the image of heartbreak in the stones are Dorothy's own version of prophecy:

> The Colours of the mountains soft & rich, with orange fern—The Cattle pasturing upon the hilltops Kites sailing as in the sky above our heads—Sheep bleating & in lines & chains & patterns scattered over the mountains. They come down & feed on the little green islands in the beds of the torrents & so may be swept away. The Sheepfold is falling away it is built nearly in the form of a heart unequally divided. Look down the brook & see the drops rise upwards & sparkle in the air, at the little falls, the higher sparkles the tallest. We walked along the turf of the mountain till we came to a Cattle track. (*DWJ* 26)

Within another week, William began work on "the sheepfold," blindly striving to compose a "semijocular" pastoral of anapestic verse, hardly associated with anything that mattered.

Wordsworth hopelessly struggled at the "crudely comic" ballad that would become "Michael."[79] Throughout the month of October 1800 Dorothy records repeatedly the difficulties William was having with the poem (15, 18, 20, 21, 22, 23, 24, 25 October). On 28 October, William composed in the fir grove, most likely where John had restlessly paced, for Dorothy claims that it was an excellent covert from the wind, which is comparable to the advantage William ascribed to it in "When to the attractions of the busy world." On 9 November, William "burnt the sheep fold," as it was called, and began again. By 26 November, Dorothy writes that William was "very well & highly poetical" (*GJ* 33). "Michael" was completed on 9 December 1800 (*GJ* 35).

In the interim between the burning of "the sheepfold" and the successful completion of "Michael," John began writing about money. Shortly after 10 November 1800, John wrote to Dorothy that

> it is an object to me to get as much money as possible I shall then get my investment upon better term{s} Captn W. is let[ting] me have 2000£ & Richd 2000£ & I have had an offer of 1500£ from a quarter that I did not expect. (*LJW* 74)

Although admitting that he had command of £5500, John wrote to Dorothy a week later asking that she contribute the meager £80 inheritance she had received from uncle Christopher Crackenthorpe in January 1800—"as it is of consequence to me to get as much ready [mone]y as possible I shall be much obliged to you for the 80£—" (*LJW* 75). As it turned out, the amounts invested by Richard and cousin Captain Wordsworth were not as high as John claimed; still, the family investment in his first voyage as captain turned out to be substantial: Dr. Cookson invested £470, William sold stock to invest £277.10, Richard finally offered £1014, Captain Wordsworth was in for £1650, and Dorothy for £80.[80]

John's importunity and an interesting reminiscence most likely catalyzed the anxiety over material values related to the divided sheepfold. The following anecdote is hearsay, but its uniqueness and source speak for its veracity. John Wilson ("Christopher North"), future editor of *Blackwood's,* resident of the Lake District, and, as Dorothy later described him, "a Friend and *adorer* of William and his verses" (*MY* 1 206), records of John Wordsworth's departure from Grasmere:

> [William] accompanied [John] across the hills on his way to join his ship for the last time, and here [Grisedale Tarn] they sat, about to part. They

had talked over their future plans of happiness when they were again to meet, and of their simple sports [fishing]. As their last act, they agreed to lay the foundation-stone of a little fishing hut, and this they did with tears.

They parted there, in that dim and solemn place, and recommended each other to God's eternal care. . . . I one sweet summer day went along with him and heard the melancholy tale.[81]

John, William, and the Reverend Joseph Sympson (1715–1807) often fished at Grisedale Tarn (see figure 1). Dorothy's description of Sympson and his wife suggest that they are the models for Michael, the hale geriatric shepherd, and Isabel, his dutiful matron whose heart "was in her home":

We are also upon very intimate terms with one family in the middle rank of life, a Clergyman with a very small income, his wife, son and daughter. The old man is upwards of eighty yet he goes a fishing to the Tarns on the hill-tops with my Brothers, and he is as active as many men of 50. His wife is a delightful old woman, mild and gentle, yet chearful in her manners and much of the gentlewoman, so made by long exercise of the duties of a wife and a mother and the charities of a neighbour, for she has lived 40 years in this vale and seldom left her home. (*EY* 299)

**1. Grisedale Tarn. Photograph by author.**

One could imagine the sorts of long conversations these fishing mates would have had—William, John, the Reverend Sympson— after becoming familiar: William, eager to stock up on stories of local color and characters, listening to Sympson reminisce about the little world of Grasmere; John, recounting his wider-world experiences in America, the West Indies, India, and China, and the rich future he foresaw as a captain; Sympson, teaching the younger men some tricks about tarn fishing, while most likely offering unrequested and unrestricted advice. William did write to Thomas Poole that he was partly a model for the old shepherd: "I had your character often before my eyes, and sometimes thought I was delineating such a man as you yourself would have been under the same circumstances" (*EY* 322). But Poole could not have been the original model for the shepherd of the first sheepfold, and Dorothy's description of Sympson and wife lead one to believe that the old vicar was on Wordsworth's mind when he began his poem:

> Perhaps the old man is a provident elf
> So fond of bestowing advice on himself
> And of puzzling at what may befall
> So intent upon baking his bread without leaven
> And of giving to earth the perfection of heaven
> That he thinks and does nothing at all.[82]

But Wordsworth, finally, could not write a jocular poem about the foundational values touching so closely upon his relationship with John.

In light of the evidence we have reviewed on the mariner captain's life, and the likelihood that William would have been aware of much of it, there is that allegorical relationship in the Wilson anecdote between life and art that we often find in Wordsworth's poetry, in this particular case, between the brothers' act and the comparably motivated scene in "Michael," during which Luke lays a foundation stone at Michael's request to symbolize his commitment to ancestral values and to his return after assuring the family's financial future:[83]

> ["]Heaven bless thee, Boy,
> Thy heart these two weeks has been beating fast
> With many hopes—it should be so—yes—yes—
> I knew that thou could'st never have a wish
> To leave me, Luke,—thou has been bound to me
> Only by links of love, . . .

> But I forget
> My purposes. Lay now the corner stone
> As I requested, and hereafter, Luke,
> When thou art gone away, should evil men
> Be thy companions, let this Sheep-fold be
> Thy anchor and thy shield; amid all fear
> And all temptation let it be to thee
> An emblem of the life thy Fathers liv'd,
> Who, being innocent, did for that cause
> Bestir them in good deeds. Now fare thee well:
> When thou return'st thou in this place wilt see
> A work which is not here, a covenant
> 'Twill be between us—but whatever fate
> Befall thee, I shall love thee to the last,
> And bear thy memory with me to the grave."
>
> The Shepherd ended here; and Luke stoop'd down,
> And as his Father had requested, laid
> The first stone of the Sheep-fold; at the sight
> The Old Man's grief broke from him, to his heart
> He press'd his Son, he kissed him and wept.
>
> (lines 407–32, LB 265–66)

The unresolved tension that propels this scene is Michael's inability to square his belief in Luke's love with Luke's desire to leave. The halted rhythms and faulted logic of Michael's speech:

> Thy heart these two weeks has been beating fast
> With many hopes—it should be so—yes—yes—
> I knew that thou could'st never have a wish
> To leave me, Luke,—thou has been bound to me
> Only by links of love

reveal that the poet has not moved beyond the affective impasse of "The Brothers." Leonard left to become rich and his reward is finding everything he worked for dead when he returns. Michael/William, now familiar with the dangers of the world Luke/John is entering, has ample reason to doubt the possibility of John's return, and here both become implicated in the future of the young. It is Michael's plan that Luke go to the city; it is William's option to be supportive of John's enterprises because of their bond.

It seems too that Michael's anxiety over Luke's commitments inspires him to enact the dramatic scene at the site of the future sheepfold. Michael admits to purposefully bringing Luke to the pile of stones. One must presume that Michael seeks to mingle Luke's desire to leave with an emotionally laden commitment to return:

> But, lay one Stone—
> Here, lay it for me, Luke, with thy own hands,
> I for the purpose brought thee to this place.
>
> . . . . . . . . . . . .
>
> Lay now the corner-stone,
> As I requested, and hereafter, Luke,
> When thou art gone away, should evil men
> Be thy companions, let this Sheep-fold be
> Thy anchor and thy shield, amid all fear
> And all temptation, let it be to thee
> An emblem of the life thy Fathers lived,
> Who, being innocent, did for that cause
> Bestir them in good deeds.
>
> (396–99; 414–22)

If the groundbreaking of their fishing hut were comparably motivated by William's anxiety, one will appreciate John's reported torment, and his suicidal passivity, as his end neared. "Let this Sheep-fold be / Thy *anchor*," indeed. An unexpectedly appropriate metaphor for a shepherd who bespeaks a poet's anxiety.[84]

Richard/Robert Bateman functions by absence as the ghost of speculators past. He is the orphaned lad in "Michael" who enters Isabel's fantasy as the unspoken model of success for her son.[85] As Michael concludes his explanation on the financial necessity of Luke's departure, Isabel drifts into a private fantasy:

> There's Richard Bateman, thought she to herself,
> He was a parish Boy—At the church door
> They made a gathering for him, shillings, pence,
> And halfpennies, wherewith the Neighbours bought
> A Basket which they fill'd with Pedlar's wares,
> And with this Basket on his arm the Lad
> Went up to London, found a Master there
> Who out of many chose the trusty Boy
> To go and overlook his merchandise
> Beyond the seas, where he grew wondrous rich,
> And left estates and monies to the poor,
> And at his birth-place built a Chapel, floor'd
> With marble which he sent from foreign Lands.

> These thoughts and many others of like sort
> Pass'd quickly through the mind of Isabel
> And her face brighten'd.
>
> (268–83, *LB* 261–62)

This exchange between Michael and Isabel is one of the most poignant moments in Wordsworth's verse. Michael believes that he sees affirmation in Isabel's brightened face for *his* plan that Luke go away for a profitable while and then return. If he knew she were musing upon the Bateman boy instead of her son's return, he might have changed his mind about risking Luke's future.

Wordsworth indicates in his note to "Michael" that the story of Bateman was well known (*LB* 403, n. to line 268). An anecdote on the chapelry of Hugil in the *Topographical Dictionary of England* (1831) reports on what was known throughout the Lake District about Robert, not Richard, Bateman. He did indeed rebuild a chapel and

> gave £1000 for purchasing an estate, and erected eight alms-houses for as many poor families, besides a donation of £12 per annum to the curate. This worthy benefactor . . . from a state of indigence succeeded in amassing considerable wealth by mercantile pursuits. He is stated to have been poisoned, in the straits of Gibraltar, on his voyage from Leghorn, with a valuable cargo, by the captain of the vessel.[86]

By introducing Isabel's fantasy of Bateman the unfortunate entrepreneur, the poet quietly acknowledges the unspoken risks for John—even if he would have been comparably successful—that he and Dorothy had on their minds.

Nevertheless, Michael/William's economic motivation for encouraging Luke/John's departure wears the mask of rationality: "If here he stay / What can be done? Where every one is poor / What can be gain'd?" (lines 263–65). But William has built into the poem the divided consciousness that he felt over John's working for him. Michael would still have one-half his land, and without risk to his son. William and Dorothy would survive without the sacrifice of John.[87]

The place and moment of John's departure was to be painfully recalled in Wordsworth's elegiac poem on John's death, "I only looked for pain and grief":

> Here did we stop, and here look round
> While each into himself descends

For that last thought of parting Friends
That is not to be found.
Our Grasmere vale was out of sight,
Our home and his, his heart's delight,
His quiet heart's delicious home.
But time before him melts away,
And he hath feeling of a day
Of blessedness to come.

Here did we part, and halted here
With One he lov'd, I saw him bound
Downwards along the rocky ground
As if with eager cheer.
A lovely sight as on he went,
For he was bold and innocent,
Had liv'd a life of self-command.
Heaven, did it seem to me and her,
Had laid on such a Mariner
A consecrating hand.

(*P2V* 612–13)

As John hurried down the hill after having lain the foundation stone of their little fishing hut—either on this occasion or another—it must have seemed that theirs and John's fate literally hung in the stars. John's comment to Mary quoted earlier is precisely summative. He speaks as Luke in applying Michael's final words to himself: "But what ever fate Befal me I shall love [thee] to the last and bear thy memory with me to the grave" (*LJW* 126). And perhaps he did.

# Part II
## Sinking Vocations

### 1. Confrontations on Land and Sea

Capt. John Wordsworth was exalted with his appointment as commodore of the 1,200-ton vessel, the second *Earl of Abergavenny*. "Never ship was like us," he wrote to Dorothy in his diffident manner: "indeed we are not a *little* proud" (*LJW* 114). Again, "We have the finest ship in the fleet she is indeed a most noble ship and is the *pride* of the fleet & the Service" (*LJW* 117). Tongue-in-cheek, he gently chastises Mary Hutchinson for not appreciating his status:

> come come my dearest Mary do not tell me again that you do not know how to direct [mail] to me . . . do you suppose that J.W Esqr & c. c is not to be found in such a place as Portsmouth— if you were to see how great a man I am on bd my great ship you would say that I have just cause to be offended— (*LJW* 121).

Considering the deference accorded East India Company captains, John's claim to attention is modest.

Nevertheless, the log entries of John's first two voyages as captain support his statement that "a more stupid place than a ship cannot well be imagined" (*LJW* 112), with attempted escapes, raucous behavior, accidents, and deaths recorded as routinely as details of wind and rain:

> Feb 13 [1801]—taking in lead and tin
> Mar 28—Company's agent came on board and mustered
> ship's company. Punished John Martin with two dozen
> lashes for insolence, drunkenness and striking
> fourth officer.
> May 9—Finding William Jones, Seaman, concealed in
> one of the shore boats for the purpose of escaping,
> confined him in irons.

June 30—Read to ship's company the abstract of the
33rd of His Majesty George the 3rd relating to
punishment of offenders on board . . .
Aug 5—Run from the ship Thomas Coffin, Seaman
Aug 7—Run from the ship James Pris, Seaman
Aug 30—at 7 PM Mr. Salisburg midshipman unfortunately
fell overboard and was drowned.
Sep 13—John Melvile Seaman fell overboard and was
drowned
Nov 9—Run from the ship Robert Hughes
Dec 20—reached China
Jan 30 [1802]—anchored in Wampoa Reach
Feb 8—Employed delivering lead
Feb 20—Employed delivering lead, flints, receiving
3 boats of Bohea [tea] for Company
Feb 28—Sent half the ship's company to Canton on
liberty
Mar 1—Received 3 loads of tea for Company
May 27—Departed this life Aquum, one of the Chinese
Committed the body to the deep.
June 2—Departed this life Thomas Cook, Seaman
June 10—Punished John Kirkman with one dozen lashes
for theft
June 16—Departed this life John Thorp, carpenter
June 21—Departed this life George Moore. Committed
the body to the deep with the usual ceremony.
June 27—Departed this life George Fieder armourer
Sep 9—Anchored in the lower part of Gravesend
Reach
Until Nove 3—Employed delivering tea and general cargo, refitting,
    cleaning etc.; at which date . . .
inspector came on board and cleared the ship.[1]

John's log for the next voyage, to Wampoa in 1803–4, is replete with
comparable entries of labor, mortality, and attempted escapes, with
insubordination worsening as worthy seamen became scarce. The
Royal Navy was assured priority in the selection of seamen during
this renewal of war with France. Indeed, the Navy had the authority
to impress sailors from merchant vessels, in any port of call, which
often left East Indiamen undermanned. The Company had to go
with the warm bodies that were left, often homegrown "trash," as
John described one of his crews, and foreign nationals. Mutinous
confrontations between officers and seamen became common. On

the voyage to Wampoa, John decisively suppressed an uprising with timely corporal punishment:

> May 30—Finding a spirit of dissatisfaction to prevail in the ship, held consultation of officers and punished Michael Gretorix with one dozen lashes. Previous to the punishment several of the people ran forward in a mutinous manner. Singled out one of the ringleaders Wm Davies and punished him with two dozen lashes, also one of the Chinese with one dozen for attempting to stab with a knife one of the boatswain's mates in the execution of his duty.

Besides attentiveness to discipline and order, John established the religious life his powerful supporters expected. Ship logs show that Sunday services were either unrecorded or unconducted on his first voyage, but logs of the second voyage make divine worship, weather permitting, a matter of record—"May 22—Sunday performed Divine Service"; "Feb 28—Wind being variable we were prevented from performing Divine Service."

As wretched as ship life might have been, John remained on board in port, living up to his reputation as the "philosopher." Writing to Mary he says, "indeed this is a most stupid place to be in—my brother *Commanders* are *dashing* away in high style on shore this I could never bear was my fortune ever so large." The resulting ostracism hardly mattered at the time, although it may have played a part in the halted rescue efforts on the night of the sinking: "I remain constantly on bd & have become quite an *alien* to them," that is, to his "brother *Commanders*." Instead of carousing with the "many impure," he read Shakespeare ("the greatest of all great men"), his brother's *Lyrical Ballads,* and Anderson's *The Works of the British Poets* (*LJW* 121, 123), with recommendations from William.

Having pledged his support to William, John felt invested in the second edition of *Lyrical Ballads,* but learned quickly that he could not force the poems on acquaintances: "the fact," he says, "is every one is so full of his own business that *even I* scarce hear them mention'd except I *lug* them in myself" (*LJW* 95). Yet, he was uncomfortable with John Stoddart's review in the *British Critic* for being "too indiscriminately flattering," shrewdly concluding that "in time they will become popular but it will be by degrees" (*LJW* 95). He accused Longman, the publisher of *Lyrical Ballads,* of being "a vile abominable and impudent Jew for only giving Wm 80£ for the 2 Editions." John was sure Longman "will clear at least 400£ or perhaps 500£" (*LJW* 95–96).

Of all the poems of *Lyrical Ballads*, "Michael" became John's favorite. At first he thought the language "rather vulgar" (*LJW* 94), but soon found the poem "superior" even to his former favorite, "The Brothers" (*LJW* 110). His judgment on the reading habits of the common reader was probably based on his own reaction to his brother's work:

> I do not think that Wms poetry will become popular for some time to come it certainly does not suit the present taste I was in company the other evening with a gentleman he read the Beggar "Why says he this is very pretty but you may call it any [thing] but poetry— I like the description but still it is very different to what I should conceive poetry to be— I said it might be true (for I like to give people their own way) & that perhaps from local circumstances I might be more interested in it than it deserved— the truth is there are few people that like, or read, poetry many who buy it—buy it for the name—read about twenty lines the language is very fine & they are content with praising extravagantly the whole poem— Most of Wms poetry improves upon 2d 3 or 4th reading now people in general are not sufficiently interested with the first reading to induce them to try a 2d.[2] (*LJW* 103)

John's nine-month visit to Grasmere not only taught him what a poet did, quite simply, think, read, and write, but more importantly, why the leisure to be materially unproductive ought to be patronized. Wallace W. Douglas is correct in saying "Wordsworth's interest in money was one of the determining factors in his life,"[3] but William admitted and proved throughout his life that he was "strangely unfit for exertion as far as it is mere labour in the way of job and money" (*EY* 555). John was not.

Life's distance between William and John had been immense before their time together. John's education ended with grammar school. He spent his seafaring years in the company of ne'er-do-wells, social misfits, and avaricious barbarians. While John had been at sea, suffering present inanity for the prospect of future riches, William finished his studies at the Hawkshead Grammar School and then Cambridge University. He lived in Revolutionary France, where he fathered a child. He spent some radical years in the intellectual circles of London, befriended Coleridge, established several domiciles with Dorothy, wrote some promising early verse.[4] There is no doubt that, with Coleridge's encouragement, he had become preoccupied with the importance of his calling. William was yet to print his rhapsody on the cultural significance of the poet and poetry—

Poetry is the breath and finer spirit of all knowledge. . . . Emphatically may it be said of the Poet, as Shakespeare hath said of man, "that he looks before and after." He is the rock of defence of human nature: an upholder and preserver, carrying every where with him relationship and love. (*Preface*, 1802)[5]—

but he had come to such convictions before 1802. John's monetary commitment to William's vocation indicates that he believed whole-heartedly in his brother's idea of "the Poet." It might be surmised that dedication to William gave John's life a higher purpose. For one needed no motivation other than greed for selling opium to China and tea to England.

John was palpably—one might almost say—present to his poet-brother and sister while on his voyages. Dorothy records that on 24 November 1801, William imagined being in a tempest in John's Grove, where "he had been surprized & terrified by a sudden rushing of winds which seemed to bring earth sky & lake together, as if the whole were going to enclose him in—he was glad that he was in a high Road" (*GJ* 41). On 26 March 1802, the day he wrote "My heart leaps up" and the day before composing the first four stanzas of the *Intimations Ode*, William wrote a beautiful conclusion for "When to the attractions of the busy world," the verse narrative inspired by John and his grove:

> Back to the joyless ocean thou art gone:
> And now I call the path-way by thy name
> And love the fir-grove with a perfect love.
> Thither do I repair when cloudless suns
> Shine hot or winds blow troublesome and strong;
> And there I sit at evening when the steep
> Of Silver-How, and Grasmere's silent Lake
> And one green Island gleam between the stems
> Of the close firs, a visionary scene!
> And while I gaze upon this spectacle
> Of clouded splendour, on this dream-like sight
> Of solemn loveliness, I think on thee
> My Brother, and on all which thou hast lost.
>
>                       (*P2V*, p. 566, 92–104)

"[A]ll which thou hast lost" is a poignant reflection on John's sacrifices. Besides experiences of transitory natural loveliness, John had given up a lifetime with Mary, which William claimed in February

1802, when he announced their marriage. Apparently without guilt, or concern for John's possible disappointment, William continues his meditation by imagining concord:

> Nor seldom, if I rightly guess, when Thou
> Muttering the verses which I mutter'd first
> Among the mountains, through the midnight watch
> Art pacing to and fro the Vessel's deck
> In some far region, here, while o'er my head
> At every impulse of the moving breeze
> The fir-grove murmurs with a sea-like sound,
> Alone I tread this path, for aught I know
> Timing my steps to thine, and with a store
> Of indistinguishable sympathies
> Mingling most earnest wishes for the day
> When We, and others whom we love shall meet
> A second time in Grasmere's happy Vale.
> (P2V 566–67, lines 105–17)

Because of compositional timing and the sharing of the key terms "gleam," "visionary," and "dream," Irene Tayler wonders whether these lines from John's Grove might not have been the "timely utterance" of *Ode* ("There was a time"): "To me alone there came a thought of grief: / A Timely utterance gave that thought relief, / And I again am strong" (*P2V* 272, lines 22–24).[6] It is a shrewd insight. The "thought of grief" might well have been a fear for John's death. The "Timely utterance" in John's fir grove can provide "relief" from mortal fears because William successfully imagines that they are stepping together to the beat of his verse. One recalls a comparably successful identification in "This Lime Tree Bower, My Prison," which affords Coleridge relief from his fears of lost experience with peripatetic friends:

> A delight
> Comes sudden on my heart, and I am glad
> As I myself were there![7]

About a month later, Dorothy records a fantasy of death occurring in John's Grove amid the sounds of waters:

Thursday 29th [April 1802]. . . . We . . . went to Johns Grove, sate a while at first. Afterwards William lay, & I lay in the trench under the fence—he

> with his eyes shut & listening to the waterfalls & the Birds. There was no one waterfall above another—it was a sound of waters in the air—the voice of the air. William heard me breathing & rustling now & then but we both lay still, & unseen by one another—he thought that it would be as sweet thus to lie so in the grave, to hear the *peaceful* sounds of the earth & just to know that ones dear friends were near. (*GJ* 92)

A few years later, this peculiar reflection on the finality of death worked its way into the *Ode,* as William mused upon the child's primitive intimation of immortality: "To whom the grave / Is but a lonely bed without the sense or sight / Of day or the warm light, / A place of thought where we in waiting lie" (*P2V* 274–75, ll. 120–23). What choice but to wait hopefully that John would return safely and successfully from risk-filled, sacrificial ventures?

More mundanely, William and Dorothy shared in John's tribulations over raising capital for his private investment. As a neophyte fund-raiser attempting to secure loans for his personal cargo, John was frazzled: "I can assure you," he writes to Mary, "I felt very strange & it will take some time { } before I shall feel easy under my new acquired title" (*LJW* 80). He writes to Dorothy, "I am employ'd all day in shipping men, & with Tradesmen of every discription {so} & being a new thing I find myself a little . . . at a loss— I do not go on so well as an old experienced Capt. would do" (*LJW* 98).

The family could not refuse to become involved. John requested that William sell his stock to bolster his first venture (*LJW* 12). He requested Dorothy's £80 inheritance. Finally, he reported that his outlay in borrowed money for his first voyage was between 9,000 and 10,000£ (*LJW* 93). "O what *a rich dog* they say I am to be," he wrote to Mary, "I have had 5000£ offer'd for my voyage" (*LJW* 90). That is, he might have sold his captaincy to another eligible officer and remained home. But John did not take the bird in the hand, and returned after an eighteen-month voyage in debt to his creditors.[8] To add insult to his financial injuries, the "vile and abominable Monsters at the India House" fined him £210 for his "sins during the voyage," which were selling the Company's monopoly item, camblets, a cloth made of silk and wool, to China (*LJW* 126, 215 nn. 32–33). Although his items of private trade brought back to England arose in value after a short while, he still found himself thousands of pounds in debt.

The positive financial news on his return was that Sir James Lowther, the infamous Earl of Lonsdale, had died on 24 May 1802 and repayment of his debts was being negotiated by his responsible successor, Sir William Lowther (*CMY* 173). But even the Lowther settlement was a mixed blessing for John: because of its promise, William proposed to Mary Hutchinson, and perhaps Mary Moorman is correct in assuming that Mary's sister Sara—whom John hardly knew—was expected to marry John.[9]

William and Dorothy learned of the momentous financial news in June 1802 when Lord Lowther advertised in *The Cumberland Pacquet* that he was accepting claims from those "with any demands on the late Earl" (*GJ* 239, n. to 18 June 1802). William and Dorothy were joyful, Dorothy especially so, for she had been particularly concerned about her welfare now that William was to marry. William candidly declared her present state to be one of "utter destitution" (*EY* 361). With her share of the settlement, however, Dorothy could stop depending on Richard and John for occasional and sometimes tardy stipends:

> Sunday 20th. . . . After tea we walked upon our own path for a long time. We talked sweetly together about the disposal of our riches. We lay upon the sloping Turf. Earth & sky were so lovely that they melted our very hearts. The sky to the north was of a chastened yet rich yellow fading into pale blue & streaked & scattered over with steady islands of purple melting away into shades of pink. It made my heart almost feel like a vision to me. (*GJ* 112)

Dorothy's tender feelings were soon bruised by an acrimonious exchange of letters with brother Richard on the quid pro quo of John's monetary demands.

The tension began when William chided Richard for speaking to him on monetary matters "as you were speaking to a Child," hoping that this would be "the last time I shall have occasion to speak on this subject" (*EY* 371). William then presumed to advise his brother—the attorney and professional man of business—on how to proceed with a suit on just compensation against the Lowther estate for their nearly twenty years of financial distress. Richard recommended that they have patience. William accused his brother of sounding like a "hackney m[a]n of business" (*EY* 372) and threatened to separate from Richard, John, and Christopher, if they decided on redress in a court of law. William became imperious:

> If without previously consulting me such step be taken, or any measures resorted to which seem manifestly to lead thereto, I apprise you that I

immediately divide from you upon the business, and shall act singly upon my own judgement. (*EY* 373)

Richard became haughty. He informed William that he had been in consultation with "Men of learning and of the soundest Judgment who are men of Experience also"; that he never intended to make their application for redress a legal disputation, not for William's fears that poor people have little chance against the rich in a court of law, but rather because their claim included charges without sound legal precedent, such as interest on principal and legal fees, which comprised over half of the family's claim of more than £10,000; and that, finally, if they split up, they were certainly to lose any hope of a satisfactory conclusion to the matter (*EY* 686–87). Richard concludes:

> One would almost suppose from your Letter that you were apprehensive I was as it is vulgarly called wanting *a Job*. No believe me I have no such wish. . . . I will be obliged to you [to] say whe[the]r you approve or disapprove of my future Proceedings. For I have no desire to act in a Matter where my exertions are thought nothing of." (*EY* 687) [10]

In December 1802, John relayed the welcome news that Richard was dealing with Lord Lowther's business agent over a settlement that would provide at least £3000–4000 by Christmas (*LJW* 131), which indicated that the Wordsworth claim would be given priority over others. Richard's computation of the family's claim on the Lonsdale estate amounted to £10,388.6.8 (*LJW* 133), but total demands were in excess of £200,000 and no promise would be made on the final amount or the date of retribution. When Christmas passed without a payment, John began looking to his interests. His next voyage being imminent, John met with Lowther's agent in February 1803 and extracted from him a promise "to pay immediately three thousand pounds on our acct," John wrote to Dorothy, "in consequence of my *speedy* departure to India this was intended by him to serve me—." He assures Dorothy that Richard will provide her "any Security you may want with respect to that part of the money I shall take out" and then discusses the wisdom of the family purchasing a share of the *Abergavenny*, that would soon be up for sale, because it will be worth "2,500£ & 2,700, to me" (*LJW* 137). The promised £3000 was passed in March from Lowther through Richard to John.

On 28 March, Richard contradicted John's assurances on security when he wrote to William that he refused to *"make myself liable to all* [John's] *creditors,"* and thus it would be up to William and Dorothy to let John know if you "will let him have your shares or not" (*EY* 384, n. 1). Silence followed. On 16 April, John wrote William a business letter:

> it is absolutely necessary that I should have the whole of the three thousand pounds or I had better resign the command of the ship for if I have not money it is not possible that I make money & it happens unfortunatly that most of the goods which we take out to China require ready money for the purchace of them— I have got the command of the ship under such favourable circumstances that if any money is to be made in the Service I must make it— With respect to the security I certainly can never ask Richd to become { ? } security for all my debts—& for this reason that I already owe him two thousand pounds & 1,500 to Captn Wordsworth—which they have lent me on . . . my own security alone— . . . I am not asking you for the whole of your property for god knows that if the whole sum which Lord L. owes us was paid & you were to offer me the whole of it I would not take it because I know there is a risque—every person who is concerned in trade must have a risque. (*LJW* 139)

John's point is clear: you who are to gain from my success owe me your support. On 20 April 1803, a few days after John's letter to William, Richard was writing to Lowther asking for an additional £1000 for John's use, as the £3000 "will not be adequate and sufficient" to compensate for John's past financial losses as well as to invest in his next voyage (*EY* 387).

Speaking for herself, Dorothy was perturbed with being ignored by Richard, who seemed always to be holding her purse strings. A year earlier, she had unsuccessfully implored him to let her know what had happened to the meager £10 John had promised to send her semiannually—and which she had already spent—but she wrote thrice to no avail. On 22 April 1803, she wrote to Richard asking if she were correct in assuming that he would underwrite her investment in John's voyage (*EY* 386). Receiving no response, she wrote again to emphasize that she refused to invest without Richard's security:

> for this reason; that if I we[re to]lose it I should forfeit my independence without having any means of reinstating myself in it. I thought you could not possibly have any objection to give me the security I desired if there

were little or no risque, and that if there *were* risque, . . . you would think me the last person in the world who ought to be called upon by my Brothers to bear it. . . . I wrote to you in order that I might be positively assured from yourself that I was right in this supposition. I received your answer yesterday. You say "the question is *who* is to support John? Am I to run all the risque? William and you seem to think that I ought—John, Christopher, and myself think otherwise." To this I reply . . . I told you that I thought I ought not to be called upon to bear *any part* of the risque. I still entertain the same opinion, . . . Having said this much I dismiss this matter entirely.

Except for one further matter, optimistically supposing that Richard will secure her investment: "As John is to take out this money, I have now only to ask, if he has provided any means for the payment of interest during his absence, and if he has not, whether you will consent that I should draw upon you half yearly for it" (*EY* 388–89).

Dorothy prepared an attachment on the matter to be forwarded to John:

I am sure, my dear Brother, that I need not speak of my affection for you, of the deep love I bear you, and you know well that there are few sacrifices that I should be unwilling to make on that score. But this is not an affair to be weighed in the balance of my affection for you, nor have I been called upon to advance the money on that score. It is an affair of prudence. As such, I have no doubt, and merely as such you have considered it, though we have come to different conclusions. (*EY* 389)

After some small talk about health and weather, Dorothy adds an anecdote that must have seemed oddly teasing:

The Sympsons and old Molly never forget to inquire after you. Molly says "if I could but see Maister John I would send all the money that ever I have for a venture with him! ["]—you must know she has more than seven pounds. (*EY* 390)

John failed to respond to any letters. William and Dorothy were understandably anxious for his safety and probably uneasy about their disagreement. The Peace of Amiens broke down 16 May 1803 and "now that the War is certain we are still more anxious to know," Dorothy wrote to Richard on 22 May 1803, "whether he has sailed or not." She also asked again if "John had made any provision for the payment of the Interest of my share of the money during his absence, and if not whether you would permit me to draw upon you for it" (*EY* 390–91). Richard did not respond. It must have become quite clear that both John and Richard were upset. John departed on 6 May 1803 on his second voyage to China. He would not return until 6 August 1804. The total investment of the family circle seems to have been about £7827 (*CMY* 212).[11]

As practical or "prudent" as Dorothy's decision to withhold her funds may have been, it was disregarded because John *would* have the money. There is no evidence of any interest being paid to Dorothy. After John's death, William admits that he did not know if their money had been insured. In response to Beaumont's anticipation of William's need for money—in case he had invested in his brother's venture too heavily—William reports *almost* candidly of the investment:

> Lord Lonsdale . . . died, and the present Lord Lowther paid to my Father's estate £8500. Of this sum I believe that 1,800 apiece will come to my Sister and my self, at least would have come: but 3,000 was lent out to our poor Brother, I mean taken from the whole sum which was about 1,200 more than his share, which 1200 belonged to Dorothy and me. This 1,200 we freely lent him; whether it was ensured or no I do not know; but I dare say it will prove to be the case; we did not however stipulate for its being ensured. (*EY* 546)

There was no need for William to tell Beaumont the entire truth about Dorothy's haggling over the issue of insurance.

The highlight of John's second voyage was a martial engagement between the East India Company's merchant convoy with a formidable French naval squadron in the Strait of Malacca off the island of Pulo A'ur. On its journey home from China and unaccompanied by the routine escort of men-of-war from the Royal Navy, the Company's laden China fleet of sixteen Indiamen and eleven India-bound country-trade vessels faced down a French squadron on 15 February 1804. The French squadron laying in wait for the promise of British booty consisted of the 74-gun *Marengo*, the 40-gun frigate *Belle Poule*, the 36-gun frigate *Semillante*, the 22-gun corvette *Berceau*, and a 16-gun brig, all under the command of Rear Admiral Charles Durand-Linois. Linois had been informed by a spy in Canton that he should expect twenty-four merchant vessels unescorted by warships of the Royal Navy, but when twenty-seven appeared Linois was

confused and consequently hesitated in his attack. The senior officer of the Company fleet, Nathanial Dance, raised the Royal Navy's
blue ensign on his three lead vessels to feign a martial presence. Linois fell for the ruse, hesitating three or four miles distant from the
fleet until about 1:00 P.M. the next day, when he decided to attack by
separating the fleet from its apparent escort. Dance then executed a
move of skill, cunning, and courage worthy of Admiral Nelson, and
made even more impressive in light of the reputation of Company
crews for sloppy seamanship and undisciplined captains[12] on their
lightly armed vessels.

Dance's description of the confrontation is found in his letter to
the Company dated 8 August 1804, which appeared verbatim in the
*Gentleman's Magazine* of October 1804:

> At one P.M. finding they proposed to attack, and endeavour to cut off
> our rear, I made the signal to tack and bear down on him, and engage
> in succession, the Royal George being the leading ship, the Ganges next,
> and then the Earl Camden. This manoeuvre was correctly performed,
> and we stood towards him under a press of sail. The enemy then formed
> in a very close line, and opened their fire on the headmost ships, which
> was not returned by us till we approached him nearer. The Royal George
> bore the brunt of the action, and got as near the enemy as he would
> permit him; the Ganges and the Earl Camden opened their fire as soon
> as the guns could have effect; but, before any other ship could get into
> the action, the enemy hauled their wind, and stood away to the Eastward
> under all the sail they could set. At two P.M. I made the signal for a gen-
> eral chase, and we pursued them till four P.M. when, fearing a longer
> pursuit would carry us too far from the mouth of the Straits, and consid-
> ering the immense property at stake, I made the signal to tack, and at
> eight P.M. we anchored. . . . I must state, that every ship was cleared and
> prepared for action; and, as I had communication with almost all of
> them during the two days we were in presence of the enemy, I found
> them unanimous in the determined resolution to defend the valuable
> property entrusted to their charge to the last extremity, with a full con-
> viction of the successful event of their exertions; and this spirit was fully
> seconded by the gallant ardour of all our officers and ships' companies.[13]

It was fortunate for Dance that his vessels did not get close enough
for the badly bluffed French admiral to realize that he was being
pursued by undermanned merchant vessels with puny eighteen-
pound cannons. Consequently, Dance lived to become a folk hero
rather than a fool who lost his head in risking an entire fleet and a
combined cargo of tea, silk, and porcelain valued at £6,000,000.

Reports of the engagement between the China Fleet and Linois reached the London papers in late July. *The Sun* confirmed on 26 July 1804 that "the whole merit . . . of this most gallant achievement, belongs to the Officers and Crews of the Indiamen," and not to the Royal Navy's men-of-war: "when it is considered with what disadvantage Ships deeply laden contend against vessels constructed solely for the purpose of War, this Victory must be allowed to add greatly indeed to our Naval reputation."[14] When the fleet returned to London in August 1804, Dance was received at Court by King George and knighted, the East India Company rewarded him with a pension of £500 per annum, and the Bombay Insurance Company presented him with an award of £5,000. John F. Timins, the captain of the lead ship, the *Royal George*, received £1,000 from the Company for his bravery in action, and the remainder of the vessel captains, including John Wordsworth, received £500 pounds each, a commemorative plate and an impressive citation (see figure 2) stressing the international, financial, and historical significance of their sensational engagement:

> The deliberate Courage and Seamanlike Conduct of Captain Dance senior officer of *Captain Timins,* who in the most gallant manner led the Fleet into action and bore the Brunt of the Engagement and all of the Commanders Officers and Men who under the favour of Divine Providence preserved the Sixteen Sail of the Honorable East India Company's Ships with Eleven more belonging to the Merchants of India, from the formidable Enemy who had sailed from the Isles of France and Batavia for the avowed and almost sole purpose of intercepting them a noble incitement to provoke his Valour and Enterprize considered either with relation to the value of the booty not less than 6 millions sterling or to the incalculable Loss when his success would have brought on the Commercial and Public Interests of the British Empire.[15]

*The Sun* commented wittily of the well-publicized affair:[16] "The French have long been admired for their excellence in *dancing,* but Admiral Linois has found that our East India Company has a better DANCE than he knows, and that British Sailors of every description are good at a *Ball.*"[17]

Across the channel, Linois was vilified for cowardice. Napoleon condemned him for showing "want of courage of mind."[18] Seeking to vindicate his judgment, Linois wrote to Dance to learn "*the number of Guns & of men* which were on board the fleet of Indiamen." Dance admitted in private conversation that there had been real

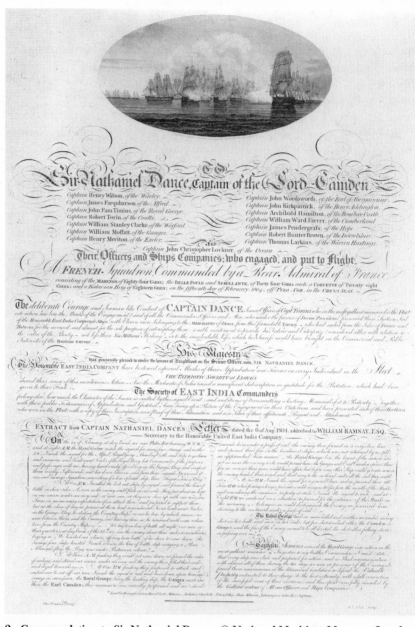

2. Commendation to Sir Nathaniel Dance. © National Maritime Museum, London. John Wordsworth's name is at the top of the second column.

danger fortunately averted: "he was convinced that Linois . . . would have been taken though He might have destroyed an Indiaman or two before He surrendered.—He said Had Linois broken through his fleet in the *night time* before the day of the action, He cannot pretend to say but that Linois might have done much mischief, but day light put an end to all apprehension."[19]

John Wordsworth's log for this worthy adventure reads:

Feby 15—Cleared ship for action. At 1 PM Commodore made signal to keep in close order. At 2 signal for forming line ahead, the strangers appearing to be a 74 [?] gun ship, frigates and a brig on the lea quarter. The chasing ships made signal for an enemy. At 5 signal to conceal all lights during night At daylight enemy on the weather beam distant about 4 miles At 11 signal to prepare for action Got two guns forward about this time enemy began to engage Royal George who was headmost ship.

Feby 16—At 1 PM we were all nearly within gunshot when the enemy bore up crowded all sail and ran to the northward. Made sail in chase as did the rest of the fleet. The Royal George who being headmost ship stood the heat of the engagement at 2 PM signal for medical assistance. Perceived several shot holes in her sails and hull. In tacking we fired two guns at the enemy supposing ourselves within gunshot. At 5 PM Commodore made signal to prepare to anchor At 6 enemy nearly out of sight At 10 PM anchored At daylight weighed and stood after Commodore.[20]

John's personal report to cousin Capt. John Wordsworth records that Linois's intention was to destroy the merchant fleet and share the spoils with his squadron (*LJW* 141). As the log for 16 February indicates, John had his gunners fire a few volleys at the tails of the French, but John was hardly bigheaded about the event.

Charles Lamb recalls John's earlier "wish that he might meet a Frenchman in the seas; & it seem'd to be accomplished, all to his heart's desire."[21] But after two unsuccessful voyages, and in despair over his financial losses, John's reaction to the nation's adulation was muted: "You will see by today's papers the flattering mention that is made of the China fleet," he wrote to Captain Wordsworth, characteristically failing to mention that he was praised by name with the other captains, while ruefully concluding; "I can assure you it gives me very little pleasure compared to the solid advantage that I might obtain by procuring a Bombay & China voyage *could I get one*" (*LJW* 143–44). Dorothy wrote on 18 July 1804, only a few days before the story appeared in the London press, that the family was "anxious" about John, fearful that, in addition to all of the natural dangers of life at sea, he might "fall into the hands of the French" (*EY* 489).


## 2. "THE WATERS OF THE DEEP / GATHERING UPON US"

William never referred to his brother's battle at sea or to John's rightful share of the nation's gratitude. Biographers have kept the silence,[22] but the incident as well as his silence will here receive consideration. One can look to the poetry William wrote during John's time at sea for more anticipations of the doom foreseen in "Michael." The practiced empathy William used to share in his brother's experience is also evidence that the many dangers of John's life were on his mind. Finally, it is unlikely that the poet of the following lines from *Home at Grasmere* could be oblivious to his brother's engagement at sea:

> I cannot at this moment [1800] read a tale
> Of two brave Vessels matched in deadly fight
> And fighting to the death, but I am pleased
> More than a wise Man ought to be; I wish,
> I burn, I struggle, and in soul am there.
>
> (MS B, lines 929–33, pp. 96, 98)

This remarkable anticipation of Whitman's famous lines from *Song of Myself*, "I am the man, I suffer'd, I was there,"[23] alerts one to pause on the significance of what Wordsworth is saying about his imagined and imaginative experience. This is not emotion recollected in tranquillity as a stimulus to composition, but rather sympathetic identification with the aggression required in John's life, which is an aggression William shares but sublimates:

> But me hath Nature tamed and bade me seek
> For other agitations or be calm,
> Hath dealt with me as with a turbulent stream—
>
> . . . . . . . . . . . . . . . . . .
>
> Her deliberate Voice
> Hath said, "Be mild and love all gentle things;
> Thy glory and thy happiness be there.
> Yet fear (though thou confide in me) no want
> Of aspirations which have been—of foes

To wrestle with and victory to complete,
Bounds to be leapt and darkness to explore.
That which enflamed thy infant heart—the love,
The longing, the contempt, the undaunted quest—
These shall survive, though changed their office, these
Shall live; it is not in their power to die."

(MS B, 934–52, p. 98)

The Vision on Mt. Snowdon, the related Analogy Passage excluded from the five-book *Prelude,* and the Dream of the Arab from Book 5 can be read as sublimated transformations of the "undaunted quest[s]" that had "not in their power to die" in the development of Wordsworth's poetic autobiography. The lines on his imaginative experience in John's Grove reveal that John's perilous time at sea aroused William. Books on the travails of sea voyagers are read for inspiration, and spots of time reveal the mind to be triumphant over literal and figurative waters.

Duncan Wu's text of the five-book *Prelude* will be a convenient editorial construct for organizing the following analysis of biographical and compositional concerns flooding upon Wordsworth during this period of John's perilous voyages. As relevant is Coleridge's imminent departure for Malta in March 1804, which would also entail a dangerous sea journey and become the immediate cause for Wordsworth's rush to complete the form of the *Prelude* he now envisioned. At an earlier stage of his autobiographical project, Wordsworth provoked himself with memories of chastisement:

> Meanwhile my hope has been that I might fetch
> Reproaches from my former years, whose power
> May spur me on, in manhood now mature,
> To honourable toil.

(*2PP,* part 1, 450–53)

Now, in late February–early March 1804, tales of voyagers reacting to mortal distress assist Wordsworth in dealing with anxieties aroused by the voyages of John and Coleridge. Although the timing of this prolific compositional period seems eerily associated with John's actual engagement at sea, this was not a matter of prophecy. Newspaper accounts provided a daily diet of hostile action on the trade routes of the East and West Indies to give anyone reasonable fears for loved ones. In Wordsworth's case, the seas threatened everything that mattered: the financial and vocational futures promised by John's voyages and Coleridge's future mentoring.

As Wu's text of the five-book *Prelude* clarifies, the passages that suggest the greatest anxiety about the dangers of water, the analogy passage and the dream of the Arab, were left out of the poem, probably for thematic redundancy. The spot-of-time on the Drowned Man, which had caused anxiety and deep compositional confusion in the Two-Part *Prelude*, becomes neutralized by the now-alledged power of the boy's imagination over the terror of water:

> At length, the dead man, mid that beauteous scene
> Of trees and hills and water, bolt upright
> Rose with his ghastly face—a spectre-shape
> Of terror even. And yet no vulgar fear,
> Young as I was (a child of eight years old),
> Possessed me, for my inner eye had seen
> Such sights before, among the shining streams
> Of fairyland, and forests of romance.
> Thence came a spirit hallowing what I saw
> With decoration and ideal grace,
> A dignity, a smoothness, like the works
> Of Grecian art and purest poesy.[24]

The Vision on Snowdon, which begins the fifth and final book of the *Five-Book Prelude,* features Wordsworth's battle of mind against the sea. Jonathan Wordsworth calls attention to its textual sources in Wordsworth's own *Descriptive Sketches* and "A Night-Piece," in Beattie's *Minstrel,* and in Coleridge's "Kubla Khan," wittily concluding that "Wordsworth . . . hardly needed to go near a mountain, let alone have a specific occasion in mind" to compose this his most famous spot-of-time.[25] There is no need to reintroduce the entire series of passages J. Wordsworth considers, but a few of the discrepancies between the primary source and the Vision—some of which he considers and some not—suggest that while mountain vision is the goal of the Snowdon passage, the power of the "enchafed flood"[26] must be overcome before a transcendent vision can be achieved.

The chief differences between the passage of origin in *Descriptive Sketches (DS)* and the Vision on Snowdon are these: the *DS* passage records a morning scene in the Alps, while the Vision records a night scene in Snowdonia, Wales; the *DS* scene's mist covers an Alpine valley; the Vision's mist obscures the Irish Sea; the *DS* passage

introduces no allegorical interpretation of the descriptive sketch,
while the Vision grandly finds an image of transcendental imagination serving as a conduit between physical and metaphysical worlds.
The point of changing locations from the Alps to Snowdon is to introduce what Wordsworth below calls "the real sea" into the experience. The related passages include the evidence to consider,
especially the imagined sea of *DS* and the Irish Sea of the Vision on
Snowdon:

*Descriptive Sketches* (1793)

'Tis morn—with gold the verdant mountain glows
More high, the snowy peaks with hues of rose.
Far stretched beneath the many-tinted hills,
A mighty waste of mist the valley fills,
A solemn sea, whose vales and mountains round
Stand motionless, to awful silence bound.
A gulf of gloomy blue, that opens wide
And bottomless, divides the midway tide;
Like leaning masts of stranded ships appear
The pines that near the coast their summits rear;
Of cabins, woods, and lawns a pleasant shore
Bounds calm and clear the chaos still and hoar.
Loud through that midway gulf ascending, sound
Unnumbered streams with hollow roar profound.

(492–505)

The associated passage from the Vision on Mt. Snowdon in the 1804
*Prelude* reads:

I looked about, and lo!
The moon stood naked in the heavens at height
Immense above my head, and on the shore
I found myself of a huge sea of mist,
That meek and silent rested at my feet.
A hundred hills their dusky backs upheaved
All over this still ocean; and beyond,
Far, far beyond, the vapours shot themselves
In headlands, tongues, and promontory shapes,
Into the sea—the real sea, that seemed
To dwindle and give up its majesty,
Usurped upon as far as sight could reach.
Meanwhile, the moon looked down upon this show
In single glory, and we stood, the mist

> Touching our very feet. And from the shore
> At distance not the third part of a mile
> Was a blue chasm, a fracture in the mist,
> A deep and gloomy breathing-place through which
> Mounted the roar of waters, torrents, streams
> Inseparable, roaring with one voice.
> The universal spectacle throughout
> Was shaped for admiration and delight,
> Grand in itself alone, but in that breach
> Through which the homeless voice of waters rose,
> That dark deep thoroughfare, had Nature lodged
> The soul, the imagination of the whole.
>
> (5BP, 5.40–65)

The majesty of the Irish Sea, "the real sea," is "usurped upon," in fact, it "dwindles," beneath the cover of mist, which "meek and silent" rests, in obeisance, at the poet's feet. The "fracture" in the vapour, the "deep and gloomy breathing place" "Through which the homeless voice of waters rose" is a displacement of the "seething breathing chasm" of "Kubla Khan." One might say that the Vision is Wordsworth's poetic interpretation of "Kubla Khan," perhaps intended as a tribute to Coleridge upon his departure for Malta, but as much a domestication of the poem's ominous cultural origins from the mysterious and threatening Orient, where John was venturing, to the familiar West. The "sacred river" erupting from the "breathing" chasm of Coleridge's poem sinks "in tumult to a lifeless ocean: / And 'mid this tumult Kubla heard from far / Ancestral voices prophesying war!" Wordsworth's "real sea" and the "homeless voice of waters" rising through the "dark deep thoroughfare" suggest a sublime bonding between "soul" and "imagination." In the 1805 *Prelude*, Wordsworth will explain:

> A meditation rose in me that night
> Upon the lonely Mountain when the scene
> Had pass'd away, and it appear'd to me
> The perfect image of a mighty Mind,
> Of one that feeds upon infinity,
> That is exalted by an underpresence,
> The sense of God, or whatsoe'er is dim
> Or vast in its own being
>
> (1805, 13.66–73)

We also learn that this "Power," which Nature displays in this wondrous mental landscape, is "a genuine Counterpart / And Brother of the glorious faculty / Which higher minds bear with them as their own; / This is the very spirit in which they deal / With all the objects of the universe" (13. 84–92). A power in nature is capable of imposing meaning upon its physical elements—sound, form, color, light—through transient shaping; the human power of imagination, as if authorized by Nature's example, likewise exercises omnipotence over the material universe of things and sensations. The Vision on Snowdon brings together those "Brother[ly]" powers to show that, as Wordsworth will claim in the 1805 poem, "the mind / Is lord and master, and that outward sense / Is but the obedient servant of her will" (11.271–73).

When Wordsworth broke from the Vision on Snowdon of the Fifth Book to compose the analogy passage[27]—as if gathering more evidence for claims of mental omnipotence over sublime landscapes—the selection of passages suggests that comparable anxieties of death by water were meant to be imagined away by aesthetic grace. The first of these records a storm that ravaged the environs of Lake Coniston:

> It was a day
> Upon the edge of autumn, fierce with storm;
> The wind blew through the hills of Coniston
> Compressed, as in a tunnel; from the lake
> Bodies of foam took flight, and the whole vale
> Was wrought into commotion high and low—
> Mist flying up and down, bewildered showers,
> Ten thousand thousand waves, mountains and crags,
> And darkness, and the sun's tumultuous light.
> Green leaves were rent in handfulls from the trees,
> The mountains all seemed silent, din so near
> Pealed in the traveller's ear, the clouds ran wild,
> The horse and rider staggered in the blast,
> And he who looked upon the stormy lake
> Had fear for boat or vessel where none was.

This imitation of an ocean storm is crowned by a border image[28] of protective, "unmutilated" mastery, "bridging the whole vale" with "colossal stride," which yet is of "substance thin as dreams":

> Meanwhile, by what strange chance I cannot tell,
> What combination of the wind and clouds,
> A large unmutilated rainbow stood

> Immoveable in heaven, kept standing there,
> With a colossal stride bridging the whole vale.
> The substance thin as dreams, lovelier than day,
> Amid the deafening uproar stood unmoved,
> Sustained itself through many minutes space,
> As if it were pinned down by adamant.
>
> (*5BP*, 33–56)

The rainbow, "thin as dreams, lovelier than day," is a rendering of God's biblical promise to save the earth from future destruction by water: "I shall sustain my covenant with you," Yahweh said to Noah, "never again will all living creatures be destroyed by the waters of a flood, never again will there be a flood to lay waste the earth" (Gen. 9:11).[29] But Wordsworth makes the image his own by making it "unmutilated" and thus potent. Perhaps it is another border image of the father promising his protection from the threatening storm with this sign of presence. The image surely bears a marked contrast with the "mutilated bower" of "Nutting," which saw the boy-child attack the passive grove of hazel trees, "with milk-white clusters hung," after which he "Exult[ed], rich beyond the wealth of kings," until pangs of conscience provoked by the "intruding sky" denied him his psychological victory.[30] For today, at least, the poet could be calmed by a rainbow above "the stormy lake" and his empathic "fear for boat or vessel where none was" could be quieted by imagination.[31]

Wordsworth then recalls incidents from travel narratives that comparably offer a lesson in mastering death with hope, such as the story of Sir Humphrey Gilbert:

> that bold voyager,
> When after one disastrous wreck he took
> His station in the pinnace, for the sake
> Of honour and her crew's engagement,
> And they who followed in the second ship,
> The larger brigantine which he had left,
> Beheld him while amid the storm he sate
> Upon the open deck of his small bark
> In calmness with a book upon his knee—
> To use the language of the Chronicle,
> A soldier of Jesus Christ, undismayed—
> The ship and he, a moment afterwards,
> Engulfed, and seen no more.
>
> (*Analogy passage*, 93–105)

Several other passages of land and sea voyagers are gathered from books that Wordsworth probably read for the first time now in late February 1804: John Churchill's *A Collection of Voyages and Travels* (1704), William Dampier's *A New Voyage round the World* (1697), Richard Hakluyt's *The Principall Navigations, Voyages, and Discoveries of the English Nation* (1589), and Mungo Park's *Travels in the Interior Districts of Africa* (1798).[32] The Dream of the Arab, however, represents a challenge to this gathered hope.

If the rainbow passage recalls the Creator's covenant "never to destroy / The Earth again by flood, nor let the Sea / Surpass his bounds, nor Rain to drown the World" (*Paradise Lost*, 11.892–94), the Dream of the Arab suggests that the deluge was permitted in the unconscious, where daytime anxieties became the realities of night. Douglas B. Wilson rightly argues that the Arab dream is a "nightmare through which the poet's unconscious discloses itself."[33]

Jane Worthington Smyser established the importance of a dream of René Descartes, reported in Adrien Baillet's biography, *Vie de Descartes* (1691), for suggesting the dichotomy between science and poetry that were to become the images of stone and shell in Wordsworth's Dream of the Arab: "Descartes, like the dreamer in *The Prelude*, beheld two books, one of which contained all scientific knowledge, while the other, which he valued more highly, contained all the inspired wisdom of poetry."[34] Perhaps this finding has been given too much importance in that it ignores the dynamism of Wordsworth's Dream. Although it is generally believed that Coleridge probably passed on the narrative of the dream to Wordsworth, and thus becomes the "Friend" of the passage who narrates the dream as his, there seems to be no evidence that either Wordsworth or Coleridge read Baillet.[35] The more important point is that the alleged influence ends with the idea of the two books: there is no danger in Descartes's dream, no deluge to threaten the existence of intellectual and imaginative creations, no altruistic mission to save human works from natural forces, and no sacrificial madness to dignify the mission. Wilson explains fully the far more important influence of Cervantes on the passage, emphasizing that Wordsworth's mission is far less quixotic than Don Quixote's jousting with windmills. But it is the pragmatism of Kenneth R. Johnston's reading of the dream that is most relevant to my argument: "For the dream is preeminently a *vocation*," Johnston says, "a story about the proper choice of one's life's work. . . . Simply put, Wordsworth's love for

poetry is closely accompanied by a feeling of its frailty (its unproduc-
tiveness, its selfishness), and this feeling, rebounding from his help-
less love, results in a fantasy of heroically saving it from apocalyptic
destruction."[36] The turn I will take with the dream being vocational
is more biographically grounded in Wordsworth's fear of the sea
being a literal threat to his financial and vocational futures and the
Arab himself being an altruistic functionary, such as brother John
Wordsworth.

William is the poet of the dream, one who produces the works
that "lodge in shrines so frail" (48) and require the protection of a
Quixote-like figure, such as John, to protect them against the nightmare of apocalypse, the fear of which, it must be emphasized, had
now a strong foothold in reality. The dreamer in the narrative is
Coleridge, who wishes to join the Arab/John in protecting the stone
of geometry and the conch of poetry:

> My Friend continued, "Strange as it may seem,
> I wonder'd not, although I plainly saw
> The one to be a Stone, th' other a Shell,
> Nor doubted once but that they both were Books,
> Having a perfect faith in all that pass'd.
> A wish was now engender'd in my fear
> To cleave unto this Man, and I begg'd leave
> To share his errand with him. On he pass'd,
> Not heeding me; I follow'd, and took note
> That he look'd often backward with wild look,
> Grasping his twofold treasure to his side.
>
> . . . . . . . . . . . . . . . . .
>
> I fancied that he was the very Knight
> Whose tale Cervantes tells, yet not the Knight,
> But, was an Arab of the Desart, too;
> Of these was neither, and was both at once.["]
>
> (*1805*, 5.110–26; p. 165)

John, like Quixote, somewhat simple and yet ennobled by sacrificing
his life on behalf of the great good of his brother's vocation, toils
selflessly against the dangers of the flood:

> ["]I saw
> A glittering light, and ask'd him whence it came;
> 'It is,' said he, 'the waters of the deep

Gathering upon us'; quickening then his pace,
He left me; I call'd after him aloud,
He heeded not; but with his twofold charge
Beneath his arm, before me full in view
I saw him riding o'er the Desart Sands,
With the fleet waters of the drowning world
In chace of him, whereat I wak'd in terror,
And saw the Sea before me; and the Book,
In which I had been reading, at my side."

                                                    (*1805*, 5.128–39)

Wordsworth recovers from the Dream of his Friend with a description of the type of Man he believes the Arab to be: one, "craz'd / By love and feeling and internal thought, / Protracted among endless solitudes" (144–47); or, like John, the "silent poet," who gave up all to work for his brother:

And I have scarcely pitied him; have felt
A reverence for a Being thus employ'd;
And thought that in the blind and awful lair
Of such a madness reason did lie couch'd.
Enow there are on the earth to take in charge
Their Wives, their Children, and their virgin Loves,
Or whatsoever else the heart holds dear;
Enow to think of these; yea, will I say,
In sober contemplation of the approach
Of such great overthrow, made manifest
By certain evidence, that I, methinks,
Could share that Maniac's anxiousness, could go
Upon like errand. Oftentimes, at least,
Me hath such deep entrancement half-possess'd,
When I have held a volume in my hand,
Poor earthly casket of immortal Verse!
Shakespeare, or Milton, Labourers divine.

                                                    (*1805*, 5.149–65)

But it was William's role to join the ranks of "Labourers divine" and to receive the full-hearted support of one crazed with love and the quest for meaning in his own life. The admiring, but far less devoted, Dreamer awakens before he or the poet learn if the Maniac Arab is successful in protecting the Stone and the Shell from extinction. The conclusion, however, would soon be revealed.

## 3. "A Young Man who was lost"

Despite the martial acclamations for the skirmish with Linois, John's second voyage was also financially unsuccessful. Thus, no money could be repaid to the family and one must conclude that William and Dorothy remained ignorant of its surety. John wrote to Capt. John Wordsworth after his return that "Opium and Quicksilver were the only things in the China market that sold to profit" (*LJW* 143), but apparently not for him. Or perhaps he was keeping his hands clean by not engaging in the drug trade, as his employers would have expected. His homebound private cargo being low-priced black and green teas, the best he could now hope to do is "make up for the great loss which I sustained last voyage" (*LJW* 143).

John's immediate campaign upon returning from his second voyage in August 1804 was to get the best voyage the Service had to offer for his third venture as captain. He got to Charles Grant's ear immediately and met with William Wilberforce, philanthropist, M.P., and friend of the family since attending Cambridge University with uncle William Wordsworth. Within a few weeks John was writing to Captain Wordworth of "succeeding in getting a voyage far beyond my expectation I could almost say my wishes":

> I have been ill and well, well and ill according as my hopes have been raisd or depressed but however it has been of this service to me that I have found and made friends that are very powerful and very willing to serve me— In the first place I must inform you that I have almost a certain . . . prospect of getting for my next voyage a Bombay and China voyage thro' Mr. Grant who will be Chairman next year Mr. Wilberforce is my great friend there and had I applied to him sooner I should have had a Bombay and China voyage on Mr. Grant's the Deputy's nomination— (*LJW* 147)

John wrote to Dorothy of his "very powerful" friends "being willing to assist me," principally, "Mr Wilberforce who is the great friend & Brother labourer in the same vineyard with Mr. Grant the Chairman of the Court of directors" (*LJW* 148). As noted in Part I, Grant and fellow Claphamites were interested in extending patronage to John to further their rehabilitative moral ends. As Grant's son, Robert, expressed his family's understanding of life: "the desire of being ascendant, and the desire of multiplying retainers and connections—

the love of power and patronage—are as consonant to human nature, as it is consonant to vegetable nature that a tree should shoot its branches into the air."[37] John was now in the shade of Grant's morality tree. Wilberforce also saw an opportunity to reclaim in John a young man for Christ. Wilberforce "called to mind," Thomas Clarkson wrote to the Wordsworth family after John's death, "your Brother[']s modest and unaffected Manner; he considered himself as the Patron of a Young Man who was lost."[38]

At least temporarily, matters looked more promising for John. He would not have to wait for his dream excursion; the powers that be were prepared to offer it to him now. One of John's less venturesome peers turned down a new voyage the East India Company had devised, because it would require navigating one of the smaller rivers of India to reach its market. While John's cautious peer believed this an unacceptable risk for a large vessel,[39] John leapt at the opportunity:

> the Chairman sent for me and . . . congratulated me on having got what he conce[i]ved to be the best voyage in the Service he told me that I should have . . . every advantage that the Bombay Ships had and the probability of a great many more . . . he has sent for me several times since I first saw him and offerd to send letters overland or to afford me any assistance in that or any other way in his power— I have the greatest confidence that this voyage will turn out something very good if not great. (*LJW* 150)

Captain John's table on the *Abergavenny* would be filled with forty paying passengers en route to India; John felt assured "of doing well with [his] outward bound investment," because comparable voyages had lately turned a 40 to 50 percent profit; he would have "as much cotton" as he wished for his private freight in addition to opium and rice; he would take on homeward bound passengers; and "as much Iron and Steel as I like upon my own terms" (*LJW* 150–51). All of this was wonderful news to everyone awaiting repayment of old money and holding hopes of making more.

John amassed almost £20,000 in investments for the upcoming voyage, including the previous investment of William and Dorothy, who were apparently content to "let it ride," as we say, without further comment or inquiry. With a cargo valued at £200,000, and some sixty-two chests of dollars weighing in at 265,000 ounces and valued at £70,000, the *Abergavenny* was to be one of the richest vessels ever to sail to India under the Company flag. With the magnitude of his investment and the unqualified support of the Company management, John and his supporters had every reason to expect, as he wrote exultantly to William before sailing on 24 January 1805 from Portsmouth: "I have no doubt but that I shall make a very good voyage of it if not a *very great* one—at least this is the general opinion" (*LJW* 155).

Prior to John's fatal voyage, then, the family situation could be described as follows: William and Dorothy were still holding an empty bag where their inheritance should have been. There is no record of their willingly investing in any of John's three voyages, except the first, and certainly not the last. William recognized an obligation to John and therefore quietly succumbed to his will. Dorothy did not, even though she would be an equal beneficiary of John's success. His campaign to get the most promising third voyage was related to this family situation. There is no reason to doubt William's report that when they met with John in London following his first voyage John kept repeating, "Oh! . . . I have thought of you and nothing but you; if ever of myself and my bad success it was only on your account."

John's third voyage was thus meaningful for returning to Grasmere. He was gambling with his dearest family relationships for business. All of their money had now taken on an emotional coloring. John would soon be meditating upon these complications during the last hours he spent at the helm. As in time-lapse photography, William would be reflecting upon the same material issues that were to underwrite his vocational future when he composed "Elegiac Stanzas."

## 4. VERSIONS OF "A DEEP DISTRESS"

Shortly after the *Abergavenny* sank at approximately 2300 hours on 5 February 1805, its story became a prominent part of a long tradition of shipwreck narratives going back to the first collection of *Mr. James Janeway's Legacy to his Friends, containing twenty-seven famous instances of God's Providence in and about Sea-Dangers and Deliverances* (London, 1675). It continues to the present day in Keith Huntress's edition of *Narratives of Shipwrecks and Disasters, 1586–1860* (Ames: Iowa State University Press, 1974) and Terence Grocott's even more recent *Shipwrecks of the Revolutionary and Napoleonic Eras* (London: Chatham, 1997).

Indeed, the *Abergavenny* story provides a typical example of the evolution of these unsinkable narratives. Within a few days of the tragedy, the *Morning Chronicle* of London published an account with several letters from one of the military passengers, Cornet Burgoyne, and the *Abergavenny*'s fourth mate, Thomas Gilpin. On 13 February, a forty-nine-page pamphlet was published in London by John Stockdale, who claimed that his chapbook was corrected from "the official returns at the East India House." On 21 February, the Minerva Press of London published another pamphlet, *An Authentic Narrative . . . by a Gentleman of the East India House. The Gentleman's Magazine* published its version in February, 1805. Between 1805 and 1810 Thomas Tegg, of 111 Cheapside London, produced a series of twenty-eight-page pamphlets on shipwrecks, each having a folding aquatint as a frontispiece. One bound and dated 1806 bore the title, *A series of narratives, with folding plates in aquatints*, etc. Included was the narrative, "Loss of the 'Duke of Abergevenny' off Portland Bill, 1805, along with the loss of the 'Bounty,' wreck of the 'Phoenix,' et al." Meanwhile Archibald Duncan, Royal Navy, edited an important anthology called *The Mariner's Chronicle*, which included the story of the *Abergavenny*. Later anthologists took their narratives from Duncan, which became the basic text for later collections.[40] *The Mariner's Chronicle* had some four thousand subscribers in New England and New York. *The Naval Chronicle* (1799–1818) also contains narratives of shipwrecks, including that of the *Abergavenny*.[41] Huntress selected his text on the sinking of John Wordsworth's vessel from Duncan to conclude: "One is left with the impression, from this perhaps faulty narrative, that the command of the ship was something less than decisive" (Huntress, *Narratives of Shipwrecks*, 131).

From a biographical point of view, only one narrative might seem to matter, the relatively favorable version that Wordsworth read carefully and annotated with annoyance. But from a wider point of view, the less favorable narratives and illustrations of the shipwreck that Beaumont and other London friends were reading become equally consequential for understanding Wordsworth's defensiveness and for appreciating the public purposefulness of Beaumont's painting, *Peel Castle in a Storm* (1806).

The facts on the sinking of the *Abergavenny* were never difficult to come by, but opinions on the effectiveness of the Captain's behavior differed between those who observed the fatality as passengers and those who served as John Wordsworth's subordinates in the ship's chain of command. Inevitably, there was a closing of ranks among surviving officers in defense of their deceased Captain's decisions. The East India Company also made certain that even this self-interested story was sanitized for public consumption. Many found the official version something of a whitewash and even insiders demanded and got a second hearing on liability.

Facts; events filtered through observers and committees with self-interests; embellished narratives with dubious anecdotes and stylistic excrescences, accompanied by aquatint engravings imagining the tragedy: all of these form an interesting case study for the romantic journalism of a sea-proud nation.[42] The material facts are that the *Abergavenny* was a relatively new vessel, built in 1789 in Gravesend to replace an older vessel, also called the *Earl of Abergavenny*. Its carrying capacity, or burthen, was 1,182 long tons, rounded off to 1,200 tons. It had twenty-six cannon for armament on its final voyage. Its hull dimensions were approximately 50 by 13 meters. Because the issue of using the vessel's boats to save lives becomes an important element of the narratives to be reviewed below, it is relevant to know that there were no lifeboats on military and merchant vessels. Four to six utility vessels of various sizes, such as a pinnace, a jollyboat, a yawl, and a longboat,[43] were carried for purposes of bringing stores to vessels at anchor in the harbor, for transport of personnel between vessels, and so forth, but ship's boats were not considered to be seaworthy. The longest utility boat for a vessel of the *Abergavenny's* size would have been the longboat at about 34 to 36 feet.[44] Nevertheless, on the side of those who claimed that many lives might have been saved in the ship's boats of the *Abergavenny*, it is to be recalled that everyone was aware that Captain Bligh of the HMS *Bounty* traveled 3,000 miles to safety in his vessel's 34-foot sloop. Finally, as was mentioned above, on this its final voyage the *Abergavenny* carried cargo valued at £200,000 and about £70,000 in silver dollars.

The circumstances of the disaster are these. The *Earl of Abergavenny* had been in convoy with the *Royal George, Henry Addington, Wexford,* and *Bombay Castle,* when the fleet was separated during a storm from their naval escort vessel, *The Weymouth,* commanded by Captain Draper. Assuming responsibility as commodore for the fleet, the senior officer of the *Wexford*, Capt. W. S. Clarke, signaled to the captains who had taken on pilots to enter Portland Roads until the convoy could be reunited. The *Abergavenny* was the last to take on a local pilot to guide her through the local Scylla and Charybdis, the Shambles and the Race of Portland.[45] The pilot, however, was unsuccessful, and the *Abergavenny* was repeatedly rocked by rough seas against the Shambles, an infamous bank of coarse sand and shingle about 2 3/4 miles in length off the coast of Portland.[46]

The *Abergavenny* sank approximately seven hours later in 65 feet of water. Being heavily laden, but with the weight of its cargo and the water it had taken on evenly distributed, the vessel rested with its hull upright on the ocean floor, its three masts and rigging partially exposed above the water line. The majority of the survivors would later cling to the exposed rigging until saved in the early morning hours of 6 February 1805. Capt. John Wordsworth and nine other victims washed ashore on 20 March 1805 and were buried with unmarked stones in the churchyard at Wyke Regis.

The East India Company reported that the passenger list included 160 crew; 159 soldiers of the King and the Company; 40 passengers at the captain's table; 11 passengers at the third mate's table; and 32 Chinese workers, for a grand total of 402. Survivors included 80 members of the crew of 160; 11 of the 51 passengers; 15 of 32 Chinese; and 50 of the 159 troops, for a grand total of 156. Thus, 246 perished, 50 percent of the crew and 69 percent of the remaining personnel (80 percent of the civilian passengers; 47 percent of the Chinese; and 68 percent of the soldiers).[47] Captain Clarke of the *Wexford* believed that the great loss of life was "in great measure attributed to so many of them [soldiers and Chinese] being below at the pumps." In other words, weariness took its toll. The soldiers and crew frantically pumping seawater out of the hull for almost seven hours in their losing battle to keep the vessel afloat[48] were too tired to save themselves.

The Survival record of the ranking ship's personnel reads as follows:

John Wordsworth, captain, age 30; drowned
Samuel Baggot, chief mate, age 30; drowned
W.G.E. Stewart, 2d mate, age 24; saved
Joseph Wordsworth, 3d mate; age 23; saved
Thomas Gilpin, 4th mate; age 24; saved
John Clarke, 5th mate, age 19; saved
H. Mortimer, 6th mate, age 20; saved
Jonathan Davie, ship's surgeon, age 28; saved
C.H. Stewart, bursar, age 54; saved
Anthony Gohan, Boatswain, age 43; drowned
Thomas Abbott, gunner, age 31; saved

Of the six midshipmen, all between the ages of sixteen and eighteen, five were saved, including Benjamin Yates, age sixteen, who would later provide problematic testimony to the Wordsworth family.

To complete the mostly factual part of the story, dredging operations were successfully concluded by John Braitwhaite.[49] By 18 May 1806, the sixty-two chests of silver dollars were reclaimed. The remainder of the valuable cargo, including thirty pipes of wine, were recovered in 1807.[50] Salvaging operations also recovered the rigging. There is some disagreement over the fate of the hull. Grocott says that it was blown up in 1812 to "prevent the wreck from forming a dangerous shoal" (195); the Larns report in their *Shipwreck Index of the British Isles* that the bottom of the *Abergavenny* survives. Beyond these facts and minor factual disagreements, the real "stories" begin.

Charles Lamb passed on to the Wordsworth family the unofficial truth unadorned. On 18 February 1805, he wrote:

> all accounts agree that just before the vessel going down, your brother seemed like one overwhelmed with the situation, & careless of his own safety. Perhaps he might have saved himself; but a Captain who in such circumstances does all he can for his ship & nothing for himself, is the noblest idea. (*Lamb Letters* 2:152)

After speaking to Thomas Gilpin, the surviving fourth mate, Lamb wrote the next day:

> Gilpin . . . has assured me that your brother did try to save himself, and was doing so when Gilpin called to him, but he was then struggling with the waves & almost dead.—G heard him give orders a very little before the vessel went down with all possible calmness, & it does not at all appear that your Brother in any absence of mind neglected his own safety. (*Lamb Letters* 2:152)

Apparently unsettled over the contradiction between the two stories, Lamb undermines Gilpin's testimony as unreliable on two counts, memory and self-interest:

> But in such circumstances the memory of those who escaped cannot be supposed to be very accurate; and there appears to be about the Persons that I have seen a good deal of reservedness & unwillingness to enter

into detail, which is natural, they being Officers of the Ship, and liable
to be examined at home about its loss. (*Lamb Letters* 153–54)

In other words, with the captain dead, the chief mate dead, the third
mate, cousin Joseph Wordsworth, out of the picture because he was
saved with the purser and several passengers before the vessel sank,
Stewart, the second mate, and Gilpin, the fourth mate, were the
highest ranking officers to answer for the catastrophe. One of the
accounts revealed that Gilpin "before he met with the Secretary [of
the East India Company], 'told many a tale of misery,' in the passages of the India House."[51] After being interrogated, as we shall see,
a corrected version of the corrected version reported the detail to
be untrue.

W. G. E. Stewart, second mate; Joseph Wordsworth, third mate;
Thomas Gilpin, fourth mate; and J. Addwater, carpenter; were the
members of the ship's company to be interrogated about the sinking
by the Committee on Shipping of the Company. On 19 February
1805, the Committee published its finding: Resolved: that the vessel
was "in every respect, complete for her intended voyage"; that "the
late commander, officers, and ship's company . . . be fully acquitted
of all imputation of neglect or misconduct, in respect to her loss";
that the vessel "was fully and sufficiently found in anchors, cables,
and other stores, and that the owners should therefore be fully acquitted of all imputation of neglect or misconduct, in respect to the
loss of the said ship."[52] It was either the pilot or an act of God that
was responsible for the sinking of the *Abergavenny*. The loss of life
is unaddressed in these findings, but will be partially excused in a
pamphlet later to be produced by an insider of the Company.

On the other hand, Cornet Burgoyne, the officer in charge of the
military personnel traveling as passengers on the *Abergavenny*, had
another story to tell that was widely promulgated. It was a tale of
maintaining impressive discipline but finally at the expense of losing
lives. As the end drew near, he charged, there was ample time to
hoist the remaining ship's boats out to save as many lives as possible,
but the captain did not give the order and his officers did not take
the prerogative to question his authority. Or, it might have been
asked, was it the intention of the ship's officers to save the boat(s)
for themselves as the end drew near? For the pamphlets indicate
without comment that after the *Abergavenny* sank, the ship's officers
made rescue efforts from her longboat.

A rendition of the sinking from one of the less histrionic versions published in *The Naval Chronicle for 1805*[53] offers a base text from which comparisons and contrasts on substance and style can be made. The account begins with comments about the ship's boats from one of the first officers to arrive at the India House, apparently Burgoyne. He reported that, at first, when the vessel hit the Shambles, most passengers and crew were free from alarm, "and no idea prevailed that it would be necessary to hoist out the Boats to be ready to take the Crew on shore in case of necessity" (124). "At Six P.M." however, "the inevitable loss of the Ship became more and more apparent." Nevertheless, Burgoyne observes,

> the Captain and Officers were far from shrinking from the perils around them. They gave their orders with the greatest firmness and coolness, and by their proper conduct were enabled to preserve subordination. As the night advanced, the situation of all on board became the more terrible; the Misses Evans, and several other Passengers, entreated to be sent on Shore [on the ship's long boat]; but this was impossible. It was as much as all the Ship's Company could do to keep the Vessel afloat. In order to induce the Men to exert their utmost powers at the pumps, the Officers stood by cheering and encouraging them, by giving them allowances of liquor. . . . One boat came off from the Shore, which took on board the Misses Evans, Miss Jackson, Mr. Rutledge, and Mr. Taylor, a Cadet, all Passengers. Mrs. Blair, companion to the Misses Evans, chose, in spite of all entreaties, to remain on board: indeed there were many who would have made the same choice, so little hope was there of the Boat contending successfully against the high Sea in so dark a night.

A more difficult and contentious issue arises about boats being heard nearby but not rendering assistance (125). The narrative continues:

> The dreadful crisis was now approaching—every one on board seemed assured of his fate; some gave themselves up to despair, whilst others endeavoured to collect themselves, and employed the few minutes they had left in the best of purposes—that of imploring the mercy of their Creator. At ten o'clock the Ship was nearly full of water, and as she began gradually to sink, confusion commenced on board. A number of Sailors begged ardently for more liquor, and when it was refused, they attacked the spirit-room, but were repulsed by their Officers, who never once lost sight of their character, and continued to conduct themselves with the utmost fortitude. One of them was stationed at the spirit-room door, with a brace of pistols, to guard against surprise, and there remained

even while the Ship was sinking. A sailor was extremely solicitous to obtain some liquor from him, saying, "It will be all as one an hour hence."—"Be that as it may," replied the Officer, "let us die like Men."

Then a judgment oft-quoted in versions of the account is made: "It is a circumstance hardly to be accounted for, that, in the midst of all this distress, the Boats were never attempted to be hoisted out. About two minutes before the Ship went down, Mr. Baggot, the Chief Mate, went to Captain Wordsworth, and said, 'We have done all we can, Sir, she will sink in a moment.' The Captain replied, 'It cannot be helped—God's will be done.'"

Brutal chaos then commenced:

When the Passengers and Crew were acquainted with their situation, they made several efforts to save their lives; some laid hold of pieces of the Wreck, and committed themselves to the mercy of the waves. A Mr. Forbes stripped off his clothes, and being an excellent swimmer, plunged into the Sea, and was one of those who were picked up by a Boat from the Shore. A great number ran up the shrouds. At about eleven o'clock a heavy Sea gave the Vessel a sudden shock, and in an instant she sunk to the bottom, in twelve fathoms water. Many of those unfortunate persons who had run up the shrouds for safety, were unable to sustain the motion of the Vessel in going down, and suffered with their unfortunate companions below. Between eighty and ninety persons, however, were still able to maintain their situation, and were ultimately saved. For some time after the Vessel had gone down, she kept gradually sinking deeper in the sand, insomuch, that several persons were under the necessity of climbing higher up the masts. The highest mast was estimated to be above the water about twenty-five feet, and the persons aloft could plainly discover the end of the bowsprit. (126)

The boats that were heard in the distance failed to stop, this narrator believes, for fear "that every person on board, being eager to save himself, the whole would attempt to jump in, overload the Boats, and sink them." One might ask, however, if John had been a buddy to his fellow captains, might not one of them have attempted to assist? Between midnight and 2:00 A.M., the rescue began with orderliness.

The focus of the narrative then returns to the captain's behavior:

Captain Wordsworth, at the moment the Ship was going down, was seen clinging to the ropes. Mr. Gilpin, one of the Mates, used every persuasion to induce him to endeavour to save his life, but all in vain; he did not seem desirous to survive the loss of his Ship. The exertions of Cornet Burgoyne, and the Mates, were most exemplary; they did all that human means could effect. (127)

In the interest of objectivity, *Naval Chronicle* prints a letter from John Clarke, a member of the ship's crew and fifth mate, that bears upon the strategy of the captain and his crew to avert disaster and loss of life. After the *Abergavenny* drifted free of the Shambles, about 7:30 P.M.:

> it was determined to run her on the nearest Shore. At eight o'clock the Wind shifted to the eastward. The leak continuing to gain upon us, having 10 or 11 feet water, found it expedient to bail at the fore scuttle and hatchway. The helm being hard a starboard, the Ship would not bear up, she being water logged; but still had a hope we could keep her up till we got her on Weymouth Sands: cut the lashing of the Boats, could not get the Long-Boat out without laying the main-top-sail aback, by which our progress would have been so retarded, that little hope would have been left us of running her aground; and there being several Sloops in sight, one having sent a Skiff on board, and took away two Ladies and four or five Passengers, and put them on board their Sloop, at the same time promising to return and take away a hundred or more people, at different trips, to the Sloop; but finding much difficulty in getting back to the Sloop, did not return. About this time the third Officer and Purser were sent on Shore in the Cutter to get assistance from the other Ships; continued pumping and bailing till eleven o'clock, when she sunk. The last heave of the lead was in eleven fathoms water, having fired guns from the time she struck till she went down. At two in the morning Boats came off and took the people from the Wreck, about seventy in number. The tops of all the masts were above water. (128–29)

There was some debate about whether the Portland Pilot was responsible for guiding the vessel into the Shambles, or whether it happened, as we have just read, when the wind calmed and the vessel was thrust forward by the sea. Most reports include John Wordsworth's comment upon the misfortune that implies pilot culpability: "O pilot! pilot! you have ruined me!"

There were many reports of heroic behavior by the ship's crew following the sinking. Baggot, the chief mate and second in command to Captain Wordsworth, drowned in the attempt to save a Mrs. Blair, the elderly passenger of the narrative who was too frightened to enter the small rescue boat that came from the shore. After the sinking, Mr. Baggot left the ship's boat that he and others were floating in to rescue the drowning woman, but "just as he was on the point of reaching [the ship's boat] a swell came on, and his strength being totally exhausted, he sank and never rose again. The unfortunate Mrs. Blair sunk after him, and this generous youth thus perished in vain."[54] Gilpin, also in the ship's boat, returned to the wreck when he noticed someone in the rigging who appeared motionless. Gilpin brought a Sergeant Hart "down on his back, and took him to the boat," but Hart had died. *Gentleman's Magazine* also published a letter in praise of Gilpin for "possessing a heart of most inestimable texture," in his assistance to others throughout the night, including his earnest efforts to keep up the spirits of the survivors. The reader's attention is called to the name of Gilpin, "in whose veins flows the milk of human kindness, not as a tardy stream, but as a torrent."[55]

The reports on John Wordsworth's behavior were dismal in comparison. The chapbook referred to here as *Authentic Narrative . . . Corrected from the Official Returns at the East-India House* provides the most devastating judgment on the issue of ship's boats: "Unfortunately, in the general distress and agony of the moment [it was then 2230 hours], the ship's boats were not hoisted out, when every soul on board might possibly have been saved" (11). Specifically on the motivation of John Wordsworth's end, *Authentic Narrative* says: "He was on his third voyage as a captain, and painful to relate, perished with his ship, disdaining to survive the loss of so valuable a cargo." Nevertheless, the narrator is sure the Court of Directors "will not fail to pass a deserving eulogium on this worthy character, who so notably stood by their property till the last extremity, and forfeited his charge with his life" (16–17). When Baggot told him of the end, this narrative dramatizes, John Wordsworth

> steadfastly looked him in the face, and, at last, with every appearance of a heart-broken man, faintly answered: "Let her go! God's will be done!"—These were the last words he uttered—from that instant he was motionless.—In a few moments the ship sunk, and many who were climbing the shrouds endeavoured to save him, but without success. In this endeavour Mr. Gilpin was foremost, and made several unsuccessful attempts, at the evident risk of his own life.—Captain Wordsworth sunk with his ship, and was seen no more!!! (21)

Unable to dismiss the captain's suicidal behavior without a diagnosis, *Authentic Narrative* speculates on rumors of symptomatic behavior that began prior to the voyage:

It is an extraordinary fact, that Captain Wordsworth felt such an unaccountable depression of spirits that he could not be persuaded to go through the usual ceremony of taking leave of the Court of Directors on the day appointed; and it was not till the Wednesday following, which was specially fixed for that purpose, that he yielded to the wishes of his friends, and reluctantly attended the Court! (49)

*Narrative of the Dreadful Loss of the* Earl of Abergavenny, *Indiaman, Wrecked February 5, 1805, on the Shingles, off the Bill of Portland, as communicated to the Directors of the India House, by one of the Survivors* (London, 1805) with frontispiece, "The Distress'd State of the Crew of the Abergavenny when she was sinking," represents John as a victim of his own premonitions. *Dreadful Narrative* says John appeared late before the Court of Directors because of a "dreadful presentiment, which often is the forerunner of some great misfortune" (26). While the vessel was beating against the Shambles, its "bell, by the motion kept tolling, as if ominous of their approaching fate, 'till the Captain ordered the clapper to be lashed. What a dreadful moment must this have been to the unfortunate sufferers; to have an awful eternity in view, and the bell, as though by instinct, tolling their departing knell" (9). Just prior to the vessel sinking, this narrative says "the First Mate told the Captain she would sink in a moment—The Captain (looking in his face; and with a look, in which was strongly depicted a true sense of their dreadful situation,) replied, 'it cannot be prevented—God's will be done.'—From that instant the Captain was motionless" (13).

*Dreadful Narrative* also makes it clear that the longboat came free when the vessel sank. It was standard practice to cut the ropes of the ship's boats prior to sinking so that they would float freely when they hit the seas. The ship's officers and others mentioned as being in the *Abergavenny*'s longboat probably climbed in before she sank. For those clinging to the sails and rigging, the "situation . . . was frightful beyond all possible description; the swell of the sea was dreadful, and every moment they perceived some friend floating around them for a while, then sinking into the abyss to rise no more. 'Down on the vale of death, with dismal cries, / The fated victims shuddering roll their eyes, / In wild despair.'——" (17).

*Dreadful Narrative* makes factual errors, including John's leaving "a wife and large family to deplore his loss" (26), and concludes: "He was a man of remarkable mild manners; and of so temperate a disposition, that he was known among his ship-mates, by the appellation of the 'Philosopher.' It may justly said of him, that: 'Tho' trained in boisterous elements, his mind / Was yet by soft humanity refined. / Each joy of wedded love at home he knew; / Abroad confessed the father of his crew! / Brave, liberal, just! the calm domestic scene / Had o'er his temper breath'd a gay serene' FINIS" (26).

The frontispiece to this chapbook, an engraving titled *The Distress'd State of the Crew of the Abergavenny when She Was Sinking, Feby 5, 1805*, suggests a sharper story about this "father of his crew" and perhaps his employers as well (see figure 3). In featuring the horrors of the sinking, the engraver highlights the women passengers frantically racing about the poop deck at the vessel's stern, arms raised in a panic; darker male figures are hanging from the rigging, climbing, falling, diving, swimming, and some—probably crew members, as the narrative makes clear—are already waiting in the longboat, with several people below the boat raising their arms for assistance or attempting to hoist themselves up. The focus of the engraving is on a half-clad, androgynous figure, stripped of garments to avoid sinking of their weight, arms spread horizontally, as if crucified in air, leap-

3. Frontispiece, *The Distress'd State of the Crew of the Abergavenny*. Reproduced by permission of Bodleian Library, University of Oxford. Reference: Harding A 191.

ing feet first into the caps of the waves. In the darker region of the poop deck (see figure 4), the captain lurks with arms folded, stoically observing the scene, while a woman kneels in supplication, begging, one imagines, that he do something—release the boats?—while another woman, who has fainted, is being lifted by a ship's officer.

A few conclusions can be drawn from this presentation. Aware of the solicitude expected of a captain toward his female passengers, one infers that the detachment of this superior officer is meant to be seen as unbecoming as well as inhumane. It seems that John is being condemned for being the "philosopher," rather than a man of decisive action required by the situation. Relatedly, although more speculatively, the leaping figure with arms spread may be a parody of Christian sacrifice unwittingly caused by the Company's Claphamites, who imprudently favored this captain with a select voyage for his moral virtues rather than for his professional competence and demeanor.

The East India Company could not allow such accounts and representations to go unanswered. An engraving to counter *Distress'd*

**4. Enlarged view of the frontispiece of *The Distress'd State of the Crew of the Abergavenny*.**

*State*, for example, is entitled *The Loss of the Abergavenny, East India Man, off the Isle of Portland*[56] (see figure 5). As "The Loss" shows, however, the orderly evacuation of survivors rather than the sinking of the *Abergavenny* is the real focus of the engraving. In direct contrast with the "Distress'd State of the Crew," there is no panic in "The Loss," but rather survivors standing tall, in uniform, including hats, as if they used the time prior to their rescue for cleaning up and wrapping the sails neatly about the beams upon which they wait— and even the sails of the highest point of the masts where no one stands—patiently awaiting for the rescue boat filled with survivors to return from the attending sloop. In contrast with the sacrifical image of "Distress'd State," the central image here is the rescue boat on its way from the *Abergavenny* to the heaving sloop.

The pamphlet representing the disaster from the Company's perspective was authored by W.D., who has been identified as William Dalmeida, an assistant clerk to the Committee of Correspondence in the Home Department of the East India Company (*EY* 560, n. 2). Its complete title is *An Authentic Narrative of the Loss of the* Earl of Abergavenny, *East Indiaman, Captain John Wordsworth, off Portland, on the Night of the 5th of Feb. 1805; drawn from official documents and commu-*

**5.** *The Loss of the Abergavenny.* © **National Maritime Museum, London.**

*nications from various respectable survivors.* By a Gentleman in the East-India House (London: Minerva Press, 1805). When Wordsworth finally received this pamphlet, he read it quite carefully and, it seems, disappointedly, for it dispelled a noble version of John's behavior that he had conjured from some of the very testimony contained in the pamphlet. He penciled marginal corrections and comments as his annoyance was aroused. And there was much indeed to arouse both concern and annoyance for a family member and poet aspiring to public prominence.

As one might expect, the Wordsworths received Richard's initial letter informing them of John's death with horror and powerful grief. In an effort to get further information, as Dorothy says, on "how it was," they had to rely upon the good offices of friends, particularly Charles Lamb, who could provide them evidence from the inside. The family decided early that the newspapers and pamphlets could not be trusted to provide the truth; thus, they must attempt to communicate with witnesses directly. Lamb persuaded William Gilpin and Benjamin Yates to respond to their pointed questions, particularly John's alleged indifference to his own survival.

Gilpin wrote to the Wordsworths:

> I will give you as correct an account as I am able, of every transaction in which your late worthy Brother bore a part, from the time the E of Abergavenny struck on the Shambles till she went down—which is 2 miles from Weymouth—at a minute or two before she struck [the Shambles] the Capt said to the Pilot, are you sure you have your marks open—he reply'd—I am—when she struck the Capt exclaim'd, O Pilot you have ruin'd me—after this time . . . I was at the Pumps. . . . When I occasionally see the Capt, he was perfectly corlacted [i.e., collected] and giving his orders with firmness. . . . I see him on the Poop, less than a minute before she went down. . . . I ran to the Poop, looking out which way to save my self, and she sinking so rapidly. . . . Sum [*sic*] minutes after this I see several men hanging by ropes, fast to the mizen Mast amongst which was Capt Wordsworth. I went down into the [?] rigging to see if I cd render them any assistance, I got within 10 or 12 feet of whare [*sic*] he was, I haild him as loud as I cd & threw him a rope, he was motionless & insensible he did not katch [*sic*] the rope or answer, Sum of the others I got into the top a short time before she went down he & the first officer (Mr Bagget) were conversing together.

Gilpin concludes with the comment that he had been on two previous voyages with John and found him "a humane good Man."[57]

The Wordsworths also received from Lamb detailed information derived from the young midshipman, Benjamin Yates. Some of the following, especially those points specifically bearing on John's decisions and final behavior, were even more troublesome than Gilpin's recollection of John failing to reach for the proferred lifeline.

On why the boats were not hoisted out:

it would have deterd the men paying that attention to the sails [pumping?] and [bailing?] in the second place the anxiety of saving life would have caused an exertion in every one the Boats from the sea most likely would have swamped alongside in last [order ?] the ship would have gone down in deep water when the distruction of every body though ever so good a swimmer would have been inevitable.

On Captain Wordsworth's last words: "Mr Y perfectly well recolects [*sic*] the last words of Capt W was to haul on board the main tack which I have every reason to suppose huried her down as it was a pressing sail."

On Captain Wordsworth's demeanor and his decisions: "Capt W appeared quite composed the whole time he repeatedly called out to haul the main tack on board Mr Baggot and the Pilot mentioned their was no occasion for any after sails as the ships head would not [p?]ay off."

On the great loss of life: "they kept pumping and bailing untill the ship sunk."

On why Captain Wordsworth did not survive:

Answer to . . . the reason why Capt W was not saved I cannot define. I have no reason to suppose he was thrown into the eddy the ship was quite full from the main mast forward the first and the second entirely covered her and from certain belief in my own mind he never had a wish to survive the loss of his property.

Lamb makes some mitigating comments in a note that has been partially torn away, saying things like "this young seaman's surmises" must be judged by you who knew "the inner man."[58]

More respectful responses on John's character came through cousin Capt. John Wordsworth, obviously not a witness, but one who could interpret a captain's responsibilities at such a time. He attempted to console, without rebutting any testimony in particular:

It will be highly gratifying to know that John was the delight of all the Passengers, had you heard his Praises from the Lips of Mr. Evans (a Man of strong sense & discrimination [?] it would have given you a melancholy Pleasure & convinced you that however flattering his Prospects of Happiness were in this Life had he compleated his Voyage, it is now secured to him effectually in the presence of his *Creator where there* is Joy for evermore—[59]

The family also received a personal letter from Evans, a senior official of he East India Company who was traveling to India with his daughters, and who was rescued by the sloop from the shore hours prior to the sinking:

> If I were to write all that to us appeared interesting relating to your Brother during the period we were in the unfortunate Ship, I should have to communicate the almost hourly occurrences of the day from our embarkation to our providential Escape. Sea sickness confining my family to the Cabin your Brother was generally with us except when the important duties of his Station engaged his time. I observed on all occasions an anxious desire to promote the comfort & happiness of all under his protection. He was sanguine in his expectation of a speedy voyage and on his future prospects we often were accustomed to dwell on. His wish was to proccedd [*sic*] as a single Ship but the orders regarding a separation from the fleet were too strict to be disobeyed, which we mutually lamented, & this adherence to his orders, resisting the temptations of self-interest, was the cause of our being led into the danger which has proved so fatal to so many. It was the well founded expectation of having a successful Voyage that he should in consequence be enabled to retire from the Service & live with his Family . . . [which] animated every exertion and in all his Conduct of which I was the witness, I only observed steadiness, judgement & ability, & in the serious hour of danger firmness, & resolution, which to the last he manfully maintained.
>
> It may be conceived that the Mild & reflecting Character of your Brother was not so well calculated for the Scenes he had to encounter as others who had less feeling which imposes the appearance of more energy, but as far as I can judge he tempered his Character with qualities that rendered him equal to the arduous struggles of the Profession he had adopted. . . .
>
> My Daughter and Niece would most gladly offer every consolation in their power to the amiable sister of one whose kindness and attention to them they are proud to acknowledge.

In a postscript, Mr. Evans concludes: "I cannot omit mentioning the last words of your Brother to me when I was quitting the Ship & was over the side, he came to me and emphatically said God bless You!"[60]

When writing to friends, William made certain that they were dis-
abused of the impression pervaded by the news organs that John was
indifferent to his survival. As William's own story developed, he al-
luded to the favorable parts of the testimony described above as evidence of increasing certainty, not just that John had acted
appropriately, but that he had acted heroically. Poignantly, Beaumont believed that Wordsworth's own poetry would help to heal his
sorrow, but he remained silent on William's correction of the public
reports. He expressed poetic condolences with quotes from Shakespeare and from Wordsworth's own verse. "To time the only physi-
cian we must leave it, & I doubt not the thoughts of your own mind
will then {?} exert itself on the account of others as well as your own."
He is certain that "that presence which has heretofore 'disturbed
you with the joy of elevated thoughts'" will finally offer sufficient
solace.[61] But being quite familiar with the water himself, it may have
been difficult for Beaumont to believe that John, an excellent swimmer, could not have saved himself had he wished.[62]

In particular, the Wordsworths were impressed by reports that
John was seen speaking "chearfully" with his first mate minutes before the vessel sank, for this was a certain indication of John's presence of mind to the last. William writes to Beaumont, "A few
minutes before the ship went down my Brother was seen talking with
the first Mate with apparent chearfulness [*sic*]" (*EY* 557); Dorothy
reports the same to her dear friend from girlhood, Jane Pollard Marshall (*EY* 559). Because this account of John's behavior seems so pat-
ently absurd on the face of it—and in such stark contrast to the
reports of natural chaos prevailing at the end—the contemporary
definition of "cheerfulness" is worth considering so as not to overlook the behavioral possibilities it might have once suggested.[63]
Johnson's *Dictionary* offers what one might expect: "1. Freedom
from dejection; alacrity. 2. Freedom from gloominess." Johnson also
offers an illustrative quote for definition 1 that concerns cheerfulness in the face of death:

> With what resolution and *cheerfulness*, with what courage and patience
> did vast numbers of all sorts of people, in the first ages of christianity,
> encounter all the rage and malice of the world, and embrace torments
> and death?

It is an outstanding example of true believers seeking martyrdom.
But can one believe that the man whose first thought was on finan-

cial loss, shouting "O Pilot Pilot you have ruined me!," that that man would seven hours later be looking forward with cheer to meeting his Maker amid the horrific panic of hundreds of passengers screaming and scrambling on the decks of his vessel?

As unlikely then as reports of John's demeanor may be, it was yet grasped by the Wordsworth family as true because the alternative was awful. The fear hinted at in their letters is that John wished to die because he had failed them and himself in disastrously losing their inheritance. And, frankly, had he survived, he would have been woefully in debt to many and not likely to get another captaincy. His career had been cursed. After learning that their money was indeed insured, Dorothy writes of the family's relief in assuming that John did not die believing he had ruined their hopes for independence:

> My Brother Richard says that there is no reason to think that we shall any of us suffer in our property. This is a great comfort to us for our poor John's sake, who I am sure would have one pleasing thought on that account when he knew that all he carried out with him would be lost. (EY 561–62)

The family's optimism on this point may be justifiable; however, the final insurance settlement offered John's creditors was 18 shillings on the pound.[64] John could not have known what the family's settlement would be. Still, being convinced that John did not commit passive suicide, William was free to imagine John's death as "a noble spectacle" because John remained at his post to the end. After reading Gilpin's testimony, Wordsworth concludes:

> From this it appears that every thing was done that could be done under the circumstances, for the safety of the lives and the Ship: my poor Brother was standing on the hen-coop (which is placed upon the Poop and is in the most commanding situation in the Vessel) when she went down: and was thence washed overboard by a huge sea which sunk the Ship, he was seen struggling with the waves some time afterwards having laid hold, it is said, of a rope. He was an excellent swimmer, but what could it avail in such a sea encumbered with his cloaths and exhausted in body as he must have been. He was seen talking with the 1st Mate with apparent chearfulness a few minutes before the Ship went down. . . . There is nothing remarkable in the courage or presence of mind which he shewed at his death, thousands would have done the same. But it is a noble object of contemplation that a man of his gentle and meek and happy temper a man in the prime of health and strength (he was only

32 years of age) with every thing in prospect which could have made life dear, beloved and honored to the height of love and honor by his nearest friends and kindred and respected and liked by every body that knew him; that such a man having the anguish which he knew he would leave behind him, should nevertheless die calm and resigned; this is surely a noble spectacle. (*EY* 564)

After querying for more evidence from Richard and Capt. John Wordsworth about how the other officers survived (*EY* 571), William irrationally concludes that John was "placed in such a situation that he could not have been saved consistent with his duty till after the Ship was gone to the bottom."

The same undaunted courage and presence of mind which kept him faithful to his Post as long as the Ship was above water did not desert him to the last, but that having done all that could be done for others, he was when the proper time came equally true to himself.

John swam as long as five minutes, William derives from Gilpin's discussions with cousin Capt. John Wordsworth, until drowning (*EY* 583). By May, Wordsworth was writing to Beaumont of John's "heroic death," from "particulars . . . accurately collected from several of the survivors" (*EY* 586).

Interestingly, Wordsworth turned to Aristotle for a definition of fortitude to apply to John's behavior, as if he wished to dispel the notion of philosophy's irrelevance—or a philsopher's inherent incapacity—in dire situations:

It is, says he, the property of fortitude not to be easily terrified by the dread of things pertaining to death: to possess good confidence in things terrible, and presence of mind in danger; rather to prefer to be put to death worthily than to be preserved basely; and to be the cause of victory. Moreover, it is the property of fortitude to labour and endure, and to make valorous exertion an object of choice; further, presence of mind, a well disposed soul, confidence, and boldness are the attendants on fortitude:—and besides these, industry and patience. (*EY* 557–58)

Except for making "valorous exertion an object of choice," Wordsworth says, John "might have sate for this picture" (*EY* 558).

William now more deeply feels their mutual commitments. He wrote to Beaumont: "there is a bond between us yet, the same as if he were living, nay far more sacred, calling upon me to do my utmost, as he to the last did his utmost to live in honour and worthiness" (*EY* 547). Sir George's response was respectful of Wordsworth's sympathies. He admires Wordsworth anew for "follow[ing] up your noble pursuits with encreasing energy—it shews a resolution worthy of your character." He also offers him money he may need at this time of crisis and closes with: "I have lived many years in the world, & I began to think, that all is selfishness was at least as true an axiom as all is vanity—I fear they in a great measure divide it betwixt them—but I now have the satisfaction of knowing there are exceptions"[65]

## 5. "*PORTRAYED* ON THE TEA-TRAY"

When William finally got his hands on the pamphlet produced by the East India Company, that is, the widely circulated narrative of W.D., he was chagrined and felt his story shaken. For it is quite obvious upon reading the whole of the story the Company had to tell that John Company was interested in distancing itself from John Wordsworth. It seems Wordsworth read it at least twice, most likely making the single annotation in ink the first time through and then underlining in pencil and sometimes making marginal comments on second and/or successive readings. He annotated its inaccuracies and speculations with annoyance, but some of its dire conclusions were incontrovertible.

W.D.'s narrative emphasizes at the outset that the general public has a justifiable interest in the sinking of the *Abergavenny*:

> It hath been well observed, on the much-lamented and never-to-be-forgotten loss of the *Halsewell,* that the misfortunes of individuals affecting only their immediate relatives, occasion no public concern—and death . . . though at all times awful, is too familiar to be tremendous; but when numbers are involved in one common fate, and that fate is attended with circumstances of unusual horror, the blow is felt by the whole community, the republic itself is convulsed by the shock, and grief, pity, and regret expand among all orders and conditions of men. With the fate of the *Halsewell* all are familiar. We too often, by a strange perversion of taste, and lapse of humanity, see the distresses of the ill-fated Captain and his passengers portrayed on the TEA-TRAY, and emblazoning the screen. (Wordsworth's underlining, without comment, p. 2)

In other words, the Wordsworth family might anticipate a commercialization of their tragedy in the hawking of domestic memorabilia.

Just as shipwreck narratives and their illustrations were a popular element of contemporary journalism, so were more ambitious oils.[66] The sinking of the *Halsewell*, East Indiaman, in particular captured the imagination of numerous artists because the vessel captain, Richard Pierce, drowned along with his beautiful and talented daughters.[67]

The fate of the *Halsewell* is mentioned in comparison because the *Abergavenny* sank 7 1/2 miles from the "spot which proved so eminently disastrous to the fortunes and the hopes of Captain Pierce and his amiable family." (4). Then praise is given to John Wordsworth as "cool and even [in the] temperature of his blood"—he was no "passion's slave"—and his gentle demeanor had given him the epithet of "the PHILOSOPHER" (4). The vessel's tonnage is correctly mentioned as being "*1200* tons burthen," which Wordsworth mistakenly comments "was 1500" (4). A comment that only an East India Company insider would be privy to is introduced: "Ships of this burthen are in general employed only for China; but the Company, ever attentive to commercial experiments, had, from their good opinion of the Commander, fixed on the *Earl of Abergavenny* to lade cotton from Bengal for the Canton market: an experiment which, from the improved method of pressing this important article of Indian traffic, promised the most complete success" (5). As an assurance of the reliability of this narrative, W.D. reveals the monetary details of the ship's invoice:

| | Pounds Sterling | s | d |
|---|---|---|---|
| For Bengal | 61,000 | 4 | 4 |
| ditto | 1289 | 0 | 4 |
| ditto | 8076 | 3 | 0 |
| China | 18,110 | 4 | 2 |
| | £89,075 | 11 | 10 |

(p. 5)

W.D. then comments that the revenue of the Company and of the nation are so interlocked, that "whenever the first shall decrease, the latter cannot fail of experiencing an alarming shock" (6). Wordsworth again bothers to miscorrect the tonnage of the ship's burthen twice on page 6.

In making one of his many comments to put the Company and the surviving officers of the *Abergavenny* in the best light, this time regarding the excessive loss of life belowdecks among the soldiers doing the pumping for seven hours, W.D. says that the Military Service of the Company is "the most enviable in the world;—where the officers find in each Director a friend and father, tremblingly alive to their interests" so, "what can be expected but the enthusiasm of gratitude, and the ardour of enterprise?" (7). The Company even provides meals on board the vessel for cadets so that the "pocket as well as the health of the young soldier is effectually preserved from impoverishment, to the no small mortification of exorbitant inn-keepers, and a certain description of persons who too often prey on the volatile and unwary" (8). The bereaved families of the deceased soldiers would now know that the Company cared for their children and, thus, could never be insensitive to their fates, even if they had pumped themselves to death.

The issue of pilot error is introduced to clear the Company of blame: "in the general opinion of those who think they 'best can tell,' the loss of the *Earl of Abergavenny* may be attributed to the ignorance of the Pilot" (9). W.D. introduces a new item on the firing of the ship's guns to signal distress, which Wordsworth finds slightly misrespresentative of the truth as he understands it. The original opinion of the captain, W.D. says, was that "the ship *might be got off* [the Shambles] *without sustaining* any material damage, and accordingly no signal guns of distress were ordered to be fired for upwards of an hour and a half afterwards, when twenty were discharged" (12). The pencil comment in the bottom margin is "had not sustained," so that the sentence would read: "the ship had not sustained any material damage"; in other words, there was no doubt in John's mind that his ship was still seaworthy and thus he did not have the guns fired, as he might have, and should have, otherwise. As we recall from other accounts of the ship's officers, Stewart and Gilpin, both agreed that the guns were fired immediately and throughout the sinking, but that was by now an unnecessary and immaterial untruth, which need not be argued against the testimony of other witnesses.

A verbatim transcription of Gilpin's testimony before the Court of Directors is then offered. Regarding the failure to use the ship's boats to save lives, Gilpin tells the same story that Clarke told above and that Benjamin Yates told the Wordsworth family in correspondence:

> Cut the lashings of the boats—could not get the long boat out, without laying the main-top-sail back, by which our progress would have been so

delayed, that no hope would have been left us of running her aground; and there being several sloops in sight, one having sent a small skiff on board, took away two ladies, and three other passengers, and put them on board the sloop, at the same time promising to return and take away a hundred or more of the people; she finding much difficulty in getting back to the sloop, did not return. (11)

It is not revealed how crew members of the *Abergavenny* could have known why the sloop assigned to rescue efforts failed to return. The third mate [Joseph Wordsworth] and the purser [Stewart] were also sent in the cutter to get assistance from the other ships, but nothing came of this either. Gilpin concludes: "Continued pumping and baling till 11 P.M. when she sunk—last cast of the lead 11 fathoms; having fired guns from the time she struck till she went down, about two A.M. boats came, and took the people from the wreck, about 70 in number. The troops, in particular the Dragoons, pumped very well" (12). And died for it.

Another comment on the splendid personnel of the Company is offered:

It has for ages been the boast of England, that her gallant sons of the Ocean, whether gaining fresh laurels for their country, in bravely combating the common foe, or enduring the all-conquering perils of winds and waves, are still, in the hour of danger, cool and collected. They fight like Heroes, and they die in the conscious pride of having discharged their duty as MEN.

"In the present melancholy instance," for example, "the behaviour of the Commander and officers proved that they were worthy of a nobler fate—that of dying in the cause of their King and Country. They knew the value of discipline, and even the frowns of the grim tyrant, Death, could not shake them from their purpose" (15–16).

The nobility of the ship's officers in the face of death is comparable to Caesar:

When Caesar met his fate in the Capitol, he folded his robe about him, that he might fall with decency—when the sailors pressed ardently for a supply of liquor on the officer who guarded the spirit-room—"Give us some grog!" exclaimed the honest Tars; "it will be all as one an hour hence!"—the reply of the officer would have done honour to the brevity of Roman fortitude—"I know we must die," cooly replied the gallant Midshipman, "but let us die like men!"—He kept his post, armed with a brace of pistols, and there staid, even whilst the ship was sinking. (16)

Wordsworth is again moved to correct the substance of the text when he reads that "Captain Wordsworth had made two *successful* trips to India:." The pencil comment in the right margin is, "for the Owners but unsuccessful for *himself.*" Then there is the reference to John's role in the battle with the French frigate, with an allusion to his citation:

> His last voyage had bestowed the full meed of FAME. His ship formed a part of that gallant fleet of merchantmen which had made *Admiral of the Marengo* tremble. He had received the noblest reward of valour—the THANKS of his employers, the PLAUDITS of a grateful nation. (25)

W.D. offers another insider's comment when revealing that uncle Captain Wordsworth "engaged in a convivial party, dwelling with honest pride on former successful voyages, expatiating with rapture on the rising prospects of his young *élève*, and circulating the cheerful glass in bumpers to the safe return of the *Earl of Abergavenny*" and "On the very instant that this melancholy accident occured" (25).

The scene of woe at the India House is then recounted:

> The Purser was so overcome by the frequent repetition of the sad—sad story, that, soon after he left the India House, he fell into a strong fit. He unhappily had more than general cause for sorrow— ... a son—his pride—his hope—had unfortunately perished in the common wreck, and under such distressing circumstances, that to relate them were to "add the death" of the survivor. (26)

Wordsworth makes another pointless pencil correction: Mr. Dent, the managing owner of the *Earl of Abergavenny,* had two *nephews* on board." The text reads. Wordsworth makes a marginal correction that changes "nephews" to "Cousins." A later correction alters the mention of a Mr. *John* Dent to "Robert" (both on p. 30).

This narrative disputes the "depression of spirits" anecdote ("that the protraction of Captain Wordsworth's taking leave of the Court arose from depression of spirits, we decidedly disallow"). W.D.'s narrative claims that John had not completed the "forms of office" and thus he was obliged to "defer his parting obeisance till another day" (29). Stories about Gilpin telling his "'tale of misery' in the passages of the India House" (29) are dismissed as nonsense, for the men who went down were "work[ing] cheerfully ... and they died in the very act of discharging their duty" (29). On the "cheerfulness" of the situation, Cornet Burgoyne, "a name deservedly dear to Englishmen" raised the spirits of those clinging to the masts by singing an appropriate "ditty," and the "passengers and crew joined cheerfully in the chorus" (29). The officers before the sinking "excited the crew to manual exertion by a *cheerful* song and the smile of encouragement" (p. 16; the pencil comment of a single word that looks like *dacre* is indecipherable). We also get another version of the final moments:

> Some minutes before the ship sunk, Mr. Baggot, the Chief Mate, went to Captain Wordsworth, and said—"We have done all we can, Sir—she will sink in a moment."—The Captain replied—"It cannot be helped— God's will be done."—The Captain and Mr. Baggot were observed to converse with apparent cheerfulness; though when the ship first struck, the former was heard to exclaim—"O pilot! pilot! you have ruined me!" (17–18)

Another comment and pencil correction is made at a very important point in the narrative where the culpability of the captain is considered:

> It has been said, that had the proper precautions been taken, not a life would have been lost; perhaps Captain Wordsworth was not, till too late, sufficiently aware of the <u>incurable state</u> [underlined in pencil] of the ship: but it is hardly probable, whatever might have been the resolution of the passengers, that *all* the crew would have deserted her—it is a well-known fact, that some sailors will not quit a sinking ship: we may instance the *London* East Indiaman, which was run down by the *Russel* man of war—the crew to a man might have been saved, but they energetically exclaimed—"No, we cannot leave our beautiful ship—we will share her fate!" and they were seen in the ACT of CHEERING as she went down. (17)

Although such behavior seems the result of not guarding the spirit room, the East India Company positing a happy martyrdom on *The Abergavenny* is preposterous.

In contradiction of its own self-serving suppositions, the narrative includes gruesome stories of people who desired to live:

> A singular circumstance happened to a Sergeant who escaped the fatal doom of so many of his comrades: his wife, who was with him in the shrouds, on quitting her hold, as the last struggle for her life, bit a large piece from the husband's arm, which is dreadfully lacerated.

This is true insider information because the passenger list does not contain the name of a woman passenger who might be related to any of the military personnel.

W.D. discusses John's end, as the other accounts do, but without coloring it favorably:

> Captain Wordsworth, at the moment the *Earl of Abergavenny* was going down, was seen clinging to the ropes. Mr Gilpin used every persuasion to induce him to endeavour to save his life; *he did not seem desirous to *survive* the loss *of his ship.*

Apparently, John's desire to die not being a matter of Company culpability, the Company does not bother to contradict the other accounts on this point, but Wordsworth finds it intolerable. He adds an asterisk in ink and makes his only marginal comment in ink:

> *Contradicted by Wm Gilpin, who spoke to Capt Wordsworth— and saw him using ["making" crossed out and "using" written above] every exertion to save his life— (24)

Thus, John's employers, who had acted so favorably on his behalf, now joined the public chorus that maligned the story of fortitude William had developed for the family. John did not do everything he could for others; for whatever reason neither did he act on his own behalf. The family could remain in a state of denial about the truth of the story, nevertheless, even this the most sympathetic of public accounts was accusatory. The most heartrending letters Wordsworth ever wrote concerned the loss of John and the struggle to understand the metaphysical truth of John's final words, "God's will be done." But John's most profound legacy was William's commitment to the memory of their bond and John's ultimate sacrifice that his brother might do something "for the world."

# Part III
## Beaumont and the Promotion of Wordsworth

SIR GEORGE HOWLAND BEAUMONT, LIKE BROTHER JOHN WORDSWORTH, requires some biographical resuscitation for his importance in the poet's middle life and work to be understood.[1] There are also interesting parallels and connections to be drawn between John Wordsworth and Sir George: both were patrons of the poet, both came into his life at about the same time, and both believed that his genius could make a difference to the world. John's patronage consisted of his life's work and ultimately his life. Beaumont's patronage was influence, support, and friendship. His painting of *Peel Castle* effects a biographical convergence among the poet, his brother, and himself in its attempt to offset the adverse publicity over the sinking of the *Abergavenny*. Ironically, as we shall see, William Wordsworth's vocational fortunes seemed comparable to his brother's misfortunes, given the unanimously hostile reception of *Poems, in Two Volumes*.

Norma S. Davis makes the observation that we see in Beaumont's relationship with Wordsworth a redefinition of the role of the aristocratic patron for his "consciously but informally" assisting selected artists "on the basis of a friendship,"[2] rather than distant respect. William Knight credits Beaumont with "the gift of calling out whatever was best in his friends."[3] In Wordsworth's particular case, Sir George went beyond the role of patron and friend in his attempt to manage Wordsworth's career.

### 1. "PATRON OF GENIUS"[4]

In the fall of 1803, Sir George Howland Beaumont (1753–1827), landscape artist, accomplished amateur actor, descendant of the Renaissance dramatist, Francis Beaumont, patron of the arts, avid collector, and luminary of London culture discreetly offered Wordsworth

113

the gift of a plot of land in Applethwaite, which was near Coleridge's residence at Keswick, so that the two poets

> might be able to communicate most frequently your sensations to each other, & that this would be a means of contributing to the pleasure & improvement of the world by stimulating you both to poetical exertions.[5]

Stephen Gill surmises that Wordsworth was embarrassed by the gift, for he and Beaumont had only recently met. The land was indirectly for Coleridge, Sir George explained, for he wanted to "oblige him & . . . soon found there was no means of doing this so effectually as by accommodating his friend." The truth was that Sir George and Lady Beaumont were Wordsworth enthusiasts. Coleridge reported to Wordsworth that "Sir G. & Lady B. . . . are half-mad to see you." After viewing Hazlitt's portrait of Wordsworth, Sir George and Lady Beaumont "both say," Coleridge went on, "that the Picture gives them an idea of you as a profound strong-minded Philosopher, not as a Poet," to which Coleridge responded, "that so it must needs do, if it were a good Portrait—

> for that you were a great Poet by inspirations, & in the Moments of revelation, but that you were a thinking feeling Philosopher habitually—that your Poetry was your Philosophy under the action of strong winds of Feeling—a sea rolling high. (*STCL* 2:957)

Wordsworth decided not to build on the land and offered it back,[6] but Sir George responded that he and his wife would prefer to "live and die with the idea the sweet place, with its rocks, its banks & mountain streams are in the posses[s]ion of such a mind as yours, & moreover let the particulars of the transaction remain unknown to all but you, Coleridge, Lady Beaumont & myself."[7]

Beaumont's interest in Wordsworth's reputation would soon follow. He and Lady Beaumont loved much of Wordsworth's poetry, but they were the exception in their influential circle. Friend and fellow artist, Joseph Farington, records in his *Diary* that

> Sir George read part of a Poem by [Wordsworth] called "Tintern abbey," which He thinks exquisite & has read it 100 times.— . . . Sir George said He was infinitely indebted to Wordsworth for the good He had recd. from His poetry which had benefitted Him more, had more purified His mind, than any Sermons had done. (Farington, *Diary*, 6:2271)

But J. Taylor expresses the common perception of Beaumont's circle in reacting to *Lyrical Ballads* much as John Wordsworth had predicted the literati would:

> Wordsworth much superior as a Poet to Coleridge & Southey; but that all of them affecting to be simple and natural, they frequently reduce their expressions to what may almost be called *clownish.*—He said Jerningham had told him that the Bishop of London, speaking of their works said, "Whatever merit there might be in them was not *legitimate Poetry.*" (Farington, *Diary*, 7:2785)

William Wilberforce, who received a signature copy of *Lyrical Ballads* (1800) and a long note from Wordsworth on the political intentions of "Michael," found the poetry contrived. Farington summarizes Wilberforce's assessment:

> Of Cowper, He sd. that what He produced, as an Author, appeared to have flowed naturally from Him on some occasion that affected His mind.—So, He added, He thought, it should always be. He would have men act only from the impulse of nature & feeling. Wordsworth, on the contrary, lives to make verses. (Farington, *Diary*, 8:2827)

Matthew Arnold would later assert that, judiciously edited, Wordsworth would be recognized as one of Europe's greatest poets.[8] Beaumont had the same goal for the poet in the making. He would have Wordsworth abandon his fearless experiments with peurile characters ("The Idiot Boy"), morbid psychology ("The Thorn"), and simplistic language (the previous two and others) so that his unparalleled works of genius ("Tintern Abbey") could stand unencumbered.

Intervening to influence an artist's development was not uncommon to Beaumont, but he was wont to attend to young painters who would accept the aesthetic principles promulgated by Sir Joshua Reynolds. To this end, Beaumont began indoctrinating John Constable in his Grosvenor Square studio. Those who opposed the dicta of Reynolds, such as J. M. W. Turner, were ostracized. The Beaumont circle pronounced Turner a madman, whereas they held hope for Constable, David Wilkie, and Benjamin Robert Haydon, if patronage and education could be counted upon.[9]

The hostility to Turner is instructive in coming to understand the challenge Sir George confronted in seeking to promote Wordsworth in a circle of likeminded aesthetes. "Turner's pictures at the British

Institution were spoken of," Farington reports, "Sir George said they appeared to Him to be like the works of an *old man* who had ideas but had lost his power of execution" (Farington. *Diary*, 7:2710). James Boaden and John Taylor looked on Turner's *Waterfall at Schaffhausen* as the work of "a Madman" (Farington, *Diary*, 7:2748). Northcote said that Turner's "desire of singularity & greatness of style, became *rhodomantade*, it was like *bombast in poetry*" (Farington, *Diary*, 7:2750). Another member of the circle praised an obscure painting by Calcott, because it contained complete figures,

> not left *blots* like Turner's.—He denounced Turner's "Water fall at Schaffhausen," as being a wild, incoherent, unnatural production, the froth of the water being like a brush of snow.—[Benjamin] West said Turner had become intoxicated, and produced extravagancies. (Farington, *Diary*, 7:2757–58)

This sort of universal and confident declamation was also to be the fate of Wordsworth's *Poems, in Two Volumes*.

Although Beaumont impressed young painters with his social status and accomplishments as a landscape artist, they did not always retain their respect after experiencing his modus operandi. Calcott speaks for Constable, Turner, Hearne, Haydon, Farington, and Wilkie when he writes of Beaumont's reputation among the young:

> the gentleman is esteemed by the world at large as the first connoisseur of the day. . . . The praise you have heard bestowed [on Haydon's "Dentatus"] is none other than what I have heard him regularly bestow upon the whole race of existing artists at their first appearance. He has deemed every one the greatest in his turn as long as he only promised well but the moment he began to fulfill his promise . . . he had made a point of pulling him to pieces, and for this simple reason, that while an artist remains below mediocrity, it is a display of his judgement to point out his beauties but directly he is above par then the tables must be turned . . . as this Gentleman has become the Demagogue of the picture Criticks so he conceived himself under the necessity of making the artists feel the weight of his power.[10]

Haydon was driven to distraction by Sir George, who hoped that Haydon would become England's first history painter in Reynolds's Grand Style, but then Sir George confronted the unpleasant reality of Haydon's ambitious works. Of being in and out of Sir George's favor, Haydon writes in his *Diary*:

L[ord] M[ulgrave] & Sir G. B. were delighted with my picture. There was then every prospect of it being hung in a good situation in the Royal Academy and attracting public approbation, and every prospect too of the People being tired of W[ilkie] and his falling [in] their estimation. All their conversation was on the beauties of my Picture, on my perseverence, how fine this was or how fine that. Poor W. was literally not spoken to. Every body's attention, Ladies and Gentlemen, was directed to me. I finished my Picture [*Dentatus*], sent it to the Exhibition, where by the rascality of Mr. West it was hung so that nobody could see it. Of course, every body pitied me, said it was a shame. . . . Wilkie, who two months ago was neglected, was now smiled on, spoken to, praised, flattered, while I, who when there was a prospect of success, was treated in a similar manner, was now unnoticed. . . . Two months since, when I shewed an inclination to speak, every body turned towards me and listened with attention and smiles, but now my observations were drowned in clamour, and every ear and eye, with a gracious *oome* and a smile were directed to Wilkie.[11]

But Sir George remained charming and Haydon could never get enough of his praise. On another day, in another year, Haydon remarks: "He is the most glorious fellow living. His touch always goes into my marrow with sensation; no being that ever lived except Phidias felt the true nature of substance like him. What they said about my Picture had double value in consequence of being so fresh from such fine things," to wit, the European paintings Sir George and Lady Beaumont had studied while abroad (Haydon, *Diary*, 2:243). Later Haydon says that Sir George is "the most delightful man in the World when he pleases" (Haydon, *Diary*, 2:393).

Haydon's private eulogy for Beaumont evaluates both the virtues and faults of his presence for the cultural life of London:

Sir George was an extraordinary man, one of the old school formed by Sir Joshua, a link between the Artist & the Nobleman, elevating the one by an intimacy which did not depress & lower the rank of the other. Born a Painter, his Fortune precluded the necessity of application for subsistence, & of course he did not apply. His taste was exquisite, not peculiar or classical, but essentially *Shakespearean*. Painting was his great delight; he talked of nothing else, thought of nothing else, and would willingly have done nothing else. His ambition was to connect himself with the Art of the country, and he has done it for ever, . . . He is justly entitled to be considered as the founder of the National Gallery. His great defect was a want of moral courage; what his taste dictated to be right he would shrink from asserting if it shocked the prejudices of others or put himself to a moment's inconvenience. With great benevolence he appeared, therefore, to be mean; with exquisite taste he seemed often to judge wrong; & with a great wish to do good he often did a great deal of harm. He seemed to believe that to bring forth unacknowledged talent from obscurity was more meritorious than to support it when acknowledged. The favorite of this year was forgotten the next.

His loss, with all his faults, will not easily be supplied. He founded the National Gallery. Let him be crowned. Peace to him. (Haydon, *Diary,* 3:183)

In Wordsworth's unique case, Sir George was interested in reorienting the energies of a major talent toward that which would, in Sir George's words, "generally please." The record indicates that Beaumont wished Wordsworth to become an historical poet in the "grand style," and he partly succeeded.

Beaumont's paintings reveal his neoclassical bias. David Wilkie said that "the beautiful style of art which he professed was abstract and general—a poetical recollection rather than a minute detail of nature; full of sentiment and feeling, and eminently successful in what was his chief delight—a rich and deep tone of colouring."[12] Beaumont's *Peel Castle in a Storm* was yet to be painted, but Wilkie's description foresees it well.

Given Beaumont's conservative aesthetic, many were mystified by his delight in Wordsworth's verse. His biographers remark that "filling the vacuum left by Reynolds's death, [Beaumont] became a spokesman for art with the uncomplicated approach of his generation which never fully understood the creative forces of the new century."[13] In an attack on the stodginess of the governing board of the Royal Academy, which included Beaumont, West, and Northcote, the Hunts wrote in the *Examiner* that "Originality . . . threatens to make them less, and they do not like it. To contradict their opinions is to let the world into the secret of their comparative insignificance." The Hunts thus expressed open puzzlement over Sir George's dismissive attitude toward the "modern painters of nature," while he thought "so highly of that very original and natural poet . . . his friend, Mr. Wordsworth."[14]

Wordsworth and Sir George did see eye to eye on painting and on the comparative importance of poetry. In commenting on Wordsworth's admiration for Charles Le Brun's *Magdalene,* Ernest De Selincourt remarks that the poet "never acquired any sound taste in pictorial art, and was able to express a genuine admiration for the canvases of his friends Haydon and Sir George Beaumont."[15] Wordsworth's taste for painting may have been colored by friendship, but he also had Sir George believing that *"Poetry was superior to Painting."*[16]

After the negative reviews of the first edition of *Lyrical Ballads* (1798) had been supplanted by the far more favorable reception of the two-volume 1800 edition, Wordsworth, Beaumont, and Lady Beaumont may have felt that the poet was but a step away from overdue acclamation. In his first letter to Beaumont, Wordsworth includes three patriotic sonnets, "Written at Needpath," "To the Men of Kent," and "Anticipation," closing with the comment: "If you think . . . that these two last sonnets are worth publication, would you have the goodness to circulate them in any way you like?" (*EY* 411). After praising the sonnets (*EY* 410–11) as "animating to a large degree," Beaumont says that he will send them to the "papers which I think will be the best mode of making them generally known." His selections were *The Poetical Register* and *The Anti-Gallican.*

Shortly, Beaumont was to send the Wordsworths his watercolor of Applethwaite as a gift, which Dorothy would ponder for "many a ten minutes" (*EY* 483) and which William found a daily pleasure, as he wrote to Sir George:

> There is not a day in my life when I am at home in which that exquisite little drawing of yours of Applethwaite does not affect me with a sense of harmony and grace which I cannot describe. (*EY* 517)

The third gift Beaumont presented to Wordsworth after the plot of land and the watercolor was Edmond Malone's edition of Reynolds's *Discourses*,[17] which included a lengthy preface on the Master's charmed life. To a near-indigent poet, Malone's preface might sound like Matthew's third temptation of Christ: "All these things will I give thee, if thou wilt fall down and worship me" (Matt. 4:9). The preface also suggests that Beaumont had the keys to the kingdom. Wordsworth read the preface with some care.[18]

Beaumont's gift of the *Discourses* enhanced the "high opinion which [Wordsworth] before entertained of Sir Joshua Reynolds" for his taste and judgment. The problem Wordsworth found with Reynolds was that he did not give "more of his time to the nobler departments of painting" (*EY* 491). Reynolds sacrificed the ideals promulgated in his *Discourses* for an opulent lifestyle. In his important fourth Discourse, Reynolds concedes that portrait painters and landscape and still-life artists moved "in these humbler walks of the profession," but "are not ignorant that, as the natural dignity of the subject is less, the more all the little ornamental helps are necessary to its embellishment" (*1803* 107). Wordsworth wrote that it "grieved" him that Reynolds "generally pass'd the time from eleven till four every day in portrait painting" because by Reynolds's own admission it was "a sacrifice of great things to little ones" (*EY* 500). Reynolds had declared that the great subjects of painting are "heroick action, or heroick suffering" (*1803*, 80), which were to be found in classical literature and the Bible and yet he spent the greater part of his genius on immortalizing the countenances of dukes and countesses.

Wordsworth also learned the specifics of Reynolds's affinity for friends and money. Malone writes that "Sir Joshua Reynolds was constantly employed in a lucrative profession, the study and practice of which afforded him inexhaustible entertainment, and left him not one idle or languid hour; and he enjoyed as much fame as the most ambitious candidate for popular approbation could desire," yet he was free from "vanity and ostentation" (*1803* lxxxvi):

> While engaged in his painting-room, Reynolds had the pleasure of seeing and conversing with all the beautiful, accomplished, and illustrious characters of his time; and when not employed in his art, his hours were generally passed in the most pleasing and enlightened society that London could produce. (*1803* lxxxvii)

Malone describes the "work" day that irked Wordsworth:

> He usually rose about eight o'clock, breakfasted at nine, and was in his painting-room before ten. Here he generally employed an hour on some study, or on the subordinate parts of whatever portrait happened to be in hand; and from eleven the following five hours were devoted to those who sat for their pictures: with occasionally short intervals, during which he sometimes admitted the visit of a friend. (*1803* xcviii)

Not only was there no anguish over ambitious works, Reynolds's practice grew tremendously lucrative. In 1755, his commission for painting "a head" was 12 guineas; by 1758, it rose to 20; by 1760, to 25; by 1770, 35; and by 1781, 50. The price of a half-length rose to 100 guineas, and for a whole-length, 200 (*1803* lxxv). The selling prices of embellished projects of important families and of nonportraiture also increased enormously over time. Malone lists the following paintings, purchasers, and selling prices of Reynolds's works, at a time when an annual income of about £400–500 would support a stylish London life:[19]

1. "Garrick, between Tragedy and Comedy," 300 Gs, purchased by the Earl of Halifax;
2. "Count Ugolino" sold for 400 Gs to the Duke of Dorset;
3. "A Gipsy telling fortunes," 350 Gs to the Duke of Dorset;
4. "The Marchioness Townshend, Mrs. Gardiner, and Hon. Mrs. Berisford, decorating the Statue of Hymen," 450 Gs to Viscount Mountjoy;
5. "The Nativity," a design for the window of New College Chapel, Oxford, 1200 Gs, to the Duke of Rutland;
6. "Cardinal Beaufort," 500 Gs, to Mr. Alden Boydell;
7. "The Cauldron Scene in Macbeth," 1000 Gs, to Boydell;
8. "Mrs. Siddons, in the Character of the Tragick Muse," 700 Gs to N. Desenfans, Esq.;
9. "Hercules, stangling the serpents," 1500 Gs, to the Empress of Russia. (lxii–lxx passim)

The fifty-four luminaries of Reynolds's Literary Club rounded off his spectacular London life. Along with Samuel Johnson, Edmund Burke, David Garrick, Oliver Goldsmith, Edmond Malone, Laurence Sterne, James Boswell, Adam Smith, Thomas Warton, Thomas Percy, Richard Brinsley Sheridan, Lord Mansfield, Charles James Fox, and a few others of equal political and literary prominence, Sir George Beaumont sat within Reynolds's circle (*1803* xxiv).

Sir George imbibed the principles of the *Discourses,* which Reynolds delivered every December from 1769 to 1790 as president of the Royal Academy. In 1779, Reynolds invited Sir George to be his guest at the Academy dinner when he delivered his very brief Discourse IX. Perhaps Reynolds invited Beaumont to audit this particular Discourse because, as a fellow artist and an aristocrat with wherewithal, Beaumont might some day play a leader's part in fulfilling the master's vision of "a School of English Artists."[20]

The cultural stakes, as Reynolds describes in Discourse IX, were high:

The estimation in which we stand in respect to our neighbours, will be in proportion to the degree in which we excel or are inferior to them in the acquisition of intellectual excellence, of which Trade and its consequential riches must be acknowledged to give the means; but a people whose whole attention is absorbed in those means, and who forget the end, can aspire but little above the rank of a barbarous nation. (*Discourses* 169)

Neighboring nations, Reynolds bemoaned, excel the English not only in the quantity and quality of great art but also in the institutions to house their treasures.

The message was heard. Or, as Wordsworth might say, its power was felt. Beaumont never shook the stardust from his shoulders and turned out to be the dedicated disciple Reynolds desired. Besides influencing the development of young British painters through financial assistance and convivial training holidays midst his private collection at Coleorton, Beaumont realized his long-held dream of establishing a national gallery in 1823.[21] Beaumont's biographers conclude that Reynolds retained a lasting influence over Beaumont, because he had given "Beaumont's life its purpose, and lent pattern and context to the various interests and friendships he had discovered thus far."[22]

Besides the grandeur of Reynolds's life, Malone's preface reveals that a beloved artist might receive the recognition of a national hero at his death. Wordsworth would also notice additional evidence of Sir George's prominence in the description of Reynolds's funeral. The Master's pall was borne by "three Dukes, two Marquisses, and five other noblemen," and Sir George sat in one of the forty-two carriages of noblemen, followed by their forty-nine empty carriages rolling solemnly through the streets of London. The Mayor locked the city gates to accommodate the procession, which he personally led to St. Paul's, where Reynolds was interred alongside Christopher Wren (*1803* cxii–cxv). Beaumont was also included in the list of legatees, receiving Reynolds's painting *Sebastian Bourdon,—the Return of the Arc* (*1803* cxvii, n. 67). He acquired several more paintings at an estate auction, including *Study of a Black Man* (1790) and *Head of a Bearded Man* (1779). When the Reynolds era ended with his death in 1792, Beaumont inherited an important responsibility.

Beaumont admired Wordsworth's dedication as a poet and grieved publically in 1808 "of the unfortunate situation of Poets compared with that of Painters." "He sd," reports Farington, "that two of our principal Portrait Painters had got more money within the last Seven Years than all the poets in this country had obtained. He sd. Wordsworth had not got £160 for all He had written & published" in more than ten years (Farington, *Diary*, 9:3288). The subtext Wordsworth must needs have read in the Malone preface is that poets need not starve, if they know how to please, as the case of lesser lights than Wordsworth, most notably Robert Southey and Walter Scott, were proving, and as Lord Byron was yet to prove.

The principal lessons of the *Discourses* as they might apply to Wordsworth's poetry are not difficult to infer: that accidental particulars must be eschewed in the interest of the whole (83); that the artist should never make his subjects mean in shape or proportion; thus, there is no virtue in keeping one's "eye on the object," to recall an aesthetic principle from Wordsworth's "Preface" to *Lyrical Ballads*. Painting, like poetry, must take license with the truth. The Dutch are the worst history painters, Reynolds writes, because "With them, a history-piece is properly a portrait of themselves" (102). They are excellent otherwise; "they are only ridiculous when they attempt general history on their own narrow principles, and debase great events by the meanness of their characters" (104). When Reynolds discusses landscape painting he finds Claude Lorrain to be the best for never copying nature but rather for seeking ideal form from an examination of many scenes (105). He concludes that there are two distinct styles in history painting, the grand and the splendid or ornamental, but the "grand style stands alone" (108).[23]

## 2. Great Events and Poetry

Admiral Nelson's death at Trafalgar several months after the sinking of the *Abergavenny* stimulated an exchange between Beaumont and Wordsworth that brought Reynolds's guidance on audience, style, and historical significance to a practical point. The Battle of Trafalgar was only the latest of Nelson's spectacular victories at sea over, in turn, the French, Spanish, Danish, and now the combined French and Spanish fleets. As a noted historian said, "To an age accustomed to indecisive naval battles, or at best modest successes, [Nelson] brought annihilating victories."[24] Nelson worship was intense following his dramatic death at Trafalgar on 21 October 1805 at the very moment of the victory that ended the threat of French invasion by sea. Here then was an epic hero awaiting his epic poet.

Dorothy reports to Lady Beaumont that William was at first incredulous upon hearing the news of Nelson's death on 9 November, although she at once "burst into tears":

> William would not believe all at once, and forced me to suspend my grief till he had made further inquiries. At the Inn [in Patterdale] we were told that there were "great rejoicings at Penrith—all the bells are ringing." "Then,["] I exclaimed, ["]he cannot be dead!" but we soon heard enough to leave us without a doubt, and bitterly did we lament for him and our Country. . . . I believe that every truly *brave* Man, in the highest sense of the word, is, as you describe Lord Nelson to have been, tender and humane in all the daily acts of life. (*EY* 650)

On 25 November 1805, Sir George wrote to Wordsworth about Nelson's extraordinary personal qualities. He recently dined with the captain of the *Thunderer*, one of the vessels at the Battle of Trafalgar, who "gave such an account of the private virtues of Nelson; as made us if possible deplore his loss with increased regret, he was by his account the very soul of generosity, & his manner of conferring benefits 'did outweigh his gifts, & yet enriched them too.'" "As a man of business," Beaumont goes on, Nelson

> was not less extraordinary, the care, accuracy, & celerity with which he transacted it was wonderful. In short he was one of those characters with which mankind are rarely indulged in any line, sanguine, & rapid without hurry, without harshness, bold, forward, & capable, for my own part & I am persuaded I feel in common with the whole nation, & never was affected in the same manner by the loss of any public man, nor do I think there ever was the same degree of concern ever manifested so generally and mean[ingfully] on any similar occasion. (*GBL* 12)

Wordsworth responded to Beaumont after composing his "Character of the Happy Warrior" sometime between December 1805 and January 1806. Nelson's death and Beaumont's information on the hero's recondite qualities afforded Wordsworth an oblique opportunity to say something publicly in John's defense, though few could know, or would care, if they had known. That Wordsworth would compose a poem on a warrior in heroic couplets might be evidence of a desire to please the multitude that Beaumont represented, but it would also be a private satisfaction to convince the reader to accept his depiction of a hero as one who need not be victorious. After praising the "happy warrior" for his "master bias [which]

leans / To home-felt pleasures and to gentle scenes (*P2V* 86, lines
59–60), which is as unlike Nelson as one could imagine, Wordsworth
concludes with contrasting generalities which implicitly intend to
make the great disparity between the fates of John and Nelson in-
consequential:

> 'Tis, finally, the Man, who, lifted high,
> Conspicuous object in a Nation's eye [Nelson],
> Or left unthought-of in obscurity [John],
> Who, with a toward [Nelson] or untoward lot [John],
> Prosperous [Nelson] or adverse [John], to his wish or not,
> Plays, in the many games of life, that one
> Where what he most doth value must be won [both],
> Whom neither shape of danger can dismay,
> Nor thought of tender happiness betray [both];
> Who, not content that former worth stand fast,
> Looks forward, persevering to the last,
> From well to better, daily self-surpast [both]:
> Who, whether praise of him must walk the earth
> For ever, and to noble deeds give birth [Nelson],
> Or He must go to dust without his fame [John],
> And leave a dead unprofitable name [John],
> Finds comfort in himself and in his cause;
> And, while the mortal mist is gathering, draws
> His breath in confidence of Heaven's applause [John];
> This is the happy Warrior; this is He
> Whom every man in arms should wish to be [Nelson or John].
>                                         (lines 65–85)

The "noblest reward of valour—the THANKS of his employers, the
PLAUDITS of a grateful nation" be damned, Wordsworth, in effect,
replies to W.D.'s sanctimonious evaluation of John's fleeting moment of glory in 1803. John's final words, "God's will be done," tes-
tify to his faith in "Heaven's applause."

On 11 February 1806, almost a year to the day that the Wordsworth family had learned of John's death, Wordsworth responded
caustically to Beaumont's praise of Nelson. John's death and his ill-
fated business ventures were certainly on Wordsworth's mind.
"[C]onsidering the matter [of Nelson's death in battle] coolly,"
Wordsworth writes, now bitterly at odds with the lamentation he
shared with Dorothy a few months earlier, "there was little to regret":

Few men have ever died under circumstances so likely to make their death of benefit to their Country: it is not easy to see what his life could have done comparable to it. The loss of such men as Lord Nelson is indeed great and real; but surely not for the reason which makes most people grieve, a supposition that no other such man is in the Country: the Old Ballad has taught us how to feel on these occasions:

> I trust I have within my realm
> Five hundred good as he.

But this is the evil that nowhere is merit so much under the power of what . . . one may call that of fortune as in the military and naval service; and it is five hundred to one that such men will [not] have attained situations where they can shew themselves so, that the Country may know in whom to trust. Lord Nelson had attained that situation; and therefore, I think, (and not for other reason) ought we chiefly to lament that he is taken from us. (*MY* 1:7)

There were enough hints in the poem, not the least of which is the devastating literalism of the Happy Warrior's "dead unprofitable name," to alert Beaumont to its hidden subject. Nevertheless, Beaumont implies in his response of 5 March 1806 that Wordsworth has squandered an opportunity to participate *as an artist* in one of the great events of the time. "Your lines are excellent & the remarks natural & just," Beaumont writes, signaling to Wordsworth his awareness of their true intent by clarifying the referent in the following passage ("him [i.e., not John], Nelson"), so that Wordsworth could not miss the point:

> I think however when the spirit moves you that an effusion may be added more particularly addressed to him, Nelson, in which his name may be mentioned with enthusiasm. I mention this more on account of others than myself, as a name so dear to the public will call the attention of every one & thereby be more likely to answer the purpose you have in view.

When Beaumont refers to a tacitly understood "purpose" Wordsworth has "in view," he acknowledges the poet's oblique attempt to change the record on the death of John.

Wordsworth never wrote the great poem to Nelson; nor did he reveal to Beaumont that he placed his disrespect for the great admiral in the praises mouthed by the drunken sailor of *The Waggoner*, composed in January 1806, but left unpublished until 1819. Referred to in the poem as a "Tar," a contemptuous synonym for a seaman, the sailor of the poem is a worthy spokesmen for the "honest Tars" of W.D.'s pamphlet, and his audience in the tavern seems to be a rendering of Nelson worshippers.

After warming up to his coming burlesque by dancing, drinking, and singing in the Cherry Tree pub, the Tar rolls in the model of Nelson's flagship, the *Vanguard,* which he has been dragging behind his donkey. He begins his illustrated war story of the Battle of the Nile, with particular focus on its quarterdeck:

> "On which brave Admiral Nelson stood—
> A sight that would have done you good.
> One eye he had which bright as ten
> Burned like a fire among his men.
> Let this be land, and that be sea,
> Here lay the French and thus came we!"[25]

The allusion to "one eye" recalls Nelson's loss of an eye at Calvi; he also lost an arm in a battle prior to his victory over Napoleon in the Nile. An anecdote of Nelson's warlike nature that often left him flirting with charges of insubordination reveals why he remained a relatively low-ranking admiral, despite his phenomenal battle record. When ordered to disengage from the Danes in 1801, Nelson placed the telescope against his blind eye and claimed he could not see the signal from the fleet commander's vessel. He entered the fray and won. Before the Battle at Trafalgar, he gave the famous signal from his flagship, *Victory,* "England expects every man will do his duty." Such is the stuff of the Nelson legend.

Not surprisingly, the house of country revelers in *Waggoner* is mesmerized by their rude historian: "[?Then all the Dancers] gather'd round, / And such the stillness of the house, / [?You] might have heard a nibbling mouse" (MS 1, 405–7). Meantime, the Sailor "through the story runs / Of Ships to Ships and Guns to Guns, / And does his utmost to display / [?The history of that wondrous day] (MS 1, 409–12). Benjamin is delighted and bellows an order for a sailor's and his heroic admiral's due reward:

> "A bowl, a bowl of double measure,"
> Cries Benjamin, "a draft of length
> To Nelson, England's pride and treasure,
> Her bulwark and her tower of strength!"
>
> (MS 1, 413–16)

The "battered Tar . . . like a hero crown'd with laurel / Back to her place the Ship he led— / Wheel'd her back in full apparel; / And so, [?Fl]ag flying at mast head, / [?He] yoked her to the Ass" (MS 1, 426–32). The Sailor, his wife, their child, and Benjamin then proceed through the night, with the donkey tethered to the wagon led by Benjamin's horse, and the trailing model of the *Vanguard* with "Sails spread as if to catch the wind" (MS 1, 547). Here then was Wordsworth's tribute to Nelson in lines not openly disrespectful, except in the telling and teller.

Published in *Poems, in Two Volumes,* "The Character of the Happy Warrior" carries the following author's note:

> The above Verses were written soon after tidings had been received of the Death of Lord Nelson, which event directed the Author's thoughts to the subject. His respect for the memory of his great fellow-countryman induces him to mention this; though he is well aware that the Verses must suffer from any connection in the Reader's mind with a Name so illustrious. (*P2V* 86)

The Fenwick Note to the poem tells the surprising truth: Wordsworth placed Nelson in the ranks of the impure. He possibly alludes to Nelson's open and adulterous affair with Emma, Lady Hamilton, when he comments that Nelson's "public life was stained with one great crime" that prohibits "satisfaction" in even thinking of him "in reference to the idea of what a warrior ought to be"; whereas, "many of the elements of the character here pourtrayed were found in my brother John who perished by shipwreck" (*P2V* 405, note to "Character of the Happy Warrior").[26] We recall the fixation on John's purity that repeatedly emerges in the family letters on his nobility, but Wordsworth's denigration of Nelson as a warrior here and in his letter to Beaumont is ludicrous.[27]

### 3. *PEEL CASTLE IN A STORM*

It seems probable that Beaumont painted *Peel Castle in a Storm*[28] because he wished to support Wordsworth in rising above the prevailing opinion of John Wordsworth's end. Living often in his London residence at 29 Grosvenor Square, rather than his seat at Coleorton, Beaumont would certainly be more aware than Wordsworth of the many pamphlets and the gossip attending the wake of the *Abergavenny*. The worst of the unsubstantiated rumors, which failed to reach the Wordsworth family, was that John Wordsworth's judgment had been affected by alcohol.

Sometime between late 1805 and early 1806, Beaumont began a study of Piel Castle that he hoped to hang at the annual exhibit of the Royal Academy. He had made several sketches of the castle, one during a tour with Thomas Hearne in 1777 from which Hearne made a drawing in 1777 that became the prototype for *Peel Castle in a Storm.*[29] Hearne's drawing was then engraved by W. Byrne and T. Medland in 1783 (see figure 6). Beaumont's oils of Piel Castle closely follow Hearne's image, but it took conjoint meditation with Wordsworth on the meaning of John Wordsworth's death, Beaumont's awareness of the public forum, and perhaps William Close's meditations on time and Piel Castle in his new edition of Thomas West's *Antiquities of Furness* (1805), all to inspire the symbolism of his finest oils. The smaller of the two oils (33.7 × 50.1 cm), a preparatory study, is owned by the Wordsworth Trust and on permanent exhibit at the Wordsworth Museum at Dove Cottage; the larger (73.5

6. **Engraving of Peel Castle from Vol. 1,** *Antiquities of Great-Britain, illustrated in views of views of monasteries, castles, and churches, now existing, engraved from drawings by Thomas Hearne,* **1786. Plate 42. Reproduced by permission of Bodleian Library, University of Oxford. Reference: G.A.Gen. top. b.12.**

× 99 cm) is in the collection of the Leicester Museum and Art Gallery.

A month after the tragedy, Wordsworth shared with Beaumont his metaphysical quandary over John's death:

> Why have we a choice and a will, and a notion of justice and injustice, enabling us to be moral agents? Why have we sympathies that make the best of us so afraid of inflicting pain and sorrow, which yet we see dealt about so lavishly by the supreme governor? Why should our notions of right towards each other, and to all sentient beings without our influence differ so widely from what appears to be his notion and rule, if every thing were to end here? Would it be blasphemy to say that upon the supposition of the thinking principle being destroyed by death, however inferior we may be to the great Cause and ruler of things, we have *more of love* in our Nature than he has? The thought is monstrous; and yet how to get rid of it except upon the supposition of *another* and a *better world* I do not see. (*EY* 556)

Beaumont's response to this and to William's tormented defense of John's final behavior is warm but tactfully evasive. "What a man your brother must have been," he writes, "but I will not dwell upon a subject which must revive your sorrow—to time & the kindness of providence you must leave it."[30] In March 1806, Beaumont ventured a further comment that provides a gloss on *Peel Castle in a Storm.* In withdrawing from a discussion with Wordsworth on William Pitts's political leadership,[31] Beaumont says:

> —But let us turn from the political world which being conducted by men, & disturbed by their passions, is vexed by useless distraction & storms which produce nothing but evil[.] [I]n the meantime it is pleasing & awful to observe the great vessel of the universe steadily measuring its course with undeviating serenity—because guided by the perfect hand which governs all & "rolls thro all things," nevertheless as nothing can be perpetrated but by his permissions—I still am confident good will ultimately arise, for I have full faith in the aphorism that "partial ill will in the end produce universal good—["][32]

The allegory of God as Captain of the Vessel Universe sailing serenely through time and space is the antithesis of the troubled sublunary vessel in the oils of *Peel Castle,* but the concluding allusion to the aphorism from the First Epistle of Alexander Pope's *Essay on*

*Man* is a comment on the Christian optimism that suffuses the paintings:

> All Nature is but Art, unknown to thee;
> All Chance, Direction, which thou canst not see;
> All Discord, Harmony, not understood;
> All partial Evil, universal Good:
> And, spite of Pride, in erring Reason's spite,
> One truth is clear, "Whatever IS, is RIGHT."[33]

Beaumont blends the "presence" of "Tintern Abbey" that "rolls through all things" with his reference from Pope because he finds them compatible. Pope's God is also described as the soul of the universe: "All are but parts of one stupendous whole, / Whose body, Nature is, and God the soul" (1.267–68).[34] Beaumont's paintings of Piel Castle would attempt to represent the lingering eighteenth-century belief in a sublimely optimistic universe.

But why did Sir George choose Piel Castle as his subject? Could he have known of its significance to Wordsworth, who had written a year earlier of his experience in the vicinity of Piel Island in book 10 of the 1805 *Prelude*? We recall the details. Wordsworth had been visiting with cousins and friends at Rampside for one of the divinest months of his life in the summer of 1794, during which he visited the grave of his boyhood schoolmaster William Taylor and learned of the death of Robespierre while walking on Leven Sands. Beaumont knew that Wordsworth had completed the poem on the "History of Your Own Mind,"[35] as he referred to it, in May 1805, but did Wordsworth ever reveal to him how deeply he felt about his experiences in the vicinity of Piel Island?

These questions are not answered by the surviving correspondence, but Wordsworth and Beaumont may have shared memories of the Revolution's gory days during their first meeting. Sir George had come close to being executed during a visit to France in the spring of 1790, while walking with Lord Algernon Percy, then Lord Beverley. A gang seized another passerby to execute, but it could have been them. As Allan Cunningham concludes, "Sir George and his companion were in a fair way of being hanged as unceremoniously as the man they pitied, when a sympathetic citizen fixed a tricoloured cockade in their hats, and aided their escape."[36] Wordsworth's experience in 1790 was quite different—"Bliss was it in that dawn to be alive, / But to be young was very heaven," he writes in *The Prelude*—but several years later he experienced the fear that afflicted Beaumont from the outset of the Revolution: "Such ghastly visions had I of despair / And tyranny, and implements of death" (*Prelude* 1805, 10.374–75).

The joy Wordsworth experienced upon hearing of Robespierre's assassination followed his visit to William Taylor's grave at Cartmell Priory, where the memory of his inspirational schoolmaster was revived:

> He loved the Poets, and if now alive,
> Would have loved me, as one not destitute
> Of promise, nor belying the kind hope
> Which he had formed, when I at his command,
> Began to spin, at first, my toilsome Songs.
>
> (*1805* 10.510–14)

When he returned to his autobiography following John's death, his song became one of personal witness to the grand historical event of the age. It seems that Wordsworth was following Beaumont's advice on the importance of historical subjects for high art, but he was also creating his self-portrait in history. Wordsworth writes of the glory of his month at Rampside in lines that he will recall when composing "Elegiac Stanzas":

> O Friend! few happier moments have been mine
> Through my whole life than that when first I heard
> That this foul Tribe of Moloch was o'erthrown,
> And their chief Regent levelled with the dust.
> The day was one which haply may deserve
> A separate chronicle. Having gone abroad
> From a small Village where I tarried then,
> To the same far-secluded privacy
> I was returning. Over the smooth Sands
> Of Leven's ample Aestuary lay
> My journey, and beneath a genial sun;
> With distant prospect among gleams of sky
> And clouds, and intermingled mountain tops,
> In one inseparable glory clad,
> Creatures of one ethereal substance, met
> In Consistory, like a diadem
> Or crown of burning Seraphs, as they sit
> In the Empyrean. Underneath this show
> Lay, as I knew, the nest of pastoral vales

Among whose happy fields I had grown up
From childhood. On the fulgent spectacle
Which neither changed, nor stirred, nor passed away,
I gazed, and with a fancy more alive
On this account, that I had chanced to find
That morning, ranging through the churchyard graves
Of Cartmell's rural Town, the place in which
An honored Teacher of my youth was laid. . . .
A week, or little less, before his death
He had said to me, "my head will soon lie low,"
And when I saw the turf that covered him,
After the lapse of full eight years, those words,
With sound of voice, and countenance of the Man,
Came back upon me, so that some few tears
Fell from me in my own despite. . . .

      Without me and within, as I advanced,
All that I saw, or felt, or communed with
Was gentleness and peace. Upon a small
And rocky Island near, a fragment stood
(Itself like a sea rock) of what had been
A Romish Chapel, where in ancient times
Masses were said at the hour which suited those
Who crossed the Sands with ebb of morning tide.
.   .   .   .   .   .   .   .   .   .   .   .   .   .   .
                  the great Sea meanwhile
Was at a safe distance, far retired. I paused,
Unwilling to proceed, the scene appeared
So gay and chearful; when a Traveller
Chancing to pass, I carelessly inquired
If any news were stirring; he replied
In the familiar language of the day
That, *Robespierre was dead.* Nor was a doubt
On further question, left within my mind
But that the tidings were substantial truth;
That he and his supporters all were fallen.

      Great was my glee of spirit, great my joy
In vengeance, and eternal justice, thus
Made manifest. . . .
                  (*Prelude* 1805, 10.466–506; 515–41)

The poet himself then has linked "eternal justice, thus / Made manifest" to the environment of Piel Castle.

Sir George's daring to impose the memory of John Wordsworth's death on this significantly joyful time in Wordsworth's life was uncharacteristically bold, but fortuitous. In painting a troubled vessel off the stormy coast of Piel Island, thrusting toward the sunset and—in the smaller oil that Wordsworth preferred—actually being touched by lightning, Beaumont established a palimpsest of experiences in the mode of "Tintern Abbey." The sweet nostalgia over Taylor's memory as the poet's earliest mentor, the joy over Robespierre's death as an indication of "eternal justice," the felt bliss of being healthy and alive amid the "gentleness and peace" of nature, the Romish Chapel, "Itself like a sea rock," all provide a providential and challenging matrix for assimilating a profoundly tragic experience. Seen aright, Beaumont's painting suggests, John's death ought to be perceived within this context of spiritual revelation.

And yet, except in their personal meaning for Wordsworth, there is nothing extraordinary about Beaumont's oils. Considered in relationship to the genre of paintings and drawings of vessels in distress, they are commonplace. Many contain the same gothic elements, and a few contain all: a raging sea, a setting sun, a gloomy castle, lightning streaking across the night sky or hitting the vessel, and almost invariably, a stern view of the vessel plunging into the stormy waters.[37] It was a formula for the maritime sublime that the general public could recognize and appreciate.[38]

William Close's meditation on time and the ruins of Piel Castle in his edition of Benjamin West's *Antiquities of Furness* is equally pertinent and, having been recently published, may have attracted Beaumont, who had toured the north of England with Thomas Hearne in 1777, and had then arranged for his drawing and the engraving of Piel Castle by William Byrne and Thomas Medland in 1783.[39] Close begins his commentary with expected observations on the "extensive shattered walls, and ruinated towers, mak[ing] a solemn, majestic appearance" (369), but then begins a discusssion on geological change that he "classif[ies]" as a "Neptunian" force remaking the shape and surface of the earth. "A small square tower has stood at the southern corner," Close begins,

> but the greatest part of it has been thrown down by the sea. The foundation of one side wall is also undermined the whole of its length; and as it in some places overhangs the precipice, formed by the waste of the sea; and as the castle is not situated upon a rock, but upon hard loamy soil, this side must inevitably fall in a few years. (370–71)

Close then says he left with his companions because the tide was rising, but several weeks later they "crossed the channel in a boat . . .
procured at Rampside; and [chose for their] station a little to the
north-west of the small ruinous tower at the north corner of the
outer yard" (374), from which the following observations were
made:

> The walls contain no decorations of art; and are equally destitute of all
> natural embelishments [sic]: the rugged outlines of delapidation [sic],
> associating with the appearance of past magnificence, are the qualities
> which principally interest the imagination, while comparing the settled
> tranquillity of the present, with the turbulent ages that are past, and con-
> templating the view of this mouldering fabric,

> > "Where all devouring Time,
> > Sits on this throne of ruins hoar,
> > And winds and tempests sweep his various lyre."

Close comments on the geological change that has worked to the
advantage of the embattled castle:

> The island of Fouldrey has certainly been much larger at the erection of
> the castle than it is at present; but the sea, having reduced it to its pres-
> ent small compass, has abated the rapid career of its destruction; it now
> wastes the western shore of Walney, and forms a new tract out of the
> ruins, which proves a barrier to its progress upon the Pile of Fouldrey,
> and, at some future period, may be an accession to this island, in place
> of the land which it has lost. (374)

He then describes the great opposite fate of the Isle of Walney:
"Every high tide, as a monument of its power, amasses a long convex
ridge or bar of pebbles to those that were there before; and so rapid
is the increase, that it is said the Haws-end has lengthened two hundred yards, in the period of sixty years" (375). "Indeed," he continues in balancing the good with the bad, "the encroachment of the
sea has of late been so rapid near the houses called Southend, and
for two miles to the northward, that the dwellings of the present inhabitants, seem destined to the fate of those of their predecessors;
and that, in the course of a few centuries, the sea will break through
the island in one or more places; and the part which is at present
accumulating, may extend so far as to join the pile of Fouldrey"
(375). The lighthouse was built in 1790 on the Haws point of the

Isle of Walney, "as shipwrecks are very frequent along the eastern shore of that island" (376). The embedded message was clear. Nature, understood now as a force of geological change either gradual or cataclysmic, is always and forever affecting the life of man and his embattled edifices. Sometimes for the good, but as often for the bad, the force is amoral and thus poignant.[10]

Figure 7 is an image of Piel Castle taken from the angle of the oils. Figures 8 and 9 reveal the paintings to be nearly identical. As a preparatory study, the smaller oil is rougher in detail, as one readily notices by examining the feature of the castle in the center of the painting. Following Hearne's drawing, it looks like it might be a large rock, as if Beaumont knew of the Romish Chapel, "Itself like a sea rock," while in the larger canvas, the rocklike image is revealed to be an outer tower. The waves of the smaller canvas beating against the shore are also more of a white smudge than the more detailed froth of the larger. The vessel of the smaller canvas is more prominent. The vessels themselves are not of the same type. One can tell from its single sail and mast that the vessel of the smaller canvas is more like a sloop or longboat. The vessel of the larger canvas is nondescript, having no sails or discernible masts, and almost entirely under water with its stern up. The lightning is making contact with

7. Piel Castle. Photograph by author.

8. *Peel Castle in a Storm,* preparatory oil painting by Sir George Beaumont. Reproduced by permission of Dove Cottage, The Wordsworth Trust.

the sloop of the smaller oil, while the bolt from the darker sky of the larger oil is well off the starboard side of the vessel. Finally, the larger canvas contains the shadow of a larger vessel just out of the darkness to the right of the lightning bolt. Its masts and sails suggest a larger, possibly commercial vessel, such as an East Indiaman. The smaller canvas does not contain a second vessel. Finally, the smaller oil contains a lighthouse. We recall that Close provides the information that the lighthouse was built in 1790 on the neighboring Isle of Walney because "shipwrecks are very frequent along the eastern shore of that island."[41]

We cannot be certain when Wordsworth saw either of the paintings or in which order,[42] but I think it more likely that he would have seen the smaller oil in Beaumont's London apartment after seeing the larger oil on 2 May 1806 at the Royal Academy exhibit. After receiving the poem his painting(s) inspired, Beaumont wrote to Wordsworth of the awkwardness he felt before the poet first viewed *Peel Castle:* "When you came to town you will recollect I did not shew you Peele Castle tho it was in the room, because I thought it might raise painful sensations in your mind. I did not sufficiently consider

**9.** *Peel Castle in a Storm,* **finished oil painting by Sir George Beaumont. Reproduced by permission of the Leicester City Museum.**

'How sweet the uses were of your adversity, & what a precious jewel it wore in its head.' "[43]

Wordsworth responds with appreciation:

> I could not but write them with feeling with such a subject, and one that touched me so nearly: your delicacy in not leading me to the Picture did not escape me. It is a melancholy satisfaction to me to connect my dear Brother with anybody whom I love much; and I knew that the verses would give you pleasure as a proof of my affection for you. The picture was to me a very moving one; it exists in my mind at this moment as if it were before my eyes. (*MY* 1:63)

Wordsworth's reference to "it," or a single painting, rather than "them," or both, does suggest that only the first viewing mattered for "Elegiac Stanzas." If he only saw one of the oils, it was certainly the finished painting on exhibit at the Royal Academy. It seems he is referring to the public viewing when he refers to Beaumont not "leading him to the picture," but allowing him, as it were, to discover it for himself amid all the other paintings on display, which included Beaumont's painting inspired by Wordsworth's "The

Thorn." When Wordsworth finally happened upon *Peel Castle in a Storm*, he apparently absorbed it with epiphanic intensity.[44]

It is important to consider what the oils do and do not contain in relationship to all of the contexts we have considered to this point, because they all set the agenda for the poem. In relationship to the sinking of the *Abergavenny* and its aftermath, Beaumont's oils lack reference to the dramatic particularities of the tragedy that had been widely publicized: the possible foibles of the pilot, Capt. John Wordsworth's disabling dismay, the panic of hundreds of innocent victims in the final moments, any suggestion of the controversy over the presence of ship's boats or who finally used them, the flawed journalism of articles and pamphlets, the self-serving witness of the East India Company, material considerations related to the value of cargo, and, significantly, no visible presence of human life. The particularity of the frontispieces is forgone, and forgotten, in lieu of the larger, religious perspective suggested by John's final words, "God's will be done." The oils also lack the heroic cast Wordsworth attempted to give his mariner brother in his letters and in "The Happy Warrior." A nondescript vessel sinking toward a general sunset effaces the tragic demise of hundreds who perhaps did not know that "All Chance, [is] Direction, which thou canst not see; / All Discord, Harmony, not understood; / All partial Evil, universal Good."

Beaumont thereby transforms human accident into destiny. No pilot misdirected Beaumont's vessel onto the shoals. The distress of the vessel is rather the result of awesome sea-force sending a frail bark toward the light of the setting sun—sinking westward, as it were—with the outer bastion of the castle standing front and center to provoke an interpretation of fortitudinous human values. Wordsworth was apparently stunned by this radical reconceiving of his tragedy, painted by the School of Reynolds, framed by the optimism of Pope.

Its power was felt, for Wordsworth had so painfully personalized the event in his poetry that *his* art could provide no therapy for himself nor solace for loved ones. He felt his uselessness to Dorothy in particular, who, at least partly because of the bickering over monetary support for John's voyages, felt the loss grievously. However powerfully poised, such lines from "To the Daisy" could be of little consolation to anyone:

> Six weeks beneath the moving Sea
> He lay in slumber quietly,

Unforc'd by wind or wave
To quit the Ship for which he died,
(All claims of duty satisfied)
And there they found him at her side,
And bore him to the grave.

Vain service! yet not vainly done
For this, if other end were none,
That he, who had been cast
Upon a way of life unmeet
For such a gentle Soul and sweet,
Should find an undisturb'd retreat
Near what he lov'd, at last:

That neighbourhood of Wood and Field
To him a resting-place should yield,
A meek man and a brave!
The Birds shall sing, and Ocean make
A mournful murmur for *his* sake;
And Thou sweet Flower! shalt sleep and wake
Upon his senseless Grave.

(*P2V* 610–11)

Besides the sobering admissions that John was unsuited for his calling and that he died vainly, there is no suggestion here of nature's
responsibility for John's demise. Indeed, "Unforc'd by wind or
wave" suggests quite the opposite, as nature fails to interfere with
John's dutiful commitment to the "Ship for which he died." Indeed,
rather than the agency of his destruction, the "Ocean [will] make /
A mournful murmur for *his* sake." Wordsworth had been absorbed
in creating a palatable truth from the gathered accidentals of the
publicly and privately reported event, but the resulting narrative of
dutiful commitment does not bear up very well under this poem's
withering irony: "Vain service!" though perhaps "not vainly done,"
if the goal were a "senseless Grave" at last.

## 4. "ELEGIAC STANZAS"

Wordsworth provided Beaumont with a copy of "To the Daisy"
in August 1805, which went unmentioned in Beaumont's response.
Wordsworth refrained from sharing with the Beaumonts the more
painfully doleful "I only look'd for pain and grief," which translates

the tragedy into a linguistic dimension of words and woe lying beyond utterance:

> All vanish'd, in a single word,
> A breath, a sound, and scarcely heard.
> Sea, Ship, drown'd, shipwreck—so it came,
> The meek, the brave, the good was gone;
> He who had been our living John
> Was nothing but a name.
>
> That was indeed a parting! oh,
> Glad am I, glad that it is past;
> For there were some on whom it cast
> Unutterable woe.

"[A] single word" from the sea dissoved the hope and mental omnipotence of the gathered passages, including the Vision on Snowdon. Unlike the great elegies of English literature, this is unripe in
its consolation. Recalling the "foundation-stone of a little fishing
hut," which the brothers had lain "with tears" before John's hope-
ful departure, Wordsworth flatly concludes:

> Well, well, if ever verse of mine
> Have power to make his merits known,
> Then let a monumental Stone
> Stand here [at Grisedale Tarn]—a sacred Shrine;
> And to the few who come this way,
> Traveller or Shepherd, let it say,
> Long as these mighty rocks endure,
> Oh do not Thou too fondly brood,
> Although deserving of all good,
> On any earthly hope, however pure!
>
> (*P2V* 613–14)

The "earthly hope" was surely the prosperous, reconstructed family
life, that was to be founded upon John's commercial success.

One cannot help comparing this stoic resignation with the defi-
ance of Shakespeare's memorial sonnet on the power of his language
over "mighty rocks": "Not marble nor the gilded monuments / Of
princes shall outlive this pow'rful rhyme, / But you shall shine more
bright in these contents / Than unswept stone, besmeared with slut-
tish time."[45] A decade passed before Wordsworth published this memorial to John in modified form in *Poems* (1815), but the naïveté to

which he here confesses will find its outlet as the professed belief in nature's benignity in "Elegiac Stanzas."

Inspired by Beaumont's metaphysical reconception of the tragedy, Wordsworth was moved to invent his own—but to some, troubling—interpretation of the significance of John's death. In so doing, Marjorie Levinson not unreasonably claims, he "violently . . . falsifies his past."[46] For when did the mature Wordsworth ever believe nature to be as benign as the poem claims? The biographical and poetic records will not support the poet's contention that he retained his youthful belief in natural goodness to the compositional moment of "Elegiac Stanzas," as if he had at the age of thirty-six awakened from a harmful fantasy. From the "calm oblivious tendencies of nature" that overcome Margaret in *Ruined Cottage* (1798) to the very recent apostrophe to the power of the "visible Presence" to support trances of "forgetfulness" that "soothe, / And steal away, and for a while deceive / And lap in pleasing rest, and bear us on / Without desire in full complacency,"[47] we know that Wordsworth was fully conscious of the difficulties and the virtues in responding to nature's otherness. And yet, under the influence of Beaumont's reinterpretation of the tragedy as an act of God working through nature, Wordsworth leaves the reader with the impression that he indeed has only now awakened from the dream, which has kept him "housed . . . at distance from the Kind."

How are we to understand what "Elegiac Stanzas" is justifiably claiming and disclaiming? The poet's experience of 1794, near Rampside, represents an illusion inferred from outer peace and inner joy:

> I was thy Neighbour once, thou rugged Pile!
> Four summer weeks I dwelt in sight of thee:
> I saw thee every day; and all the while
> Thy form was sleeping on a glassy sea.
>
> So pure the sky, so quiet was the air!
> So like, so very like, was day to day!
> Whene'er I look'd, thy Image still was there:
> It trembled, but it never pass'd away.
>
> How perfect was the calm! it seem'd no sleep;
> No mood, which season takes away, or brings:
> I could have fancied that the mighty Deep
> Was even the gentlest of all gentle Things.

Wordsworth attributes to his earlier self the glowing naivete of youthful idealism:

> Ah! THEN, if mine had been the Painter's hand,
> To express what then I saw; and add the gleam,
> The light that never was, on sea or land,
> The consecration, and the Poet's dream;
>
> I would have planted thee, thou hoary Pile!
> Amid a world how different from this!
> Beside a sea that could not cease to smile;
> On tranquil land, beneath a sky of bliss:
>
> Thou shouldst have seem'd a treasure-house, a mine
> Of peaceful years; a chronicle of heaven:—
> Of all the sunbeams that did ever shine
> The very sweetest had to thee been given.
>
> A Picture had it been of lasting ease,
> Elysian quiet, without toil or strife;
> No motion but the moving tide, a breeze,
> Or merely silent Nature's breathing life.

One accepts that Wordsworth means exactly what he says about the origin and limitations of this magnificent illusion: it belongs to a very specific past ("Ah THEN"), that is, at that specific time in my life, and not up to the time I wrote "Salisbury Plain" or "Ruined Cottage."

But obviously this is half the story. His rejection of naivete occurs in the compositional present, suggesting that nature's beneficence might well be a cover for something else. As we learn from "I only looked for pain and grief," his most recent experience of genuine naïveté was believing in John's promise. The figurative language of "Elegiac Stanzas" suggests economic disappointment, with nature worship serving as a screen for mundane materialism. Even the problematic economic history of Piel Island and its castle supports the material dross underlying this golden poem.

The castle was built in the fourteenth century as a fortified warehouse for cargo against pirates and invaders. But the "Pile of Fotheray," as it was called, also kept the king's custom's men at a distance, and soon Piel Island and its castle became a haven for smugglers. High tariffs on many items caused a lucrative trade in contraband to flourish. The monks of neighboring Furness Abbey had built the castle in 1327 to improve some kind of wooden fortification in place since the reign of King Stephen (1135–1154). It seems that smuggling began at the outset as the monks themselves were so accused. In 1423 the merchants at Calais made a petition to Parliament to stop the smuggling of wool by Abbot Robert to Zealand. In alluding to this charge, Beck says, "Piel harbour became afterwards a place of great resort for those who sought to evade payment of the royal duties, as the abbot had done from the period of his elevation to that dignity."[48] The island remained the focal point of a thriving smuggling trade that went on into the eighteenth century. Records show that as many as 250 ships were anchored in the vicinity of the island at any one time. As the iron industry grew in neighboring Furness, shipping became important at Piel. Houses for pilots and a public house were built by the late eighteenth century.[49]

Adverting to the language of the poem, the fluorishing trade and the prominent trafficking in contraband make the Castle "a treasure-house." Overlaying the historical treasure-house is the fancied haven promised by John's dangerous voyaging and trading in both legal and illegal commodities. Piel's association with Furness Abbey makes appropriate the poem's reference to it as "a chronicle of heaven," as does the leisurely, godlike existence a successful voyage would have guaranteed:

> A Picture had it been of lasting ease,
> Elysian quiet, without toil or strife;
> No motion but the moving tide, a breeze,
> Or merely silent Nature's breathing life.

This is the Wordsworthian version of Gonzalo's Commonwealth of the Golden Age from one of the poet's favorite Shakespearean plays, *The Tempest*: "No occupation, all men idle, all; / And women too, but innocent and pure" (2.1.155–56). The golden age would proceed from the fruits of "That Hulk which labours in the deadly swell," that is, John's vessel working for the family.

It is a painful irony that John's tempest was not controlled by the white magic of a Prospero. Unlike Ariel's metaphorical rendering of Alonso's "sea-change" ("Full fathom five thy father lies"), John literally drifted under the sea until washed ashore six weeks later. William underwent the sea change. Unlike Prospero to Miranda, Wordsworth could not advise Dorothy to "Tell [her] piteous heart /

There's no harm done"; John's death was not a scene in a romance, and Wordsworth was at a loss for power. In "I only look'd for pain and grief," he indulges in a fantasy of what might have been, if life could imitate art. Viewing a buzzard alighting at the scene of his parting with John, he laments:

> The Buzzard mounted from the rock
> Deliberate and slow;
> Lord of the air, he took his flight;
> Oh could he on that woeful night
> Have lent his wing, my Brother dear!
> For one poor moment's space to Thee—
> And all who struggle with the Sea
> When safety is so near.
>
> Thus in the weakness of my heart
> I said (but let that pang be still)
> When rising from the rock at will,
> I saw the Bird depart.
>
> (*P2V*, 611–12, lines 23–34)

There is no "pageantry of fear" represented in Beaumont's oil—except from the poet's knowledgeable perspective—because there are no human figures. Wordsworth's imagining of the "pageantry of fear" onboard the sinking *Abergavenny*, had shaken, as McFarland says, every fiber of his being, but the "pageantry" is not *in* the painting. A "deep distress," as the poet says, has imbued his soul with a newfound tenderness for those suffering creatures that shared John's fate, which was a fortune exacerbated by his culpability:

> A power is gone, which nothing can restore;
> A deep distress hath humaniz'd my Soul.

*Distress* is a rich word for gathering relevant associations at the multiple levels of Wordsworth's experience. In its primary sense for the poem it refers to the calamity. A phrase in the *OED* from Burke's *Speech on the East India Bill* is pertinent to Wordsworth's transformation: "Want of feeling for the distresses of mankind." In its nautical sense, distress is "a term used when a ship requires immediate assistance from an unlooked-for damage or danger" (Smyth *Sailor's Word-bk*). In a legal sense, distress refers to seizing property in lieu of repayment of a debt, as in *Caleb Williams,* "The squire . . . took the earliest opportunity of seizing on his remaining property in the mode of a distress for rent." Faintly, this definition of distress recalls the awkward monetary relationship between the brothers and their sister over financing John's final voyage and the hostility that smoldered over insuring their inheritance. More directly, the economic distress John was suffering included the loss of investor's money, the loss of cargo, and ultimately the loss of his career. In its meteorological sense, distress refers to "the overpowering pressure *of* some adverse force, as anger, hunger, bad weather; stress (of weather)." For example, 1793: "Driven westward, by distress of weather." We also recall the title of the pamphlet frontispiece, *The Distress'd State of the Crew of the Abergavenny when she was sinking Feby 5, 1805.* All of these connotations of "distress"—the emotional, the meteorological, the nautical, the legal/economic, even the journalistic—in addition to its being literally "deep," that is, submerged under eleven fathoms of salt water, represent the depth of Wordsworth's response to John's death, now recalled by the suggestive images of Beaumont's painting.

In sum, the poet's naivete toward nature as a young man is a screen for his more recent domestic and economic naivete. Even the epithets for the castle—"thou rugged Pile!," "thou hoary Pile!"—which, as Levinson remarks, function as a homonym for the pronunciation of the real name of Piel Castle, plays with the definition of *pile* as a heap of money. The accumulated double entendres and associations related to money are quiet but telling: the castle itself as the center of a flourishing but mostly dishonorable trade, "pile," "treasure-house," "mine," "toil," a "trust," "my loss," "work," "labours." The loss of John is equivalent to the loss of the Elysium Grasmere would have become.

The poet's "deep distress" humanizing his soul has its closest literary counterpart in Alonso's sea change from *The Tempest.* The pain of Alonso's sea change is intense. Being informed by Ariel that nature is seeking vengeance for the murder of Prospero and Miranda through the drowning of his beloved son Ferdinand, Alonso speaks of the justice that demands his suicide:

> O, it is monstrous, monstrous!
> Methought the billows spoke and told me of it,
> The winds did sing it to me, and the thunder,
> That deep and dreadful organ-pipe, pronounced

> The name of Prosper. It did bass my trespass.
> Therefor my son i'th'ooze is bedded, and
> I'll seek him deeper than e'er plummet sounded,
> And with him there lie mudded.
>
> (3.3.95–102)

After the suffering fired by the pressure of his great guilt, Alonso is awarded with the discovery that all are still alive. As a grain of sand under the water pressure of ocean becomes a pearl within the oyster's shell, his transformation from a Machiavellian to a humane, gentler man, is complete. Wordsworth's story is no comparable romance, except in the employ of deep psychological transformation catalyzed by guilt as a precedent to humanization. No romantic naivete, but rather succumbing to the risk of material rewards results in the sacrifice of a younger brother, with whom the poet's imagination "lie[s] mudded."

With belief in fantasies gone, Wordsworth concludes that the "spirit" of Beaumont's painting is "well-chosen," for its castle standing sublimely in the night storm represents the fortitude that John possessed on that stormy night in February and that William now requires in the emotional storm in his heart. Loss is not a new experience for mankind, but neither is the religious defense against its pain associated with old Christianity, now blended with the optimism of eighteenth-century rationalism. Cleanth Brooks once observed that a "great many eighteenth-century modes of thought linger in Wordsworth's poetry," but found that early poems such as *Ruined Cottage* to be moving from the "quasi-deistic poetry of the Age of Reason."[50] "Elegiac Stanzas" marks a reversal in that as well.

And what of the ambiguous "power" that we began this inquiry by questionning?

> I have submitted to a new controul:
> A power is gone, which nothing can restore.

Its vagueness would seem to lure us into the paradigm of Romantic discourse in which Clifford Siskin says we too often indulge—we have "gloried in the gaps" is his clever inditement.[51] But one might attempt to understand the poem in its own spirit, while remaining at a critical distance from the speaker.

Most interpretations of "power" find it to be an internal agency of the speaker. It follows as logically from its preceding line—"I have submitted to a new controul"—that one "power" is being replaced by another, a "new" external "controul." In keeping with the monetary undercurrent of the language, one notes that Johnson's *Dictionary* offers as a note on etymology that the noun *control* means a "register or account kept by another officer, that each may be examined by the other." In this sense, control is related to *controller* (nowadays usually spelled as *comptroller*), an officer who keeps the "counter roll" against the treasurer to keep honest track of expenditures. If John Wordsworth were not in the employ of the East India Company, one might ignore or overlook an association with the Board of Control established by Pitt in 1784 to oversee the East India Company's government of British India. Taking this association into consideration brings in the inevitable disassocation between the family and the Company. Not to ignore its primary and most obvious meaning, control generally means a "check; restraint." Taking these definitions together, "controul" in the poem means something like "I have submitted to a new check upon my material aspirations, which used to be associated with commercial ventures." The previous "power" refers not to John Wordsworth per se, but something like the function of Christ as God's "effectual might" in *Paradise Lost,* who goes out into the world to live and to die to fulfill the Father's divine plan,[52] just as the poet's Arab functions in the Dream of waters "gathering upon us." Relatedly, the extension of the poet's power is to send John out into the world to act on his behalf, while he remains at home to create poetry. The power to fulfill grandiose wishes that resided in John's career was lost at sea. At our figurative level, the "new controul" is associated with modest material aspirations, perhaps now coming from the Beaumonts and patronage.

Sir George may have believed after reading "Elegiac Stanzas" that Wordsworth had been converted to his aesthetic. His painting in the eighteenth-century sea-sublime had inspired a poem of confident declarations—a poetry of statement, as it were—about a stoic faith in philosophical optimism:

> But welcome fortitude, and patient chear,
> And frequent sights of what is to be borne!
> Such sights, or worse, as are before me here.—
> Not without hope we suffer and we mourn.
>
> ("Elegiac Stanzas," 57–60)

But *Poems, in Two Volumes* also includes poems in the idiosyncratic vein that distressed the poet's supporters and enervated his enemies. The attacks were particularly disturbing to Sir George and Lady Beaumont.

## 5. POEMS, IN TWO VOLUMES

Wordsworth put a great deal of time into organizing *Poems, in Two Volumes,* which was published on 28 April 1807. There has been some recognition of his efforts in the criticism. Richard Cronin finds *P2V* to be

> a collection addressed, to use a distinction that became important to Wordsworth at this time, not to the "public" but to the "people," not to the nation as a hierarchically ordered entity, held together by a system of difference, but to the nation as a "solemn fraternity" that will recognize the variousness of Wordsworth's volumes as a proper representation of the spaciousness of its own heart. The collection wills such a people into being, but it dares to do so because the war has given Wordsworth a "firmer faith" that his countrymen's "virtue and the faculties within" remain "vital."[53]

On the irony of Wordsworth speaking to a people, in the "real language of men," who would scoff at his use of their language, more will be said later. Cronin is surely correct, however, in emphasizing the public purpose of the patriotic sonnets and the audience Wordsworth hoped to reach.

Of the volumes' seven sections, the final grouping entitled "The Blind Highland Boy; with other Poems" ends with "Elegiac Stanzas" and "Ode" [Intimations of Immortality]. Wordsworth's guidance to Lady Beaumont on reading his poems in *Poems, in Two Volumes* gives one confidence that this section's prominent positioning in the collection, its framing poems, and perhaps its internal development are intended to be as meaningfully organized as the sonnets, whether or not we succeed in perceiving it.[54] Jared Curtis's description of this section as a "loose combination of poems," except for an "elegiac mood enter[ing] midway in the grouping" (*P2V* 37), is not inaccurate, but, to give Wordsworth the benefit of a doubt, it may be incomplete in ignoring the opening poem as well as some of the earlier poems of the sequence.

The occasion for the reading lesson Wordsworth provided Lady

Beaumont was her concern that the reception of *Poems, in Two Volumes* was not going well among the readers she knew. A Mr. Rogers complained that the shorter, trifling poems were distracting. Wordsworth responded immediately on his utter disregard for the opinion of the "Public," even apart from "the envious and malevolent," because of "pure absolute honest ignorance" of "all worldlings of every rank and situation," with some focus on the cultural elite of the metropolis:

> The things which I have taken, whether from within or without,—what have they to do with routs, dinners, morning calls, hurry from door to door, from street to street, on foot or in Carriage; with Mr. Pitt or Mr. Fox, Mr. Paul or Sir Francis Burdett, the Westminster Election of the Borough of Honiton; . . . what have they to do (to say all at once) with a life without love? in such a life there can be no thought; for we have no thought (save thoughts of pain) but as far as we have love and admiration. (MY 1:145–146)

From the moral elevation of Grasmere, Wordsworth sees the critical Mr. Rogers as one of a class "who would be pleased if they could . . . but their imagination has slept; and the voice which is the voice of my Poetry without Imagination cannot be heard" (MY I 146). A prepared reader would see that the sonnets on liberty, for example, "have a connection with, or a bearing upon, each other, and therefore, if individually they want weight, perhaps as a Body, they may not be so deficient":

> Again, turn to the "Moods of my own Mind," There is scarcely a Poem here of above thirty Lines, and very trifling these poems will appear to many; but, omitting to speak of them individually, do they not taken collectively, fix the attention upon a subject eminently poetical, viz., the interest which objects in nature derive from the predominance of certain affections more or less permanent, more or less capable of salutary renewal in the mind of the being contemplating these objects? This is poetic, and essentially poetic, and why? because it is creative. (MY 1:147)

His last and most important point is a reminder to Lady Beaumont of Coleridge's comment that "every great and original writer, must himself create the taste by which he is to be relished; he must teach the art by which he is to be seen" (MY 1:150). For all of these reasons, Wordsworth says that his "ears are stone-dead to this idle buzz, and [his] flesh is insensible as iron to these petty stings." He has "an invincible confidence that [his] writings . . . will co-operate with the benign tendencies in human nature and society, wherever found; and that they will, in their degree, be efficacious in making men wiser, better, and happier" (MY I 150). One might assume from this that Wordsworth would be well-prepared for the reviews, with ears "stone dead," and flesh as "insensible as iron."

The section entitled "The Blind Highland Boy" consists of twenty-four poems, with several of those composed after John's death positioned to offer mitigation for the pain of "Elegiac Stanzas" and a path to the transcendent force of the Ode.[55] "The Blind Highland Boy" opens the section with a narrative of a blind child's longing for the sea. The child is something of a musical prodigy who makes the sweetest melody on the bagpipes (lines 41–45) and finds enchantment in the sound of waters from the sea-fed lake near the family cottage. But he enjoys most the tales of passing sailors on "wonders of the Deep" (75), and the sounds of sealife and comaraderie, "the shouting, and the jolly cheers, / The bustle of the mariners / In stillness or in storm" (78–80). His mother forbids his dreams of sea adventure, for "The danger is so great" (90). At the age of ten the boy makes his move.

If the poem were not being narrated for a child's amusement (1–4), the blind boy setting sail in a washing tub found near the shore of Loch Levin would be silly, even if it were based on fact, as Wordsworth argued when Coleridge sought, successfully, to have him change the vessel to a turtle's shell for the edition of 1815. But for now the poet's "tale of a tub" moves on in a manner redolent of the Idiot Boy, his hapless mother shrieking, the sightless boy "in the triumph of his joy" (137), being carried towards the open sea by the ebb tide. The poet sympathizes with the child's dream of escape:

> And let him, let him to his way,
> Alone, and innocent, and gay!
> For, if good Angels love to wait
> On the forlorn unfortunate,
>     This Child will take no harm.

(141–45)

A rescue boat finally catches up with him. The boy hears it "in his darkness," and shouts "*Lei-gha—Lei-gha,*" interpreted by the poet as "Keep away, / And leave me to myself" (161–65), or more literally, as "Let me go," "Let me go," but the boy's adventure is ended, as the poet feelingly recounts:

> So all his dreams, that inward light
> With which his soul had shone so bright,
> All vanish'd;—'twas a heartfelt cross
> To him, a heavy, bitter loss,
>     As he had ever known.

(171–75)

Nevertheless, the villagers and the boy's mother are wildly glad, and the boy of former "fancies . . . wild," spirit now broken, eventually learns to be "pleased, and reconciled / To live on shore" (204–5).

One can conclude that "The Blind Highland Boy" is an innocent poem of wish-fulfillment, an antithesis, of sorts, to "Elegiac Stanzas." A child can harmlessly follow his heart and be dragged from danger by wiser heads. A narrative poet seeking to teach his youthful auditor a lesson can both sympathize with the child's yearning and acknowledge that—to return to a poem like "The Brothers"—the desire to follow the Sirens of the sea must be suppressed on behalf of family and community.

One recalls that Wordsworth had a related interest in the state of consciousness available to Highland dwellers. On their walking tour of Scotland, he and Dorothy witnessed the "half-articulate Gaelic hooting" of a boy when calling in the cows, about which Wordsworth comments that the whole misty scene "was a text . . . containing in itself the whole history of the Highlander's life—his melancholy, his simplicity, his poverty, his superstition, and above all, that visionariness which results from a communion with the unworldliness of nature" (*DWJ*, 1:286). He, too, now listens for the "unworldliness," which might fulfill his expressed desire in the final poem of the preceding sequence to "step beyond [his] natural race / . . . might one day trace/ Some ground not mine; and, strong her strength above, / [His] soul, an Apparition in the place, / Tread there, with steps that no one shall reprove!" ("It is no Spirit who from Heaven hath flown," *P2V*, p. 217, lines 13–17).

Toward the conclusion of the "Blind Highland Boy" sequence, the poet hears in the Cuckoo's echo something "Like her ordinary cry, / Like but oh how different!" in the preternatural analogy it suggests:

> Hears not also mortal Life?
> Hear not we, unthinking Creatures!
> Slaves of Folly, Love, or Strife,
> Voices of two different Natures?

> Have not We too? Yes we have
> Answers, and we know not whence;
> Echoes from beyond the grave,
> Recogniz'd intelligence?
>
> Such within ourselves we have
> Oft-times, ours though sent from far;
> Listen, ponder, hold them dear;
> For of God, of God they are!
>
> (9–24)

In "Loud is the Vale," the poem immediately prior to "Elegiac Stanzas," we learn that Fox's imminent death has the poet "ev'n to pain depress'd" during a walk reminiscent of the opening of "The Leech Gatherer." Following a storm that has the "mighty Unison of streams!" shouting as with one voice throughout the Vale of Grasmere, even as "this inland Depth / In peace is roaring like the Sea," the poet discovers a "Comforter" in the image of "Yon Star upon the mountain-top / . . . listening quietly" (1–8). Unlike the "many thousands" who await "the fulfilment of their fear; / For He must die who is their Stay," the poet can draw a calming influence from the placid star to understand its message:

> A Power is passing from the earth
> To breathless Nature's dark abyss;
> But when the Mighty pass away
> What is it more than this.
>
> That man, who is from God sent forth,
> Doth yet again to God return?—
> Such ebb and flow must ever be,
> Then wherefore should we mourn?
>
> (lines 13–24)

Such preparatory solace modifies for the reader the conflicts and intensity of "Elegiac Stanzas" as a poem in context, as if we and the poet are now awaiting the next poem with metaphysical resolve and with metaphorical anticipation of the "ebb and flow [that] must ever be"; rather than open to the hard-earned discovery of mortal hope in the poem's development. Not a single reviewer, however, paid attention to the structural features of the volumes.

6. DISTRESSING REVIEWS OF *POEMS, IN TWO VOLUMES*

It has taken so long for only some of the poems in *Poems, in Two Volumes* to receive their just acclaim that we cannot be too hard on its contemporary reviewers, who were unanimous in rejecting the poet's effort to memorialize his personal experience with large claims made simply, especially in the notorious section, "Moods of My Own Mind." Wordsworth's main concern was protecting his economic interests. Bad reviews would predictably undermine sales, and money was needed for domestic necessities. He wrote a letter to Francis Wrangham on 12 July 1807 asking him to keep *Poems, in Two Volumes* out of the hands of LeGrice so that a more sympathetic reviewer for the *Critical Review* might be found. Dorothy reiterates the message to Catherine Clarkson a week later, bemoaning the poor income of a poet and their hope that the edition will sell as they have to meet "expenses of fitting up our new house and the high rent" (*MY* 156–57).

Nevertheless, month by month for about a year the most distressing reviews of the poet's career poured forth. Byron published the first review of record in July 1807 and established the pattern for much of the commonplace criticism: appreciation for the poet's former works, distress now with "language not simple, but puerile," and the waste of the poet's talent on "trifling subjects."[56] In August 1807, Wordsworth received the dreaded judgment of *Critical Review* that he should "undergo a certain term of rigid penance and inward mortification; before he can become what he once promised to be, the poet of the heart; and not the capricious minion of a debasing affectation" (313–401). In October, *Beau Monde* reproved him for his "affectation of simplicity," which "imitates the lisp of children" (44; 142). Francis Jeffrey's important attack in *Edinburgh Review* also appeared in October 1807. In reflecting upon earlier reviews of *Lyrical Ballads*, Jeffrey says he found it necessary to criticize the poet earlier for seducing others to his poetical principles of "alarming innovation" (429; 214). Now he is sure that he did not criticize too severely, for the present poems are worse, especially in their diction:

> With Mr. Wordsworth and his friends, it is plain that their peculiarities of diction are things of choice, and not of accident. They write as they do, upon principle and system; and it evidently costs them much pains to keep down to the standard which they have proposed to themselves. (431; 217).

Another problem important to Jeffrey is the weird associations the poet makes of his simple observations:

> It is possible enough . . . that the sight of a friend's garden-spade, or a sparrow's nest, or a man gathering leeches, might really have suggested to such a mind a train of powerful impressions and interesting reflections; but it is certain, that, to most minds, such associations will always appear forced, strained, and unnatural; and that the composition in which it is attempted to exhibit them, will always have the air of parody, or ludicrous and affected singularity. (431; 218).

Jeffrey selects the following poems for censure: "To the Daisy," "Louisa," "The Redbreast and the Butterfly," "To the Small Celandine," "The Beggars," "Alice Fell," "Resolution and Independence," "Rob Roy," "Address to the Sons of Burns," and "Yarrow Unvisited." He then lambasts "Moods of My Own Mind," in general and finds "Ode" incomprehensible. He quotes some good verses to prove that Wordsworth can write when he is not in thrall to his system and closes with the hope that Wordsworth's extravagance may be now spent and that he might now recognize the "established laws of poetry" (438; 231).

The lesser reviews maintained these themes unabated. In *The Satirist* (November 1807), the anonymous reviewer scoffs at a system of poetry and theory of diction unknown to Homer, Virgil, Shakepeare, Milton, and Dryden, which is fallacious because language is "entirely factitious and arbitrary." On the level of object, rather than social class, this reviewer observes "Almost a ludicrous contrast . . . produced between the swelling self-sufficiency of the writer, and the extreme insignificance of the object described" (846; 189).

The poet James Montgomery might have been expected to provide a fair-minded critique in *Eclectic Review* (January 1808), for he was almost unique in appreciating Wordsworth's "system" and language, complimenting Wordsworth as "one of the boldest and most fortunate adventurers in the field of innovation" (333; 35). He also had praise for Wordsworth's awakening feelings in "Tintern Abbey," "The Old Cumberland Beggar," and "Verses on the Naming of Places," "the existence of which in our nature had scarcely been intimated to us by any preceding poet," and reminds the poet that he accomplished this effect with "diction of transcendent beauty," as illustrated with a long quote from "Tintern Abbey" (334; 37). But now *Poems, in Two Volumes* is filled in inverse proportion with bad work. In "these incomparable, and almost incomprehensible volumes," Montgomery continues, "[a] more rash and injudicious speculation on the weakness of the depravity of the public taste has seldom been made." He hopes that this great failure will bring the poet back to his senses, or more importantly "of the respect due his readers" (335; 39). In contrast with *Lyrical Ballads,* where the purpose of each poem in the volume was obvious, "most of [these poems] seem to have been written for no purpose at all, and certainly to no good one" (337; 43).

In February 1808, or shortly after the appearance of what should have been Montgomery's sympathetic review, Beaumont wrote Wordsworth a letter on the singularity of his verse. The occasion for the letter was Lady Beaumont's faux pas in sending to Wordsworth earlier in the month a friend's criticism of "I Wandered Lonely as a Cloud." Because of unfamiliarity with the 1807 text over the received text of 1815, which is so justifiably admired that it is presently the most anthologized poem in the English language, I will here provide the contemporary text of ridicule:

> I wandered lonely as a Cloud
> That floats on high o'er Vales and Hills
> When all at once I saw a crowd
> A host of dancing Daffodils;
> Along the Lake, beneath the trees,
> Ten thousand dancing in the breeze.
>
> The waves beside them danced, but they
> Outdid the sparkling waves in glee:—
> A Poet could not but be gay
> In such a laughing company:
> I gaz'd—and gaz'd—but little thought
> What wealth the shew to me had brought:
>
> For oft when on my couch I lie
> In vacant or in pensive mood,
> They flash upon that inward eye
> Which is the bliss of solitude,
> And then my heart with pleasure fills,
> And dances with the Daffodils.

(P2V 207–8)

We can infer the content of the friend's criticism from Wordsworth's response. "Thanks for dear lady B.'s transcript from your Friend's Letter," Wordsworth writes to Sir George:

it is written with candour, but I must say a word or two not in praise of it. "Instances of what I mean," says your Friend, "are to be found in a poem on a Daisy" (by the bye, it is on *the* Daisy, a mighty difference). "and on Daffodils *reflected in the Water*" Is this accurately transcribed by Lady Beaumont? If it be, what shall we think of criticism of judgement founded upon and exemplified by a Poem which must have been so inattentively perused? My Language is precise, and, therefore, it would be false modesty to charge myself with blame.

> —Beneath the trees,
> Ten thousand dancing in the *breeze.*
> The *waves beside* them danced, but they
> Outdid the *sparkling waves* in glee.

Can expression be more distinct? And let me ask your Friend how it is possible for flowers to be *reflected* in water where there are *waves.* They may indeed in still water—but the very object of my poem is the trouble or agitation both of the flowers and the Water. I must needs respect the understanding of every one honoured by your friendship; but sincerity compels me to say that my Poems must be more nearly looked at before they can give rise to any remarks of much value, even from the strongest minds. (*MY* 1:194–95)

Wordsworth then goes on to infer larger consequences on the depravity of the reading public and consequently the misfortune to which his poetry seems hopelessly doomed:

> The fact is, the English *Public* are at this moment in the same state of mind with respect to my Poems, if small things may be compared with great, as the French are in respect to Shakespear; and not the French alone, but almost the whole Continent. In short, in your Friend's Letter, I am condemned for the very thing for which I ought to have been praised; viz., that I have not written down to the level of superficial observers and unthinking minds. — — Every great Poet is a Teacher: I wish either to be considered a Teacher, or as nothing. (*MY* 1:195)

Wordsworth stated early in his relationship with Beaumont that "There can be no valuable friendship where the parties are not mutually capable of instructing and delighting each other; I am sure that you and I have both lived long enough to be convinced of this truth, these qualities I have found in you and Lady Beaumont" (*EY* 499). Thus, when Wordsworth received the following response from Beaumont, he is likely to have taken it seriously.

Beaumont begins by tactfully apologizing for his wife's indiscretion in passing on their friend's criticism, "for as my friend[']s permission had not been obtained or asked it was not fair to communicate what was written in a hurry & imparted in confidence." The irony of the situation is that the friend "is a most ardent admirer of your works in general," Beaumont writes, "& in common with us was nettled to perceive them not relished as they deserved, & so illiberally treated his sincere wish is that they may become generally read, not only on your account but for the sake of the good they are so well calculated to produce," which

> induced him to consider in his mind what could be the reason they were not more popular. & this produced the observation which if not well founded was at least well meant, and wishing to illustrate his criticism & nor having the book by him was the cause of the inaccuracy of his reference, had he intended it for publication or any other way than in confidence between himself & me, he would of course have been more careful, but as an additional proof how easy it may be to overlook a circumstance of that kind, when possessed by a certain spirit of investigation, the inaccuracy escaped both Lady Beaumont & myself, altho the two poems are great favorites of ours, & she has them by heart.

"[T]he fact is," Sir George says, readers do not know how to read biographical poetry of recondite experience:

> we did not apply the observation to the poems in question but equally anxious with my friend to find out any cause which might be an impediment to their general circulation our mind, never engaged in considering whether you never were induced to select subjects so peculiarly the offspring of your own observation that people in general could not feel their whole force & beauty without the advantage of your illustration—

He then goes on to assuage what he knows will be a serious case of wounded feelings with a scene of adulation for the poet:

> If you were to see how earnestly Lady Beaumont & Mrs. Fermor are now reading your poems in the next room & observe the delight in both their countenances it would make you some amends for this criticism which I hope as we had no right to communicate it, you will not suffer to go out of your family[!]

Beaumont then inserts some small talk and concludes with an allusion to Wordsworth's commentary on Shakespeare by misquoting

Shakespeare—whom he has acted many times as a young man—so that Wordsworth could better understand the life of real readers reading:

> Shakespear who could not be mistaken observes somewhere that there never was [a] philosopher who could endure the toothache patiently—but as I quote from memory I strongly suspect I am quite as inaccurate as my friend.[57]

Beaumont and his friend were not alone in identifying the particular challenge offered by "I Wandered Lonely as a Cloud." Anna Seward concluded of the poem: "Surely if his worst foe had chosen to caricature this egotistic manufacturer of metaphysic importance upon trivial themes, he could not have done it more effectually."[58] However, Beaumont was a friend, as disappointed for the poet as he was for his efforts at having him accepted into polite London society. It had seemed possible, even probable, during Wordsworth's 1806 visit to London, when Beaumont introduced him to the artists of his circle and to the political elite of his acquaintance. But Wordsworth was now an object of either disappointment or derision.

Wordsworth visited London again in early 1808 to look to the ailing Coleridge. Apparently, the universality of negative criticism and conference with Coleridge caused him to reconsider his immediate publication plans for *The White Doe of Rylstone*. Dorothy wrote him in March of her great disappointment. "As to the Outcry against you, I would defy it," she wrote, "what matter, if you get your 100 guineas into your pocket?" Besides, it would be as if the critics, "had run you down, when it is known you have a poem ready for publishing, and keep it back" (*MY* 1:207).

It may be that the cool reception given *White Doe* in a private reading at the Lambs, with Hazlitt in attendance, aroused Wordsworth's insecurity. Wordsworth said that Lamb had no mind worth considering when it came to poetry, for he has neither a "reasoning mind, and therefore cannot have a comprehensive mind, and, least of all, has he an imaginative mind" (*MY* 1:223). Of course, worse could be said about almost every other reader in London. He bothered to mention to Coleridge, as if it were exceptional, that one Dubois was one of the anonymous reviewers who "abused my last Poems, and this, too, in a most disingenuous manner!" (*MY* 1:223)

The criticism continued relentlessly for the rest of the year. Under the weight of all of this dis-sympathy, Wordsworth wrote Beaumont in April of walking about London in a state of melancholy, when he looked up and saw the "majestic form of St Paul[']s, solemnised by a thin veil of falling snow." His "sorrow was controlled, and [his] uneasiness of mind not quieted and relieved altogether, seemed at once to receive the gift of an anchor of security" (*MY* 1:209). In addition to this spot-of-time, he concludes with some comments made to him by a grocer of Lancaster, as if he were one of the border figures of earlier years, who could give him strength when needed. Not knowing he was talking to Wordsworth, the grocer said that the poet had written "some very beautiful Poems; The Critics do indeed cry out against them, and condemn them as *over simple*, but for my part I read them with great pleasure, they are natural and true" (*MY* I 210). However the only positive published comment appeared in an omnibus review in the *Annual Register* with dubious praise for the poet: one of "[t]he Minor Poets of the year . . . who has given us two small additional volumes of 'Poems,' for the most part lyrical, and possessing his common ease and simplicity" (782; 378).

Also in April, Wordsworth wrote to Wrangham a letter about the currency of his feelings for John. Apparently, Wrangham had offered to purchase a home for the Wordsworths near the ocean, to which Wordsworth responds that

> I could not be easy under the thought of any Body having the trouble of building a House for me, and since the loss of my dear Brother, we have all had such painful and melancholy thoughts connected with the ocean that nothing but a paramount necessity could make us live near it. (*MY* 1:212)

In May 1809, Dorothy makes a bald admission on the status of her brother's career, especially its profitlessness. In a letter to De-Quincey, suggesting that he might send some letters to the Edinburgh and London newspapers on Wordsworth's behalf, especially since Jeffrey had attacked him yet again in a review of Burns's works, Dorothy mentions that his poems weren't selling.

She also comments that "he intends to blend the 4 volumes together whenever they are re-printed—or should I say *if* ever? for we hear no more from Longman, and I believe that the two last volumes scarcely sell at all" (*MY* 1:326). She believes that it was Jeffrey's malice that has destroyed William's reputation and ruined his sales.

Reflecting on *Poems, in Two Volumes* in 1812, Sir George admitted disappointedly that "Wordsworth's reputation as a poet wd. have stood higher had the two volumes of His poems contained only those which would be generally approved." He judged that Wordsworth was as superior to the far more popular Walter Scott as the great Claude Lorrain was to himself; thus it was painfully regrettable that the critics were given poems "puerile in their simplicity" to attack.[59] But perhaps no criticism could have aroused the disappointment Wordsworth must have felt when he recalled John's sacrifice on his behalf: John would work for him so that he might do something "for the world." They were now brothers in failure, or of success defined so privately that not even a much-beloved sister could acknowledge it.

# Postscript

As I suggested in the section "*PORTRAYED* on a tea-tray," Wordsworth held concerns about the notoriety the family would suffer from John's disaster at sea. The pamphlet Wordsworth annotated, "*An Authentic Narrative of the Loss of the* Earl of Abergavenny, *East Indiaman, Captain John Wordsworth*, . . . By a Gentleman in the East-India House,"[1] drew his special attention for its anticipation of enduring public interest, because of the inevitable comparison between the sinking of the *Abergavenny* and the sinking of the *Halsewell,* East Indiaman, just seven miles distant, in January 1786.

He correctly highlighted the likely endurance of his brother's story, as proven by its most recent appearance in Terence Grocott's *Shipwrecks of the Revolutionary and Napoleonic Eras* (1997) and Keith Huntress's edition of *Narratives of Shipwrecks and Disasters, 1586–1860* (1974). But the most unnerving and galling reminder of his brother's death was to come from Lord Byron in the work that Wordsworth found his most offensive, *Don Juan.* In the shipwreck incident from canto 2 (1819), Wordsworth would find Juan heroically mouthing the lines from the pamphlets on the sinking of the *Abergavenny* as Juan defends the spirit-room from the crew, just as John's unidentified midshipman had done that fateful night of 5 February 1805. The pamphlet Wordsworth read stated:

> When Caesar met his fate in the Capitol, he folded his robe about him, that he might fall with decency—when the sailors pressed ardently for a supply of liquor on the officer who guarded the spirit-room—"Give us some grog!" exclaimed the honest Tars; "it will be all as one an hour hence!"—the reply of the officer would have done honour to the brevity of Roman fortitude—"I know we must die," cooly replied the gallant Midshipman, "but let us die like men!"—He kept his post, armed with a brace of pistols, and there staid, even whilst the ship was sinking. (16)

It was noted above that this and other anecdotes of heroic behavior performed by Captain Wordsworth's subordinate officers served as a devastating contrast to his inaction. The best that Wordsworth's pamphlet could make of John's behavior was that perhaps John was dilatory in not saving lives, but it was "hardly probable, whatever might have been the resolution of the passengers, that *all* the crew would have deserted her—it is a well-known fact, that some sailors will not quit a sinking ship." For example, the account goes on, when the *London*, East Indiaman, sank at sea, the crew were "seen in the ACT of CHEERING as she went down" (17).

Byron must have savored the irony of this bumptious nationalism. With Juan's vessel in distress, matters proceed more candidly, and for Wordsworth as reader—if he could have gotten through it— more critically:

### 35

Perhaps more mischief had been done, but for
    Our Juan, who, with sense beyond his years,
Got to the spirit-room, and stood before
    It with a pair of pistols; and their fears,
As if Death were more dreadful by his door
    Of fire than water, spite of oaths and tears,
Kept still aloof the crew, who, ere they sunk,
Thought it would be becoming to die drunk.

### 36

"Give us more grog," they cried, "for it will be
    All one an hour hence." Juan answer'd, "No!
'Tis true that death awaits both you and me,
    But let us die like men, not sink below
Like brutes:" —and thus his dangerous post kept he,
    And none like to anticipate the blow;
And even Pedrillo, his most reverend tutor,
Was for some rum a disappointed suitor.[2]

Wordsworth had more obvious and serious criticisms to level against Byron and his "infamous publication" than this painful borrowing. But perhaps his fear of its potential for convenient fragmentation did speak to the point of set pieces and the awful fate of John associated provocatively with Juan. "I am persuaded," Wordsworth wrote to Henry Crabb Robinson in January 1820, "that Don Juan will do more harm to the English character, than anything of our time; not so much as *Book*;—But thousands . . . will batten upon choice bits of it, in the shape of Extracts."[3]

The devastating reception afforded *Poems, in Two Volumes*, however, made for the greater anguish. Even though Wordsworth had confidence that his work would finally, at some time in the future, prevail, his "do[ing] something for the world" was an immediate failure. We today continue to favor *Lyrical Ballads* (1798) as the poet's most radical as well as most influential collection. After having reviewed the criticism of *Poems, in Two Volumes*, including the disappointment of many reviewers over what they perceived to be its falling off from the level of excellence in *Lyrical Ballads*, it is quite obvious that Wordsworth's contemporaries would have been baffled with our current assessment of which collection offered the greater challenge to prevailing taste and aesthetics. It remains to be seen whether 2007, the two-hundredth anniversary of *Poems, in Two Volumes*, will be celebrated with the same enthusiasm as the bicenntenial of *Lyrical Ballads*, but it would be of some importance to rectify the matter for a more accurate perspective of literary history.

# Appendix

### Narrative of the Loss of the
### EARL OF ABERGAVENNY, EAST INDIAMAN,

*Captain John Wordsworth, which drove on the Shambles, off the Bill of Portland, and sunk in twelve fathoms Water, February 5, 1805.*

The universal concern occasioned by the recent loss of the Earl of Abergavenny, has induced us to lay before our readers an accurate statement of this melancholy disaster, chiefly collected from the accounts which were given at the India-House, by Cornet Burgoyne, of his Majesty's 8th regiment of light dragoons, who had the command of the troops on board the above vessel, and by Mr. Gilpin, fourth officer of the ship, (who were among the few who fortunately escaped from the wreck), and from the best information afterwards received.

On Friday, February the 1st, the Earl of Abergavenny, East-Indiaman, Capt. Wordsworth, sailed from Portsmouth, in company with the Royal George, Henry Addington, Wexford, and Bombay Castle, under convoy of his Majesty's ship Weymouth, Captain Draper,

The Earl of Abergavenny was engaged in the Company service for six voyages, and this was the fourth on which she was proceeding. Her company consisted of

| | |
|---|---:|
| Seamen, &c. . . . . . . . . . . . . . . . . . . . . | 160 |
| Troops, King's and Company's . . . . . . . . . | 159 |
| Passengers at the Captain's table . . . . . . . . | 40 |
| Ditto at the Third Mate's . . . . . . . . . . . . | 11 |
| Chinese . . . . . . . . . . . . . . . . . . . . . . . | 32 |
| Total | 402 |

In going through the Needles they unfortunately separated from the convoy. The fleet, in consequence, lay to nearly the whole of the next day; but seeing nothing of the Weymouth, proceeded under moderate sail towards the next port, in hopes of being joined by the convoy. On the 5th, the convoy not appearing, it was deemed expedient to wait her arrival in Portland Roads, particularly as the wind had become rather unfavourable, having shifted several points from the N. E. Captain Clarke, of the Wexford, being the senior commander, and consequently commodore, made the signal for those ships that had taken pilots on board to run into the Roads.

The Earl of Abergavenny having at about half past three P.M. got a pilot on board, bore up for Portland Roads with a steady wind, when on a sudden the wind slackened, and the tide setting in fast, drove her rapidly towards the Shambles. The nearer she approached the less she was under management; and being at last totally ungovernable, was driven furiously on the rocks, off the Bill of Portland, about two miles from the shore. She remained on the rocks nearly an hour, beating incessantly with great violence, the shocks being so great, that the officers and men could scarcely keep their footing on the deck. At four P.M. the shocks became less violent, and in about a quarter of an hour she cleared the rocks. The sails were immediately set, with an intention to run for the first port, as the ship made much water; but the leak increased so fast, that the ship would not obey the helm. In this situation, it was considered necessary to fire signal guns of distress. Twenty were fired: the danger did not, however, appear to those on board sufficient to render it necessary for the ship's boats to be hoisted out of this moment, as the weather was moderate, and the ship in sight of the fleet and shore.

The leak increased fast upon the pumps at 5 P.M. Soon after striking, the hand pumps started above six inches, and shortly after the water increased from six to eight feet in spite of every exertion at the pumps. All endeavours to keep the water under were found in vain, and night setting in rendered the situation of all on board melancholy in the extreme: the more so, as it was then ascertained that the ship had received considerable damage in her bottom, immediately under the pumps. All hands took their turn at the pumps, alternately baling at the fore hatchway. At eight o'clock their situation became still more dreadful, when it was found impossible to save the ship, which was eventually sinking fast and settling in the water. Signal guns were again discharged incessantly. The purser, with the third officer, Mr. Wordsworth, and six seamen, were sent on shore, in one of the ship's boats, to give notice to the inhabitants of the distressed state of the ship and crew. At this time a pilot boat came off, and Mr. Evans, with his daughter, Miss Evans, Mr. Routledge, Mr. Taylor, a cadet, and Miss Jackson, passengers, embarked for the shore, notwithstanding a dreadful sea, which threatened them with almost instant loss.

For a few moments the general attention of the crew was diverted in observing the boats leave the ship; but these unfortunate people were soon reminded of their own approaching fate, by a heavy swell, which baffled almost every attempt to keep the ship above water. Every one seemed assured of his fate, and notwithstanding the unremitting attention of the officers, confusion commenced on board, as soon as it was given out that the ship was sinking. At 10 P.M. several sailors intreated to be allowed more liquor, which being refused, they attacked the spirit-room, but were repulsed by the officers, who never once lost sight of their character, or that dignity so necessary to be preserved on such an occasion, but continued to conduct themselves with the utmost fortitude till the last. One of the officers, who was stationed at the door of the spirit-room, with a brace of pistols to guard against surprise in so critical a moment, at which post he remained even while the ship was sinking, was much importuned by a sailor, while the water poured in on all sides, to grant him some liquor. The man said he was convinced "it would be all one with them in an hour hence." The officer, however, true to his trust in this perilous moment, had courage enough to repulse the man, and bid him go to his duty with his fellow comrades, observing, "that if it was God's will they should perish, they should die like men."

At half past ten the water had got above the orlop deck, in spite of the endeavours of the officers and crew, who behaved in the most cool and exemplary manner. All on board were now anxiously looking out for boats from the shore, many wishing they had taken refuge in those that had already left the ship, as their destruction on board appeared inevitable. The utmost exertions became necessary to keep the ship above water till the boats came off from the shore. Unfortunately in the general distress and agony of the moment, the ship's boats were not hoisted out, when every soul on board might possibly have been saved. At eleven o'clock, a fatal swell gave the ship a sudden shock: she gave a surge, and sunk almost instantaneously, two miles from Weymouth beach; with scarce five minutes warning, she went down by the head in twelve fathom water, after a heavy heel, when she righted and sunk with her masts and rigging standing. Many clung to loose spars, and floated about the wreck, but the majority took refuge in the shrouds. The severe shock of the ship going down, made several let go their hold, whilst others, by the velocity of the ship's descent, had not power to climb sufficiently fast to keep above the water. The Halsewell East Indiaman was wrecked within a few miles from this spot.—See Vol. II. p. 19.

When the hull of the ship touched the ground, about one hundred and eighty persons were supposed to be in the tops and rigging: their situation was beyond all description wretched: the yards only were above water, and the sea was breaking over them, in the dead of a cold and frosty night. In about half an hour their spirits were revived, by the sound of several boats beating against the waves at a short distance; but, alas! how vain their hopes, when on hailing the boats, not one of them came to their assistance. The sound of them died away, and they were again left to the mercy of the rude waves. By twelve o'clock their numbers had much decreased: the swell had swept some off, whilst others were, from the piercing cold, unable longer to retain their hold. Every moment they perceived some friend floating around them, for a while, then sinking into the abyss to rise no more,

About this time a sloop was discovered; she had fortunately heard the signal guns, and came to an anchor close by the ship. The weather was moderate, and those who had survived were now promised a speedy delivery. The sloop's boat was immediately manned, and proceeded to the rigging that remained above water, when every person was taken off. The boat returned three times, taking twenty each turn. Nothing could be more correct than the conduct of the crew on this occasion: they coolly got into the boat, one by one, and those only as they were named by their officers. When it was supposed that every one was brought off, and the boat was about to depart for the last time, a person was observed in one of the tops: he was hailed to but did not answer. Mr. Gilpin, the fourth officer, (whose extraordinary exertions on this occasion, as well as throughout the whole of this unfortunate affair, entitle him to the highest commendation), returned to the wreck, and there found a man in an inanimate state, exhausted from the severe cold. He most humanely brought him down on his back, and took him to the boat; the man proved to be serjeant Heart of the 22d regiment. Every possible care was taken of him, but to no effect: he died about twelve hours after he was landed. The sloop having now, as was supposed, taken on board all the survivors of the ship, returned to Weymouth. She had not, however, proceeded far, before it was perceived that Mr. Baggot, the chief officer, was close astern. The sloop immediately lay too for him; but this noble spirited young man, although certain of securing his own life, disregarded his safety, on perceiving Mrs. Blair, an unfortunate fellow passenger, floating at some distance from him. He succeeded in coming up with her, and sustained her above water, while he swam towards the sloop; but just as he was on the point of reaching it, a swell came on, and his strength being totally exhausted, he sunk and never rose again. The unfortunate Mrs. Blair sunk after him, and this generous youth thus perished in vain. It was nearly two o'clock before she weighed anchor from the wreck, but the wind being favourable she soon reached the port. On mustering those who had landed, it appeared that only 139 persons had reached the shore out of 402 who had embarked!

The greatest attention was paid to the unfortunate sufferers by the mayor and aldermen, as well as the principal inhabitants of Weymouth; and the purser was immediately despatched to the India House with the melancholy intelligence.

At day-light, February the 6th, the top-masts of the ship were seen from Weymouth. During the time the passengers and crew remained in the tops she appeared to have sunk eight feet, and was considerably lower in the morning; it was therefore conjectured, that she had sunk on a mud-bank. The Greyhound cutter was immediately stationed to guard the wreck, and the boats from the Rover succeeded in stripping the masts of the rigging. On the 7th her decks had not been blown up, and she appeared to remain in exactly the same state in which she had sunk. Her sinking so steadily is attributed to the great weight of her cargo, her floorings consisting chiefly of earthen-ware. The cargo of the ship was estimated at 200,000l. besides which she had on board dollars to the amount of 275,000 ounces, and is supposed to have been one of the richest ships that ever sailed for India. She was of the largest tonnage, and inferior only to the Ganges in the service, being at least 1500 tons burthen, and built for the China trade.

About 80 officers and seamen were saved, 11 passengers, 15 Chinese, five out of 32 cadets, and 45 recruits. The captain was drowned. He was nephew to the Captain Wordsworth, who formerly commanded the Earl of Abergavenny, and was considered one of the first navigators in the service. He was on his third voyage as captain, and painful to relate, perished with his ship, disdaining to survive the loss of so valuable a charge: his conduct, throughout the distressing scene, has been spoken of in terms of the highest praise. It is an extraordinary fact, that he felt such an unaccountable depression of spirits, that he could not be persuaded to go through the usual ceremony of taking leave of the Court of Directors on the day appointed; and it was not till the Wednesday following, which was specially fixed for that purpose, that he yields to the wishes of his friends, and reluctantly attended the Court! He was a man of remarkably mild manners: his conduct was, in every instance, so well tempered, that he was known, among his shipmates, by the title of "the Philosopher." As soon as the ship was going down, Mr. Baggot, the chief officer, went on the quarter-deck, and told him, "that all exertions were now in vain; the ship was rapidly sinking." Captain Wordworth, who, no doubt, expected it, steadfastly looked him in the face, and, at last, with every appearance of a heart-broken man, faintly answered: "Let her go! God's will be done." These were the last words he uttered—from that instant he was motionless. In a few moments the ship sunk, and many who were climbing the shrouds endeavoured to save him, but without success. In this endeavour Mr. Gilpin was foremost, and made several unsuccessful attempts, at the evident risk of his own life.

# Notes

## INTRODUCTION

1. The text of "Elegiac Stanzas" and other poems from *Poems in Two Volumes* (1807) will be taken from *Poems, in Two Volumes, and Other Poems, 1800–1807*, by William Wordsworth, ed. Jared Curtis (Ithaca: Cornell University Press, 1983), 266–68. Hereafter cited as *P2V*. The lines quoted here are 34–40.

2. For an interesting discussion of Wordsworth's ambivalent desire for popularity and influence see Peter T. Murphy, *Poetry as an Occupation and an Art in Britain, 1760–1830* (Cambridge: Cambridge University Press, 1993), 182–228.

3. Much was made of the tragic similarities of the sinking of *The Earl of Abergavenny* and the sinking of *The Halsewell*, East Indiaman, a decade earlier, in almost the same spot off Portland Bill in southern England. Public interest especially focused on the death of the *Halsewell*'s captain and family, who had been traveling together. The significance of the relationship will be discussed later.

4. My computation from the passenger list is that 246 drowned or died of exposure: 80 out of 160 crew members; 40 out of 51 paying passengers; 17 out of 32 Chinese laborers; and 109 out of 159 of His Magesty's soldiers, who were en route to India.

5. *The Letters of William and Dorothy Wordsworth, The Early Years 1787–1805*, ed. Ernest de Selincourt. 2nd ed. rev. by Chester L. Shaver (Oxford: Clarendon, 1967), 560. Hereafter cited as *EY*.

6. *P2V*, 266–68, lines 35–36.

7. Most recently, Kenneth R. Johnston has affirmed the prevailing opinion that John Wordsworth's "behavior as captain was unimpeachably heroic throughout the seven agonizing hours it took for the ship to sink." *The Hidden Wordsworth: Poet Lover Rebel Spy* (New York: Norton, 1998), 815. Also see *The Hidden Wordsworth* (New York: Norton, 2001), 584.

8. Hirsch writes, "The divinatory moment is unmethodical, intuitive, sympathetic; it is an imaginative guess without which nothing can begin. The second, or critical, moment of interpretation submits the first moment to a 'high intellectual standard' by testing it against all relevant knowledge available. Thus, although the critical moment is dependent and secondary, it has the indispensible function of raising interpretive guesses to the level of knowledge." *Validity in Interpretation* (New Haven: Yale University Press, 1967), x.

9. Karl Kroeber, *Romantic Landscape Vision: Constable and Wordsworth* (Madison: University of Wisconsin Press, 1975), 46.

10. Geoffrey H. Hartman, *Wordsworth's Poetry, 1787–1814* (1964; New Haven: Yale University Press, 1971), 285.

11. Ernest Bernhardt-Kabisch, "Wordsworth's 'Elegiac Stanzas,' 35–36," *Explica-*

*tor* 23 (May 1965): 71. The author comments: "it is conceivable that the word 'power' in 'Elegiac Stanzas' refers not to the poet's idealizing imagination but to the poet's brother, whom Wordsworth surely would have included among the 'higher minds'" (unnumbered page).

12. Leon Waldoff, *Wordsworth in His Major Lyrics: The Art and Psychology of Self-Representation* (Columbia: University of Missouri Press, 2001), 148.

13. *The Norton Shakespeare*, ed. Stephen Greenblatt (New York: Norton, 1997). *King Lear* (The Conflated Text), 5.2.11. Future quotations from Shakespeare will be taken from this edition.

14. Marjorie Levinson, *Wordsworth's Great Period Poems: Four Essays* (Cambridge: Cambridge University Press, 1986), 102.

15. Thomas McFarland, *William Wordsworth: Intensity and Achievement* (Oxford: Clarendon, 1992), 30–31.

16. Thomas McFarland, *Romanticism and the Forms of Ruin: Wordsworth, Coleridge, and Modalities of Fragmentation* (Princeton: Princeton University Press, 1981), 162.

17. *The Letters of Mary Wordsworth 1800–1855*, ed. and sel. by Mary E. Burton (Oxford: Clarendon, 1958), 2–3.

18. *P2V*, 150, No. 18, lines 1–4. I have accepted Mark L. Reed's conjecture on the dates of composition. See *Wordsworth: The Chronology of the Middle Years 1800–1815* (Cambridge: Harvard University Press, 1975), 29.

19. The smaller oil, which Beaumont painted as the preparatory study for the finished painting, was preferred by Wordsworth. The larger oil was the one displayed in the Royal Academy exhibit for 1806. The significant distinctions between the two paintings will be discussed later. The smaller painting is owned by the Wordsworth Trust and hangs on permanent display at the Wordsworth Museum, Grasmere. The larger painting is owned by the Leicester Art Museum and is presently in storage.

## I. Capt. John Wordsworth and the Prophecy of "Michael"

1. Ketcham's biography of John Wordsworth introduces his edition of *The Letters of John Wordsworth* (Ithaca: Cornell University Press), 1–64. The *Letters* will be cited as *LJW*.

2. *The Collected Letters of Samuel Taylor Coleridge, II, 1801–1806*, ed. Earl Leslie Griggs (Oxford: Clarendon, 1956), 1170. Hereafter cited as *STCL*.

3. *An Authentic Narrative of the Loss of the* Earl of Abergavenny, *East Indiaman, off Portland, on the Night of the 5th February 1805 . . . corrected from the Official Returns at the East-India House* (London: Printed for John Stockdale, Piccadilly, and Blacks and Parry, Leadenhall Street. February, 1805), 16–17. Hereafter cited as *AN*.

4. *The Notebooks of Samuel Taylor Coleridge*, ed. Kathleen Coburn (Princeton: Princeton University Press, 1957– ), 2: 2856. Hereafter cited as *STCNB*.

5. *Letters of Mary Wordsworth*, 3.

6. *LJW* 25.

7. Mary Moorman, *William Wordsworth: A Biography. The Early Years 1770–1803* (New York: Oxford University Press, 1957), 473–74. Stephen Gill makes no comment on the matter in *William Wordsworth: A Life* (Oxford: Clarendon, 1989).

8. The definition of *ibex* provided by the *OED* reads: "A species of wild goat . . . inhabiting the Alps and Appennines, the male of which has very large strongly ridged recurved, diverging horns, and hair of a brownish or reddish grey becoming grey in winter."

9. Basil Lubbock makes the point that the Merchant Service of the East India Company was one of five careers worthy of a younger son of the nobility and landed gentry, the others being the Royal Navy or Army, the bar, and the church. "Seamen," in *The Trade Winds: A Study of British Overseas Trade During the French Wars, 1793–1815*, ed. C. Northcote Parkinson (London: Allen & Unwin, 1948), 106.

10. This is also an unsupported point made by Joan Baum in *Mind-Forg'd Manacles: Slavery and English Romantic Poets* (New Haven: Archon Books, 1994), 78, where she says: "While Wordsworth's captain brother John Wordsworth might have testified in 1804 that the East India Company had never been engaged in the slave trade, clever questioning might have elicited from him the degree to which the company's complex subcontracting operations with 'company ships' close to shore made slave trading possible, particularly near East India Company stations in Madagascar, Bombay, and Ceylon."

11. The captains of Company vessels were often referred to as commodores to avoid the misunderstanding that they held the very high military rank of a naval captain. Military officers in general did not have much respect for Company officers, who were untrained in leadership, and members of Her Majesty's Navy scoffed at the mundane responsibilities of a Company vessel and crew; to wit, sailing the same routes repeatedly. It would be something like a comparison between a pilot for a commercial airline and a fighter pilot for an aircraft carrier.

12. Basil Greenhill, *The Life and Death of the Merchant Sailing Ship, 1815–1965* (London: Her Majesty's Stationary Office, 1980). Volume 7 in the National Maritime Museum series, *The Ship* (1980).

13. *Home at Grasmere*, Part First, Book First of *The Recluse* by William Wordsworth, ed. Beth Darlington (Ithaca: Cornell University Press, 1977), 92. MS B, lines 863–68. Hereafter cited as *HG*.

14. Lyrical Ballads *and Other Poems, 1797–1800 by William Wordsworth*, eds. James Butler and Karen Green (Ithaca: Cornell University Press, 1992), 144, lines 41–62. Hereafter cited as *LB*.

15. *Letters of Mary Wordsworth*, lines xxv.

16. *Coleridge: The Early Family Letters*, ed. James Engell (Oxford: Clarendon, 1994), 63–64.

17. Francis Coleridge's suicide note is included in the "Records of Francis S. Coleridge," *Early Family Letters*, 97.

18. Mark L. Reed, *Wordsworth: The Chronology of the Middle Years*, 1800–1815 (Cambridge: Harvard University Press, 1975), 82–83, n. 42. Hereafter cited as *CMY*.

19. "Song for the Wandering Jew," lines 19–20; *LB* (1800), 190.

20. *Dorothy Wordsworth*, The Grasmere Journals, ed. Pamela Woof (New York: Oxford University Press, 1993), 22–23. Hereafter cited as *GJ*.

21. Henry David Thoreau, Walden *and Civil Disobedience: Authoritative Texts, Background, Reviews and Essays in Criticism*, ed. Owen Thomas (New York: Norton, 1966), 20.

22. The phrase "significant group" is used in Thomas McFarland's *Romanticism and the Forms of Ruin*, chapter 3, "The Significant Group: Wordsworth's Fears in

Solitude," 137–215. The quote from *The Prelude* (1805) is in 10.968. *William Words-worth:* The Prelude *1799, 1805, 1850,* eds. Jonathan Wordsworth, M. H. Abrams, and Stephen Gill (New York: Norton, 1979), 412.

23. William Griggs, *Relics of the Honourable East India Company: A Series of Fifty Plates* (London: Bernard Quaritich, 1909), 80.

24. Hosea Ballou Morse, *The Chronicles of the East India Company, trading to China 1635–1834.* 4 vols.(Oxford: Clarendon, 1936).

25. Charles Lamb, "The Superannuated Man," from *The Last Essays of Elia* (1833). *Elia and the Last Essays of Elia* vol. 2 in *The Works of Charles and Mary Lamb,* ed. E. V. Lucas (London: Methuen, 1903–5), 194.

26. For example, the Shipping Interest that owned the *Abergavenny* built to re-place John Wordsworth's vessel consisted of twelve members: William Dent, who was in for 1/8th ownership; eight who bought 1/16th shares, including Captain John Wordsworth, and three, who invested in a 1/32 share. In C. Northcote Parkin-son, *Trade in the Eastern Seas* (Cambridge: Cambridge University Press, 1937), 186–87.

27. A long ton is 2,240 pounds; a short ton is 2,000.

28. C. Northcote Parkinson, "The East India Trade" in *The Trade Winds,* 141–56. Parkinson also provides the approximate value of the merchant fleet as 500 T at £20–30K; 800 T at £30–50K; and 1,200 T at £50–70K.

29. The Madras presidency was 49,607 square miles and governed a native popu-lation of 3,941,021; the Bombay presidency was 59,438 square miles and governed a population of 6,251,546; and the great Bengal presidency covered an area of 149,782 square miles, which held a population of 32,206,806. This data is from *The Report from the Select Committee on the Affairs of the East India Company; with Minutes of Evidence in Six Parts, and an appendix and Index to each.* British House of Commons, 1832.

30. *English Historical Documents, 1783–1832,* eds. A. Aspinall, and E. Anthony Smith (London: Eyre and Spottiswoode, 1959), doc. 562, p. 910. vol. 11 in the series *English Historical Documents,* gen ed. David C. Douglas.

31. Michael Greenberg, *British Trade and the Opening of China, 1800–1842* (Cam-bridge: Cambridge University Press, 1951), 8. From 1811–1828, the Company shipped £72,680,541 worth of Chinese goods, primarily tea, to England, and £13,244,702 worth of British goods to China.

32. *Report from the Select Committee,* 70.

33. David Edward Owen, *British Opium Policy in China and India* (New Haven: Yale University Press, 1934), 18.

34. Quoted in ibid., 23.

35. John William Kaye, *The Administration of the East India Company: A History of Indian Progress* (London: Richard Bentley, 1853), 688.

36. One of the great scandals of the embattled administration of Warren Hast-ings was his granting contracts without open bidding and transgressions of the pa-tronage system. In the latter case, he provided a friend's son with a very remunerative position as business agent for the opium trade, but the young man sold the position to another for £40,000 who in turn resold it for £70,000 (Owen, *British Opium Policy,* 32–33).

37. David Spurr, *The Rhetoric of Empire: Colonial Discourse in Journalism, Travel Writ-ing, and Imperial Administration* (Durham, N.C.: Duke University Press, 1993), 31.

38. Thomas Ainslee Embree, *Charles Grant and British Rule in India* (London: George Allen & Unwin, 1962), 127. The quote is from *Parliamentary Papers*, 1810, vol. 11, paper 300, p. 26, quoted in Embree.

39. J. J. Higginbotham, *Men Whom India Has Known: Biographies of Eminent Indian Characters*, 2d ed. (Madras: Higginbotham, 1874).

40. Ernest Marshall Howse, *Saints in Politics: The "Clapham Sect" and the Growth of Freedom* (London: George Allen & Unwin, 1952), 65–94 passim.

41. The clause inspired by Charles Grant and introduced into Parliamentary debate by William Wilberforce reads: "it is the opinion of this Committee that it is the duty of this country to promote the interest and happiness of the native inhabitants of the British dominions in India, and that such measures ought to be adopted as may tend to the introduction among them of useful knowledge and of religious and moral improvement. That in furtherance of the above objects, sufficient facilities shall be afforded by law to persons desirous of going to and remaining in India for the purpose of accomplishing these benevolent designs." Quoted in Henry Morris, *The Life of Charles Grant: Sometime Member of Parliament for Inverness-shire and Director of the East India Company* (London: John Murray, 1904), 329. The clause was finally approved in 1813 after a great crusade by Grant, Wilberforce, and other members of the Clapham Sect.

42. Quoted in C. Silvester Horne, *The Story of the L[ondon] M[issionary] S[ociety], 1795–1895* (London: London Missionary Society, 1894), 91.

43. Richard Lovett, *The History of the London Missionary Society* (London: Frowde, 1899), 40, 48.

44. "Speech on Fox's India Bill" in *The Writing and Speeches of Edmund Burke*, gen. ed., Paul Langford, vol. 5, *India: Madras and Bengal 1774–1784*, ed. P. J. Marshall (Oxford: Clarendon, 1981), 402.

45. W. H. Carey reports the *Calcutta Gazette* commenting on "sewage of an enormous native population [lying] festering under an appalling sun in open trenches." *The Good Old Days of Honourable John Company, being curious reminiscences illustrating manners and customs of the British in India during the rule of the East India Company from 1600–1858* (Calcutta: R. Cambray, 1906), 349.

46. *Hookah* is the bottle through which fumes of smoking tobacco pass through water, but more generally, all of the implements of smoking associated with India, i.e., the tube, the vase, and later the luxurious idler who spent the night in smoking. (*OED*).

47. The *Calcutta Gazette* reported on 6 September 1817 that "Scarce a week has elapsed for a considerable period past, that our newspapers have not announced one or more shocking instances of suicide, either among Europeans or Natives." Quoted in Carey, *The Good Old Days*, 349.

48. Carey, *The Good Old Days*, 172.

49. Quoted in Howse, *Saints in Politics*, 66–67.

50. Quoted in Morris, *The Life of Charles Grant*, 322–23.

51. Quoted from the Vedes Code in Charles Grant's astonishing attack on the depravity of Hindu Culture, *Observations on the State of Society among the Asiatic Subjects of Great Britain, particularly with respect to Morals; and on the means of improving it.— Written chiefly in the Year 1792*. A text of Grant's *Observations* can be found as General Appendix I of *A Report to the Select Committee on the Affairs of the East India Company; with Minutes of Evidence in Six Parts, and an appendix and index to each*. British House of Commons, 1832.

52. Carey, *The Good Old Days,* 93.

53. Parkinson, *Trade in the Eastern Seas,* 35.

54. Carey, *The Good Old Days,* 93–95.

55. Parkinson, *Trade in the Eastern Seas,* 372–73.

56. Ibid., 294.

57. Ibid., 253.

58. John Wordsworth's sword was recovered from his body after he was washed ashore and it is now encased under glass in the Wordsworth house and museum at Rydal Mount.

59. Parkinson, *Trade in the Eastern Seas,* 294.

60. Quoted from *The Court-Partial of 18—. A tale of military life.* 2 vols. London, 1844, in Parkinson, *Trade in the Eastern Seas,* 388–89.

61. Quoted in Morris, *The Life of Charles Grant,* 213.

62. The text of *Observations* used here appears as General Appendix I to the *Report to the Select Committee on the Affairs.*

63. In his "Third Anniversary Discourse, delivered 2 February, 1786 from *Discourses Delivered at the Asiatick Society, 1785–1792,* Vol. 3 of the *The Works of William Jones* (1807 reprint, London: Routledge, 1993), William Jones comments: "nor can we reasonably doubt, how degenerate and abased so ever the *Hindus* may now appear, that in some early age they were splendid in arts and arms, happy in government, nice in legislation, and eminant [*sic*] in various knowledge" (32). After further praise of their invention of instruction by *apologues,* the *decimal scale,* the game of chess, numerous works on grammar, logic, rhetoric, music, poetry, and philosophy, Jones goes on, "nor is it improbable, that the names of planets and Zodiacal stars, which the *Arabs* borrowed from the *Greeks,* but which we find in the oldest *Indian* records, were originally devised by the same ingenious and enterprising race, from whom, both *Greece* and *India* were peopled; . . . the Hindus" (45).

64. Quoted in Embree, *Charles Grant and British Rule,* 143.

65. Edward W. Said's basic argument in both *Culture and Imperialism* (London: Chatto and Windus, 1993) and his great earlier study, *Orientalism* (London: Penguin Books, 1985), is to show that Europeans established an intellectual dominion over the Orient in cultural tracts that predisposed their societies toward imperialism—the intellectual acceptance of the right to dominate another people—and then colonialism—the actual geographical and physical possession of land. For example in *Culture and Imperialism* he argues quite interestingly for the power of literary arts, especially the novel, as "almost unnoticeably sustaining that society's consent in overseas expansion" (12). While heeding the scalpel, Said fails to notice the sledgehammer of Grant's effectual impact.

66. See my "Hindoo/Yahoo: Charles Grant and the Christianizing of the Hindus" in *Swift: The Enigmatic Dean: Festschrift for Hermann Josef Real,* eds. Rudolf Freiburg, Arno Loffler, and Wolfgang Zach (Tubingen: Stauffenburg Verlag, 1998): 113–25.

67. *English Historical Documents,* vol. 11, Document 529, pp. 847–48.

68. The Marine Records c. 1600–1879 of the British Library's Oriental and India Office Collections (OIOC) show that Captain John Wordsworth's last four voyages, all on the *Abergavenny,* occurred during the following periods: 1 December 1789–23 September 1791; 16 March 1793–13 February 1795; 6 January 1797–6 February 1799; and March 1799–10 December 1800.

69. A pipe is a cask that holds 105 imperial gallons.

70. It is left vague in maritime documents of the period whether measurement or long tons are being referred to. A measurement ton is 40 cubic feet.

71. Parkinson, *Trade in Eastern Seas,* 300.

72. See A. N. Porter's *Atlas of British Overseas Expansion* (London: Routledge, 1991), 55–65, for a lucid exposition and analysis of imperialism.

73. The import of Opium into England was not illegal but it is rarely mentioned in studies of the East India Company. Virginia Berridge and Griffith Edwards maintain that Indian opium accounts for no more than 12 percent of British domestic use, and usually accounted for no more than 3 percent. They claim that Persia and Turkey were the principal suppliers of the substance. See their *Opium and the People: Opium Use in Nineteenth-Century England* (New Haven: Yale University Press, 1987), 271–73.

74. *Papers,* Box 3, Document 17, Mr. JW in Account with RW, 26 September 1796–December 16 1801. Gordon Graham Wordsworth also mentions this early opium deal in his unpublished biography of John: "as far as can judge from Richard's Accounts, [the voyage] was not a financial success, the sole item to John's credit at the end of it being £100 for a consignment of opium." *Papers,* Box 3, Item 22, unnumbered page.

75. The oiling of the naked body prevented the thieves from being grabbed and held, if detected. They usually struck British residences in the early morning hours.

76. Terence Grocott, *Shipwrecks of the Revolutionary and Napoleanic Eras* (London: Chatham, 1997), vii.

77. See Morse, *Chronicles,* "Opium Prohibited: The *Providence* Affair: 1799," 2:332–35.

78. Shakespeare, *The Winter's Tale* 4.4.566–67.

79. The phrase is Stephen Maxfield Parrish's in *"Michael* and the Pastoral Ballad," *Bicentenary Wordsworth Studies in Memory of John Alban Finch,* ed. Jonathan Wordsworth (Ithaca: Cornell University Press, 1970), 53. Parrish's essay also includes a transcription of the first text of "Michael."

80. GGW's biography of Captain John Wordsworth, Box 3, Item 22.

81. Mrs. M. W. Gordon, *Christopher North: A Memoir of John Wilson* (Edinburgh: Edmonston and Douglas, 1863), 1: 134. See also Eric Sutherland Robertson, *Wordsworthshire: An Introduction to A Poet's Country* (London: Chatto & Windus, 1911), 325. Ketcham rejects the anecdote as a "fantasy based on 'Michael'" but without explanation (*LJW,* 174, n. 102). Butler and Green also leave room for doubt, commenting that "if [the anecdote] were based on fact and not on John Wilson's imaginings, [it] might have contributed to the account in *Michael* of the ritual laying of the cornerstone" (Lyrical Ballads *and Other Poems, 1797–1800,* 403, n. 396–427. Here too there is no justification given for the skepticism.

82. Parrish's transcription of one of the stanzas from the aborted ballad on the sheepfold. *"Michael* and the Pastoral Ballad" 52.

83. See, for example, my *Poetry of Relationship* throughout for detailed explications of the intertextuality of Wordsworth's art with his life. See also Charles J. Rzepka's "A Gift that Complicates Employ: Poetry and Poverty in 'Resolution and Independence,'" *SIR* 28 (1989): 225–47 and David V. Erdman's "Wordsworth as Heartsworth; or, Was Regicide the Prophetic Ground of those 'Moral Questions'?"

in *The Evidence of Imagination: Studies of Interactions between Life and Art in English Romantic Literature,* eds. Donald H. Reiman, Michael C. Jaye, and Betty T. Bennett (New York: New York University Press, 1978), 12–41, for comparably established insights on this phenomenon in Wordsworth.

84. I would like to thank my colleague, Beth Sweeney, for speculating that *anchor* also supports the identification of Luke with John Wordsworth.

85. See Matlak, *The Poetry of Relationship,* 202–208, for a more fully considered interpretation of Isabel's values at odds with Michael's.

86. Quoted from *The Poetical Works of William Wordsworth,* ed. William Knight, vol. 2 (Edinburgh: William Patterson, 1882), 143. The anecdote is found in Samuel Lewis, *The Topographical Dictionary of England,* 4 vols. (London: S. Lewis, 1831), 2: 431.

87. In *The Hidden Wordsworth,* 746–47, Kenneth R. Johnston finds Wordsworth's own experience reflected in the creation of Luke and the disappointment he brings to the family. Johnston reads the stones of the unfinished sheepfold as an allegorical representation of the poet's frustrated efforts on *The Recluse* (749). John Wordsworth is not an important figure in Johnston's narrative of life at Grasmere. Rather his importance lay in the financial blessings he might offer through a lucrative career and thus he becomes as minor as the Robert Bateman of "Michael" (747).

## II. Sinking Vocations

1. Copy of the Log of the *Earl of Abergavenny,* India Office Library Marine Records, extracted by Miss Peggy Sichel. Box 3, Item 37, Dove Cottage Papers.

2. Just as his common reader reacted to William's poetry, so John does to Coleridge's *Ancient Mariner.* Being a mariner himself one might have expected a more sympathetic response from John than: "you say," he writes to Mary, "that the antient M—— is now . . . void of obscurity as for my part it is a poem that I could never bear to read— I dare say it is beatiful [*sic*] but I cannot see the beauty" (*LJW* 102).

3. Wallace W. Douglas, "Wordsworth as Business Man," *PMLA* 63 (1948): 641.

4. See also Johnston, *The Hidden Wordsworth,* chapter 21.

5. *Wordsworth and Coleridge:* Lyrical Ballads, eds. R. L. Brett and A. R. Jones, 2d ed. (London: Routledge, 1991), 259.

6. Irene Tayler, "By Peculiar Grace: Wordsworth in 1802," in *The Evidence of Imagination,* 133.

7. "This Lime-Tree Bower My Prison," lines 20–26; 43–45; pp. 138–39 in *Samuel Taylor Coleridge: The Complete Poems,* ed. William Keach (London: Penguin, 1997).

8. Graham Gordon Wordsworth. Unpublished manuscript of the life of Captain John Wordsworth in the Dove Cottage Papers, Box 3, Item 22.

9. Moorman, *William Wordsworth,* 1:473–74.

10. This quote is taken from a draft of the letter Richard sent to William. The actual letter has not survived.

11. When Richard drew up John's accounts with him shortly after his departure, the total deficit amounted to £1919/7/1 owed to Richard alone. Box 3, Document 18, "Captain John Wordsworth in Account with Richard Wordsworth, April 18, 1802—June 18, 1803." Debits = £3582.8.1, Assets = £1663.1.0, leaving a deficit of £1919.7.1.

12. Russell Miller, *The Seafarers: The East Indiamen* (Alexandria, Va.: Time-Life Books, 1980), 60–85 passim.

13. Letter of 8 August from Capt. Nathanial Dance to the Court of the East India Company, printed in *The Gentleman's Magazine* (October 1804): 963–64.

14. *The Times* (London), 26 July 1804.

15. Text from item number PAH 8009, National Maritime Prints and Drawings. Original size 74cm length x 53cm width.

16. The National Maritime Library, Greenwich, England, holds at least a dozen prints and drawings celebrating Dance's embarrassment of the French, with titles such as "The Signal Defeat of the French Admiral Linois Squadron. By the Honorable East India Company Ships, commanded by Nathanial Dance, Esqr . . . on the 15th Feby 1804."

17. *The Sun*, 10 August 1804.

18. Quoted in Miller, *The East Indiamen*, 156.

19. Kenneth Garlick and Angus Macintyre, eds. *The Diary of Joseph Farington*, 14 vols. Vols. 7–14 ed. by Kathryn Cave (New Haven: Yale University Press, 1978–83). Vol. 8, entry for 7 August 1806, p. 2834.

20. John Wordsworth, Box 3, entries from copy of *Abergavenny* Log.

21. Edwin W. Marrs Jr., ed., *The Letters of Charles and Mary Lamb*, vol. 2 1801–1809 (Ithaca: Cornell University Press, 1976), 152–53. Hereafter cited as *Lamb Letters* 2.

22. For example, there is no mention of the confrontation with Linois in Moorman, Gill, or Johnston. Ketcham deals with the matter briefly in *LJW* (38–39).

23. *The Collected Writings of Walt Whitman*, eds. Harold W. Blodgett and Sculley Bradley (New York: New York University Press, 1965), 66, line 832.

24. *William Wordsworth: The Five-Book Prelude*, ed. Duncan Wu (Oxford: Blackwell, 1997), 4.552–63. Cited as *5BP*.

25. Jonathan Wordsworth, *William Wordsworth: The Borders of Vision* (Oxford: Clarendon, 1982), 310–19; the quotation is on 312.

26. Shakespeare, *Othello*, 2.1.16–17: "I never did like molestation view / On the enchafed flood."

27. Wu says that Wordsworth begins the Analogy Passage after line 65, "The soul, the imagination of the whole," but then abandons it and continues with line 66, "To this one scene which I from Snowdon's breast." *The Five-Book Prelude*, 136, n. 11.

28. I am using here Jonathan Wordsworth's concept of the border image as suggestive of numinous experience. See *Borders of Vision*, 15–20.

29. Wu hears in the passage an echo of Prospero's comment "We are such stuff / As dreams are made on": 200, n. 18.

30. "Nutting," Lyrical Ballads, *and Other Poems, 1797–1800*, ed. James Butler and Karen Green (Ithaca: Cornell University Press, 1992), 218–20. The bower is first described as "mutilated' in the 1836 version of the poem. See 220, note to line 48.

31. Mary Jacobus identifes the missing vessel as Noah's Ark in a reading comparable to mine, but drawing upon Milton's account of the deluge in *Paradise Lost* (11, passim). See the extract of her argument in Wordsworth, *The Five-Book Prelude*, 186–96.

32. Duncan Wu, *Wordsworth's Reading*, 2:61, 68, 100, 162.

33. Douglas B. Wilson, *The Romantic Dream: Wordsworth and the Poetics of the Unconscious* (Lincoln: University of Nebraska Press, 1993), 174. Wilson's reading of the

Arab's dream very usefully associates chief texts of Freud with Wordsworth to illustrate their surprising agreement on imaginative creation and dreaming to conclude that "Imagination requires a descent into the 'awful lair' of madness to become fully itself" (191). Although the title of his chapter on the Arab's dream is "Wordsworth Self-Analysis: The Arab Dream," Wilson does not provide a psychobiographical reading of the dream.

34. Jane Worthington Smyser, "Wordsworth's Dream of Poetry and Science," *PMLA* 71 (1956): 271–72.

35. Wu, for example, follows Jonathan Wordsworth in assuring us that Coleridge was the source of the Cartesian dream (Wu, *Wordsworth's Reading*, 2, entry 135, p. 174), but Ralph J. Coffman's *Coleridge's Library: A Bibliography of Books Owned or Read by Samuel Taylor Coleridge* (Boston: G. K. Hall, 1987) fails to mention Baillet's *Vie de Descartes* in his entries on Descartes.

36. Kenneth R. Johnston, *Wordsworth and* The Recluse (New Haven: Yale University Press, 1984), 140.

37. Quoted in Ainslee T. Embree, *Charles Grant and British Rule in India* (New York: Columbia University Press, 1962), 127.

38. Box 3, Document 8: Letter of Thomas Clarkson at Purfleet to William Wordsworth, Grasmere . . . 1 March 1805.

39. A Captain Hamilton had been offered the voyage John finally received, but Hamilton turned it down fearing that navigating the Hooghly River, an arm of the Ganges, up to Calcutta would be an unacceptable risk.

40. See Appendix A for the Narrative that appeared in Duncan's *Mariner's Chronicle.*

41. Most of this brief publishing history is from Keith Huntress, ed. *Narratives of Shipwrecks and Disasters, 1586–1860* (Ames: Iowa State University Press, 1974), x, 232.

42. This point is visually made by James Barry, R.A., in his *The Thames or the Triumph of Navigation,* painted May 1791. See Prints and Drawings PAH 7365, National Maritime Library.

43. This inference of boats on board the *Abergavenny* is drawn from a description of boats on the *Hindostan*, East Indiaman, a comparably sized vessel that sank in 1803. "The Loss of the Hidostan, East Indiaman, off Margate, January 11th, 1803," *Mariner's Chronicle*, 2:81–90.

44. Boats lined with cork designed specifically for saving lives were developed just about this time by Henry Greathead, but at a cost of nearly ten times more than the standard ship's boat, even the Admiralty lost interest. See Brian Lavery, *The Arming and Fitting of English Ships of War, 1600—1815* (London: Conway Maritime Press, 1987), 211–24 passim.

45. Johnston speculates that the *Abergavenny* was the last to take on a pilot because she had been so far ahead of the convoy due to John's quest to be first to the markets of India.

46. Derived from the text of *A Chart of the Isle, Roads, and Race of Portland, with the Shambles &c.* (London: Laurie & Whittle, 1794). Dove Cottage Collection.

47. One of the cadets drowned on the *Abergavenny* was Walter Scott's cousin, John Rutherford (*EY* 533, n. 2).

48. Appendix #4907 to the "Committee on Shipping Meeting of 19 February 1805 on the Loss of the *Abergavenny*"; letter from Capt. W. S. Clarke of the *Wexford* to the Court of Directors.

49. Richard and Brodget Larn, *Shipwreck Index of the British Isles: Isles of Scilly, Cornwall, Devon, Dorset.* Volume 1. (London: Lloyd's Register of Shipping, 1995), section 6.

50. Terence Grocott, *Shipwrecks of the Revolutionary and Napoleonic Eras*, 195.

51. An *Authentic Narrative of the Loss of the* Earl of Abergavenny, *East Indiaman, off Portland, on the Night of the 5th February 1805 . . . corrected from the Official Returns at the East-India House* (London: Printed for John Stockdale, Piccadilly, and Blacks and Parry, Leadenhall Street. February, 1805), 6.

52. Minutes of the Committee on Shipping for 19 Feb 1805, 2493.

53. *Naval Chronicle for 1805: containing a General and Biographical History of the Royal Navy of the United Kingdom; with a variety of original papers on nautical subjects: under the guidance of several literary and professional men*, vol. 13. (January–June, 1805). London: I. Gold, 1805.

54. *Authentic Narrative*, 14–15.

55. *Gentleman's Magazine* 75 (March 1805): 232.

56. National Maritime Library, Prints and Drawings PAI 5923.

57. DCP, Box 3, Item 11: Letter *Gilpin*, Thomas at Comet, Portsmouth to William Wordsworth, 25 April 1805.

58. DCP, Box 3, Item 15: Letter *Yates*, B. at Gravesend to his cousin B. Yates, no. 6 [Chapel] Street, [  ] near Islington, March, sent on by C. Lamb to William Wordsworth, . . . (Postmark, 1 and 2 April 1805) with a postscript.

59. DCP, Box 3, Item 14: Letter *Wordsworth*, Capt. John [sen] at Brougham Hall to William Wordsworth, Grasmere, Ambleside, Kendal, 18 March 1805.

60. DCP, Box 3, Item 10: Letter *Evans*, T. at No. 2 Maddox Street, Hanover Square to William Wordsworth, 9 April 1805.

61. DCP, Letter 5. 17 February 1805. SGB TO WW.

62. Beaumont was nicknamed Otter at Eton because he was always in the water, hoping to lose weight. One of his classmates reported he might have been "amphibious, living almost as much in as out of that element." After Eton, Sir George was tutored by Reverend Charles Davy, whose home was in walking distance of Suffolk beach, where Sir George would often swim to the horizon with a rope around his waist, so he might be pulled back by his servant should he become endangered. See Felicity Owen and David Blayney Brown, *Collector of Genius, A Life of Sir George Beaumont* (New Haven: Yale University Press, 1988), 7–9.

63. McFarland develops an interesting discussion of the "stoic cheerfulness" Wordsworth developed as a result of John's death and that then stood him in good stead when confronted with the deaths of his children and beloved friends: "The ideas of 'joy' and 'cheer' and 'happiness' more and more accreted to the idea of stoic endurance; it was not enough simply to bear, but to bear proudly and even gladly" (*Romanticism and the Forms of Ruin* 162). As noble as this might sound when applied to one's personal acknowledgement of mortality, one hopes that "stoic cheerfulness" did not apply to John Wordsworth when he faced the hundreds of simultaneous deaths of those he was responsible for.

64. DCP, Box 3, Item 22. Gordon G. Wordsworth's manuscript copy of his life of Captain John Wordsworth, 1772–1805. Pages unnumbered.

65. DCP, Letter 8, 3 March 1805. SGB TO WW.

66. The National Maritime Library, Greenwich, contains hundreds of shipwreck paintings in its extensive microfiche collection and even more off-site in its archival warehouses.

67. See, for example, National Maritime Prints and Drawings, PAH 0502, "The Loss of the *Halsewell,* East Indiaman, Capt Richard Pierce. This rich laden ship (outward bound) was wreck'd off Seacombe in the isle of Purbeck in Dorsetshire, on the 6th Jan 1786" and PAH 7421, "To the Directors of the Hon'ble East India Company this Print representing the Loss of their Ship *Halsewell* in the Night between the 5th & 6th of January 1786 with precarious situation of the Survivors in a cavern of the rock."

## III. Beaumont and the Promotion of Wordsworth

1. Mary Moorman paid Sir George Howland Beaumont the dubious but lasting distinction of "assist[ing] Wordsworth's progress towards political conservatism, and especially towards faith in the landed gentry as a class, which is so marked a development of his middle life." Stephen Gill does not go much further, but correctly asserts that the poet's relationship with Beaumont was "one of the most important friendships of Wordsworth's life." Beaumont is hardly a presence in Johnston's *Hidden Wordsworth.*
2. Norma Davis, "Wordsworth, Haydon, and Beaumont: A Change in the Role of Artistic Patronage," *Charles Lamb Bulletin* 55 (July 1986): 211.
3. William Knight, Introduction to *Memorials of Coleorton* (Edinburgh: David Douglass, 1887), xi.
4. This subheading is derived from the title of the fine biography by Felicity Owen and David Blayney Brown, *Collector of Genius, A Life of Sir George Beaumont* (New Haven: Yale University Pres, 1988).
5. Dove Cottage Papers, Beaumont Letters 1803–1831. Letter 1, Sir George Beaumont to William Wordsworth, dated 24 October 1803. Hereafter cited as *GBL* followed by the letter number.
6. Although he never built on the property, Wordsworth retained it.
7. *GBL* 1.
8. Arnold's comment from his essay on Wordsworth is: "To be recognized far and wide as a great poet, to be possible and receivable as a classic, Wordsworth needs to be relieved of a great deal of the poetical baggage which now encumbers him." *Poetry and Criticism of Matthew Arnold.,* ed. A. Dwight Culler (Boston: Houghton Mifflin, 1961), 336.
9. Davis, "Wordsworth, Haydon, and Beaumont," 211.
10. *Collector of Genius,* 166; quoted from papers on deposit in the Ashmolean Museum, Oxford.
11. Willard Bissell Pope, ed. *The Diary of Benjamin Robert Haydon* (Cambridge: Harvard University Press, 1963), 1:60–61.
12. Margaret Greaves, *Regency Patron: Sir George Beaumont* (London: Methuen, 1966), 99.
13. Owen and Brown, *Collector of Genius,* 227.
14. Quoted in ibid., 182.
15. William Wordsworth *The Prelude, or Growth of a Poet's Mind,* ed. Ernest De Selincourt, 2d ed. rev. by Helen Darbishire (Oxford: Clarendon, 1959), 587, n. 77.
16. Farington 9:3289.
17. Edmond Malone, ed. *The Works of Sir Joshua Reynold, containing His Discourses,*

*Idlers, A Journey to Flanders and Holland, and his Commentary on Du Fresnoy's Art of Painting . . . to Which is Prefixed An account of the Life and Writings of the Author.* 3 vols. 3rd ed. corrected (London: Cadell, 1803), xxiv. Hereafter cited in the text as *1803.*

18. Chester Shaver describes Wordsworth's edition as having been annotated, but I have been unable to locate it or to identify anyone who knows of its whereabouts.

19. Extrapolated from Kenneth R. Johnston's "A Note on Money," *The Hidden Wordsworth,* xix–xx. The guinea (G) was worth a pound and a shilling. There were 20 shillings to the pound. See "British Money" in *The Norton Anthology of English Literature,* eds. M. H. Abrams et al., 6th ed. (New York: W.W. Norton, 1993), 2:2497.

20. *Sir Joshua Reynolds: Discourses on Art,* ed. Robert R. Wark (New Haven: Yale University Press, 1975), 169. This edition will now be referenced for the text of *Discourses.*

21. *Sir George Beaumont of Coleorton, Leicestershire: A Catalogue of works by Sir George Beaumont at Leicester Museum and Art Gallery* (Leicester: Leicester Museum and Art Gallery, n.d.) contains a listing of all of Beaumont's own paintings, his collection of the paintings and drawings of the British School, and the paintings from his collection contributed to the National Gallery.

22. Owen and Brown, *Collector of Genius,* 29.

23. Interestingly, Coleridge did not disagree with these basic principles of neoclassicism. Farington reports that Coleridge agreed with Sir George in conversation that "in Sculpture to make a *perfect form* it was necessary not to Copy any individual figure for nothing human is perfect, but to make a selection of perfect parts from various figures & assemble them together & thereby constitute a perfect whole." Coleridge found the description apt for the poetic process as well: "Nature was the basis or original from which all should proceed. He said that perhaps there was not in any poem a line which separately might not have been expressed by somebody, it was the assembling so many expressions of the feelings of the mind and uniting them consistently together that delighted the imagination" (Farington, 8:2275–76).

24. N. A. M. Rodger, "Nelson, Horatio" in *A Dictionary of Eighteenth-Century World History,* eds. Jeremy Black and Roy Porter (Oxford: Blackwell, 1994), 504.

25. *Benjamin The Waggoner,* ed. Paul F. Betz (Ithaca: Cornell University Press, 1981), MS 1, lines 398–402.

26. Mary Moorman believes that the "great crime" was Nelson's execution of the Neapolitan patriot, Carocciolo, on board his flagship (*MY* 1:154, n. 2).

27. The National Maritime Museum's permanent exhibit of Nelson's life, times, and amours and, of course, the Nelson column at Trafalgar Square are profound commemorations of England's fondness for an heroic past.

28. The correct spelling of the castle and island is *Piel,* which Beaumont spells as *Peel* in his title of the painting *Peel Castle in a Storm,* and which Wordsworth spells *Peele* in the extended title of "Elegiac Stanzas, Suggested by a Picture of Peele Castle, in a Storm, painted by Sir George Beaumont." I will use whichever spelling or misspelling applies.

29. *Antiquities of Great-Britain, Illustrated in Views of Monasteries, Castles, and Churches, Now Existing.* Vol. 1. Engraved from Drawings made by Thomas Hearne. London, 1786.

30. *GBL* 9.

31. Wordsworth had said that the flaw in Pitt's attitude toward government was that "His first wish (though probably unknown to himself) was that his Country should prosper under his administration; his next, that it should prosper: Could the order of these wishes have been reversed, Mr. Pitt would have avoided many of the grevious mistakes into which, I think, he fell" (*Middle Years* I, 7).

32. *GBL* 13.

33. Lines 289–94, Epistle One, *Essay on Man*, from *The Poems of Alexander Pope*, ed. John Butt (New Haven: Yale University Press, 1963), 515.

34. See Robert Griffin, *Wordsworth's Pope: A Study in Literary Historiography* (Cambridge: Cambridge University Press, 1995) for an excellent analysis, often surprising in its details, of Pope's wide influence on Wordsworth.

35. *GBL* 4.

36. Owen and Brown, *Collector of Genius,* 72.

37. See the National Maritime Library, Prints and Drawings collection, esp. item numbers: PAF 7440, PAD 7543, PAG 8418, PAG 8416, PAG 8417, PAG 8421, PAH 7397, PAH 7393, PAF 7311, et al. The NML librarians have gathered photocopies of many of the shipwreck paintings and drawings in looseleaf binders.

38. Adele M. Holcomb's insightful study of Romantic maritime iconography, "John Sell Cotman's *Dismasted Brig* and the Motif of the Drifting Boat," points out that the "storm-whelmed" boat even outlasted "the castle . . . as an image of the artist's proud, embattled spirit" (*Studies in Romanticism* 14 [Winter 1975]: 29). Of course, Beaumont's painting combines both symbols, but as I commented above, the combination was common.

39. Thomas West, *The Antiquities of Furness.* A New Edition with Additions by William Close (London: 1805). Hearne's drawing of Piel Castle can be found in *Antiquities of Great-Britain, Illustrated in Views of Monasteries, Castles, and Churches, Now Existing.* Vol I. Engraved from Drawings made by Thomas Hearne. London, 1786. See figure 6, p.    .

40. Of course, this is also Percy Shelley's philosophical assessment of nature's deterministic course in "Mont Blanc."

41. West, *Antiquities of Furness,* 376.

42. Mark Reed suggests that Wordsworth viewed both on his visit to London in the spring of 1806 (*CMY* 321–22).

43. *GBL* 14.

44. There is evidence that Wordsworth preferred the smaller painting of *Peel Castle,* which leads to the vexed question of which canvas inspired "Elegiac Stanzas." As one might expect, the Trustees of Dove Cottage believe the smaller oil, which they now own and beautifully display in the Wordsworth Museum at Dove Cottage, is the inspiration; the Leicester Museum and Art Gallery, owners of the Beaumont collection, believe that their masterpiece, the larger oil, is the inspiration. Beaumont writes to Wordsworth from London in November 1806:

> I have seen both the Peel Castles since I came here, & the foolish fondness of a parent having subsided, I agree with you that the small one is on the whole the best—tho I still think parts of the other are superior—I must ever value it as the prompter of those lines—& the lines, by no means exclusively for the comp[liment] elegant as it is—& such is the taste of it that I could relish it without pain. I never received a comp[liment] before which did not make me "blush restlessly [?]"

Although this clarifies Wordsworth's preference for the smaller oil, the rough logic between the clauses set off in dashes makes ambiguous to the reader, although not to the correspondents, which painting was the "prompter of those lines." One might suspect that Beaumont would not have shown Wordsworth the smaller oil first, because he originally preferred the larger and would not out of indelicacy confront Wordsworth with the smaller oil in his apartment. It would also spoil the surprise and impact of the larger painting when Wordsworth visited the Royal Academy Exhibit.

Fifteen years later, Beaumont makes another reference to the paintings based on Wordsworth's now long-held estimation. In response to Wordsworth's request for a small landscape to hang alongside a pencil sketch, Beaumont writes:

> I was about to send the Peel Castle, which besides being so immortally recorded I shall ever consider as the best work in many respects I have ever produced, when Lady Beaumont suggested that it would be too large for your room & that it would be better for me to paint it upon a smaller scale on my return, there were two or three reasons which induced me to listen to this—first I saw faults which I thought I could remedy & then I resolved in justice to your opinions, & the honors you have done it, to have a print engraved from it as soon as I return—I think this operation a test of its merits as a work of art or rather of science for colour is out of the question—& I have the vanity to think it will not make a bad one, indeed one, not the *libel* inserted in your book, but one Reynolds took *some pains* in beginning, convinces me I am right—I have however sent you down the little picture *suggested* by the banks of the Greta, which I remember you liked at Coleorton, this was done only the day before I left London.

This continues to be less exact in expression than one would like for indisputably resolving this matter, but, on balance, suggests that although Wordsworth may continue to prefer the smaller oil, the larger had inspired "Elegiac Stanzas." Beaumont must be referring to the large oil in agreeing with Lady Beaumont that it would be too large for Wordsworth's room; the small canvas at roughly 13 x 20 inches could hardly be too large for any of the rooms at Rydal Mount, where Wordsworth was residing, and Beaumont could hardly paint the smaller canvas on a "smaller scale." Left noticeably unstated is the location of the smaller oil, which Beaumont would certainly have sent Wordsworth if he retained it and if Wordsworth preferred it anyway. Nevertheless, it becomes clear that the larger canvas is associated with the poem in being "so immortally recorded." Finally, Sir George expresses dismay at the "libel" of *Peele Castle* that S. W. Reynolds had engraved as a frontispiece for the second volume of *Poems* (1815), but believes Reynolds has lately proven he is capable of more accuracy of representation. The key point, however, is that the frontispiece is derived from the larger oil. It is noteworthy that the engraving includes with greater clarity the vessel in the distance to the right of the thunderbolt. One might ask, Why was the larger oil the subject of the engraving if Wordsworth preferred the smaller? The most reasonable explanation is that the larger had inspired the poem and deserved to be memorialized with its poem in *Poems 1815*. The only distinguishing detail of the paintings that "Elegiac Stanzas" makes reference to is the "Hulk which labours in the deadly swell" (47). The sloop of the smaller canvas does not suggest a large ship of burden.

45. Sonnet 55, lines 1–4, *Shakespeare's Sonnets*, ed. Stephen Booth (New Haven: Yale University Press, 1977), 48.

46. Marjorie Levinson, *Wordsworth's Great Period Poems,* 110.

47. *Home at Grasmere*, Ms B, 352 ff.

48. John F. Curwen. Art. xii. "Piel Castle, Lancashire." Read at the site, 9 September 1909. *Transactions of the Cumberland & Westmorland Antiquarian & Archaeological Society*. X. New Series. Ed. W. G. Collingwood (Kendal, 1910), 274.

49. From "The Story of Piel Island and Castle." Undated Pamphlet published by the Tourist Information Center, Barrow-in-Furness.

50. Cleanth Brooks, "Wordsworth and Human Suffering: Notes on Two Early Poems," in *From Sensibility to Romanticism: Essays Presented to Frederick A. Pottle*, eds. Frederick W. Hilles and Harold Bloom (New York: Oxford University Press, 1965), 386.

51. Clifford Siskin, *The Historicity of Romantic Discourse* (New York: Oxford University Press, 1988), 34.

52. God addresses Christ as follows: "O Son, in whom my soul hath chief delight, / Son of my bosom, Son who art alone / My Word, my wisdom, and effectual might" (III.168–70).

53. Richard Cronin, "Wordsworth's Poems of 1807 and the War Against Napoleon," *Review of English Studies*, n.s. 48 (1997): 39.

54. Neil Freistat calls attention to the prominence of framing poems especially in collections with "sophisticated arrangements." *The Poem and the Book: Interpreting Collections of Romantic Poetry* (Chapel Hill: University of North Carolina Press, 1985), 39. Jared Curtis also says that the volume was the first that Wordsworth "deliberately shaped" (*P2V* 35).

55. The poems composed after John's death are "The Blind Highland Boy" (1804–06), "Pleasure Is Spread Through the earth" (1806), "Star Gazers" (1806), "Power of Music" (1806), "Incident" (1806), "Tribute to the Memory of the Same Dog" (1806), "A Complaint" (1806–07), "Yes! full surely 'twas the Echo" (1806), "To the Spade of a Friend" (1806), "Loud Is the Vale!" (1806), and "Elegiac Stanzas."

56. Donald H. Reiman, *The Romantics Reviewed: Contemporary Reviews of British Romantic Writers*, Part A, *The Lake Poets*, 2 vols. (New York: Garland, 1972), 662; 66.

57. *GBL* 26. Ironically, Beaumont's quotation from *Much Ado About Nothing* is near accurate: "There was never yet a philosopher / That could endure the toothache patiently" (5.1.35–36).

58. Quoted in Geoffrey H. Hartman, *Wordsworth's Poetry: 1787–1814*, 2d ed. (1964; New Haven: Yale University Press, 1971), 4.

59. Quoted in Owen and Brown, *Collector of Genius*, 138.

## POSTSCRIPT

1. The pamphlet is listed as Document 1, in Box 3, Dove Cottage Papers. Its complete title is *An Authentic Narrative of the Loss of the* Earl of Abergavenny, *East Indiaman, Captain John Wordsworth, off Portland, on the Night of the 5th of Feb. 1805; drawn from official documents and communications from various respectable survivors*. By a Gentleman in the East-India House. London: Minerva Press, 1805. Carl Ketcham makes passing reference to Wordsworth's pencil and pen annotations in *LJW* 178.

2. *Lord Byron: The Complete Poetical Works*, ed. Jerome J. McGann, vol. 5, *Don Juan* (Oxford: Clarendon, 1986), 99–100. Evidence on Byron's specific borrowing from

accounts of shipwrecks, including one of the pamphlets on the sinking of the *Abergavenny*, was described in Willis W. Pratt, *Byron's* Don Juan, *Volume IV, Notes on the Variorum Edition* (1957; 2d ed., Austin: University of Texas Press, 1971), 62–63.

3. *The Letters of William and Dorothy Wordsworth*, 2d ed. III. *The Middle Years, Part 2, 1812–1820*, ed. Ernest De Selincourt, revised by Mary Moorman and Alan G. Hill (Oxford: Clarendon, 1970), 579.

# Bibliography

## PRIMARY WORKS

*Narratives of the Sinking of the Abergavenny* and Related Works

*An Authentic Narrative of the Loss of the* Earl of Abergavenny, *East Indiaman, Captain John Wordsworth, off Portland, on the Night of the 5th of Feb. 1805; drawn from official documents and communications from various respectable survivors.* By a Gentleman in the East-India House. London: Minerva Press, [21 February] 1805.

*An Authentic Narrative of the Loss of the* Earl of Abergavenny, *East Indiaman, off Portland, on the Night of the 5th February 1805 . . . corrected from the Official Returns at the East-India House.* London: Printed for John Stockdale, Piccadilly, and Blacks and Parry, Leadenhall Street. [13] February 1805.

*A Chart of the Isle, Roads, and Race of Portland, with the Shambles &c.* London: Laurie & Whittle, 1794. Dove Cottage Papers.

"Committee on Shipping Meeting of 19 February 1805 on the Loss of the *Abergavenny.*"

*Correct Statement of the Loss of the* Earl of Abergavenny, *East Indiaman, John Wordsworth, Commander, Which was driven furiously on the Rocks off the Bill of Portland,* And lost near the spot where the *Halsewell* was wrecked, *February 5, 1805, when near Three Hundred Persons Perished, with a Cargo of About 200,000£ value. Also the Shipwreck of* Occum Chamnan; *A Siamese Noble,* London, 1805. Frontispiece "Part of the Crew of the *Abergavenny,* East Indiaman, delivered from their Perilous Situation," dated 24 December 1808, publisher T. Tegg. Dove Cottage Papers, Box 3, Document 2.

Larn, Richard, and Bridget. *Shipwreck Index of the British Isles: Isles of Scilly, Cornwall, Devon, Dorset.* Vol. 1. London: Lloyd's Register of Shipping, 1995.

Log of the *Earl of Abergavenny,* India Office Library Marine Records, extracted by Miss Peggy Sichel. Box 3, Item 37, Dove Cottage Papers.

Marine Records c. 1600–1879 of the British Library's Oriental and India Office Collections (OIOC).

*A Narrative of the Dreadful Loss of the* Earl of Abergavenny, *Indiaman, Wrecked February 5, 1805, on the Shingles, off the Bill of Portland, as communicated to the Directors of the India House, by one of the Survivors,* with frontispiece, *The Distress'd State of the Crew of the Abergavenny when she was Sinking.* London: J. Scales, [1805]

*Narrative of the Loss of the* Earl of Abergavenny, *East Indiaman, Captain John Wordsworth, which drove on the Shambles, off the Bill of Portland, and sunk in twelve fathoms Water, February 5, 1805.* In the *Mariner's Chronicle, Being A Collection of the Most*

*Interesting Narratives of Shipwrecks, Fires, Famines, and Other Calamaties Incident to a Life of Maritime Enterprise.* Edited by Archibald Duncan. 4 vols. Philadelphia: James Humphreys, 1806. Vol 4. Reprint of Narrative printed in London, 1805.

*Naval Chronicle for 1805: containing a General and Biographical History of the Royal Navy of the United Kingdom; with a variety of original papers on nautical subjects: under the guidance of several literary and professional men.* Vol 13. (January–June, 1805). London: I. Gold, 1805.

## Wordsworth Family Documents and Poetry

Beaumont, Sir George Howland. Unpublished letters of Sir George Howland Beaumont to William Wordsworth, 1803–31. Dove Cottage Papers.

Dove Cottage Papers. Box 3. Materials related to Capt. John Wordsworth.

Wordsworth, Dorothy. *Dorothy Wordsworth: The Grasmere Journals.* Edited by Pamela Woof. New York: Oxford University Press, 1993.

Wordsworth, Graham Gordon. Unpublished manuscript of the life of Capt. John Wordsworth in the Dove Cottage Papers, Box 3, Item 22.

Wordsworth, John. *The Letters of John Wordsworth.* Edited by Carl H. Ketcham. Ithaca: Cornell University Press, 1969.

Wordsworth, Mary. *The Letters of Mary Wordsworth 1800–1855.* Edited and selected by Mary E. Burton. Oxford: Clarendon Press, 1967.

Wordsworth, William. Benjamin the Wagonner *by William Wordsworth.* Edited by Paul F. Betz. Ithaca: Cornell University Press, 1981.

———. *"Descriptive Sketches" by William Wordsworth.* Edited by Eric Birdsall. Ithaca: Cornell University Press, 1984

———. *Fenwick Notes of William Wordsworth.* Edited by Jared Curtis. London: Bristol Classical Press, 1993.

———. Home at Grasmere, *Part First, Book First, of* The Recluse *by William Wordsworth.* Edited by Beth Darlington. Ithaca: Cornell University Press, 1977.

———. *Lyrical Ballads, and Other Poems, 1797–1800.* Edited by James Butler and Karen Green. Ithaca: Cornell University Press, 1992.

———. *Poems in Two Volumes, and Other Poems, 1800–1807, by William Wordsworth.* Edited by Jared Curtis. Ithaca: Cornell University Press, 1983.

———. *William Wordsworth: The Five-Book Prelude.* Edited by Duncan Wu. Oxford: Blackwell, 1997.

———. *William Wordsworth: The Prelude 1799, 1805, 1850.* Edited by Jonathan Wordsworth, M. H. Abrams, and Stephen Gill. New York: Norton, 1979.

Wordsworth, William, and Dorothy Wordsworth. *The Letters of William and Dorothy Wordsworth: The Early Years, 1787–1805.* Edited by Ernest De Selincourt, 2d ed. revised by Chester L. Shaver. Oxford: Clarendon Press, 1967.

———. *The Letters of William and Dorothy Wordsworth, II. The Middle Years, Part 1, 1806–1811.* Edited by Ernest De Selincourt. 2d ed. revised by Mary Moorman. Oxford: Clarendon Press, 1969.

———. *The Letters of William and Dorothy Wordsworth, III. The Middle Years, Part 2,*

*1812–1820.* Edited by Ernest De Selincourt. 2d ed. revised by Mary Moorman and Alan G. Hill. Oxford: Clarendon Press, 1970.

Wordsworth, William, and Samuel Taylor Coleridge. *Wordsworth and Coleridge: Lyrical Ballads.* Edited by R. L. Brett and A. R. Jones. 2d ed. London: Routledge, 1991.

Wu, Duncan. *Wordsworth's Reading: 1800–1815.* Cambridge: Cambridge University Press, 1995.

## Other Primary Works

*Antiquities of Great-Britain, Illustrated in Views of Monasteries, Castles, and Churches, Now Existing.* Vol. 1. Engraved from Drawings made by Thomas Hearne. London, 1786.

Arnold, Matthew. *Poetry and Criticism of Matthew Arnold.* Edited by A. Dwight Culler. Boston: Houghton Mifflin, 1961.

Burke, Edmund. *The Writing and Speeches of Edmund Burke.* Edited by Paul Langford. Vol. 5, *India: Madras and Bengal 1774–1784,* edited by P. J. Marshall. Oxford: Clarendon Press, 1981.

Byron, George Gordon, Lord. *Byron's Don Juan, Volume 4, Notes on the Variorum Edition.* Edited by Willis W. Pratt. 1957; 2d ed., Austin: University of Texas Press, 1971.

———. *Lord Byron: The Complete Poetical Works.* Vol. 5, *Don Juan.* Edited by Jerome J. McGann. Oxford: Clarendon Press, 1986.

Coffman, Ralph J. *Coleridge's Library: A Bibliography of Books Owned or Read by Samuel Taylor Coleridge.* Boston: G. K. Hall, 1987.

Coleridge, Samuel Taylor. *Coleridge: The Early Family Letters.* Edited by James Engell. Oxford: Clarendon Press, 1994.

———. *The Collected Letters of Samuel Taylor Coleridge, II, 1801–1806.* Edited by Earl Leslie Griggs. Oxford: Clarendon Press, 1956.

———. *The Notebooks of Samuel Taylor Coleridge.* Edited by Kathleen Coburn. Vol. 2. Princeton: Princeton University Press.

———. *Samuel Taylor Coleridge: The Complete Poems.* Edited by William Keach. London: Penguin, 1997.

Farington, Joseph. *The Diary of Joseph Farington.* 14 vols. Vols. 1–6 edited by Kenneth Garlick and Angus Macintyre. Vols. 7–14 edited by Kathryn Cave. New Haven: Yale University Press, 1978–83.

*English Historical Documents, 1783–1832.* Edited by A. Aspinall and E. Anthony Smith. Vol. 11 of *English Historical Documents,* ed. David C. Douglas. London: Eyre and Spottiswoode, 1959.

*The Gentleman's Magazine* 75 (1805): 174–75, 232.

Gordon, Mary W[ilson], ed. *Christopher North: A Memoir of John Wilson.* Vol. 1. Edinburgh: Edmonston and Douglas, 1863.

———. *Memoir of Christopher North.* 2 vols. Edinburgh, 1862.

Grant, Charles. *Observations on the State of Society Among the Asiatic Subjects of Great Britain, Particularly with respect to Morals; and on the means of improving it.* 1792. Printed as Appendix I to *Report to the Select Committee,* 1797.

Haydon, Robert. *The Diary of Benjamin Robert Haydon*. Edited by Willard Bissell Pope. Cambridge: Harvard University Press, 1963.

Hutchinson, Sara. *Letters of Sara Hutchinson, from 1800–1835*. Edited by Kathleen Coburn, London: Routledge, 1954.

Jones, William. *Discourses Delivered at the Asiatick Society 1785–1792*. London: Routledge, 1993. Reprint of Vol. 3 of *Works of William Jones*, 1807.

Knight, William Angus, ed. *Memorials of Coleorton: being letters from Coleridge, William Wordsworth, Dorothy Wordsworth, Southey, etc.* Boston: Houghton Mifflin, 1887.

Lamb, Charles, and Mary Lamb. *The Last Essays of Elia* (1833). *Elia and the Last Essays of Elia*. Vol. 2 in *The Works of Charles and Mary Lamb*. Edited by E. V. Lucas. London: Methuen, 1903–5.

———. *The Letters of Charles and Mary Anne Lamb*. 3 vols. Edited by Edwin W. Marrs Jr. Ithaca: Cornell University Press, 1975–78.

Lewis, Samuel. *The Topographical Dictionary of England*. Vol. 2. London: S. Lewis, 1831.

Malone, Edmond, ed. *The Works of Sir Joshua Reynolds, containing His Discourses, Idlers, A Journey to Flanders and Holland, and his Commentary on Du Fresnoy's Art of Painting. . . . to Which is Prefixed An account of the Life and Writings of the Author*. 3 vols. 3d. ed. corrected. London: Cadell, 1801.

Milton, John. *Milton: Complete Shorter Poems*. Edited by John Carey. 2d ed. New York: Longman, 1997.

Reed, Mark L. *Wordsworth: the Chronology of the Early Years, 1770–1799*. Cambridge: Harvard University Press, 1967.

———. *Wordsworth: The Chronology of the Middle Years, 1800–1815*. Cambridge: Harvard University Press, 1975.

Reiman, Donald H. *The Romantics Reviewed: Contemporary Reviews of British Romantic Writers*. Part A. *The Lake Poets*. 2 vols. New York: Garland, 1972.

*Report from the Select Committee on the Affairs of the East India Company; with Minutes of Evidence in Six Parts, and an Appendix and Index to Each*. Printed for the House of Commons, 1832.

Reynolds, Sir Joshua. *Sir Joshua Reynolds: Discourses on Art*. Edited by Robert R. Wark. New Haven: Yale University Press, 1975.

Shakespeare, William. *The Norton Shakespeare*. Edited by Stephen Greenblatt. New York: Norton, 1997.

———. *Shakespeare's Sonnets*. Edited by Stephen Booth. New Haven: Yale University Press, 1977.

*The Sun*, 10 August 1804.

Swift, Jonathan. *Gulliver's Travels*. Edited by Herbert Davis. Oxford: Basil Blackwell, 1965.

Thoreau, Henry David. *Walden and Civil Disobedience: Authoritative Texts, Background, Reviews and Essays in Criticism*. Edited by Owen Thomas. New York: Norton, 1966.

*The Times* (London). 26 July 1804.

Whitman, Walt. *The Collected Writings of Walt Whitman*. Edited by Harold W. Blodgett and Sculley Bradley. New York: New York University Press, 1965.

## SECONDARY WORKS

Arac, Jonathan and Harriet Ritvo, eds. *Macropolitics of Nineteenth-Century Literature.* Durham, N.C.: Duke University Press, 1995.

Aspinall, A., and E. Anthony Smith, eds. *English Historical Documents 1783–1832. Vol. 11 in the series English Historical Documents*, gen ed. David C. Douglas. London: Eyre and Spottiswoode, 1959.

Atton, Henry, and Henry Hurst Holland. *The King's Customs.* Vol 1. *An Account of Maritime Revenue & Contraband Traffic in England, Scotland, and Ireland From the Earliest Times to the Year 1800.* 1908: New York: Augustus M. Kelley, 1967, Reprints of Economics Classics.

Baron, Michael. *Language and Relationship in Wordsworth's Writing.* New York: Longman, 1995.

Bate, Jonathan. *Shakespeare and the English Romantic Imagination.* Oxford: Clarendon, 1986. [corrected paperback ed., 1989]

Baum, Joan. *Mind-Forg'd Manacles: Slavery and English Romantic Poets.* New Haven: Archon, 1994.

Beeching, Jack. *The Chinese Opium War.* London: Hutchenson, 1975

Bernhardt-Kabish, Ernest. "Wordsworth's 'Elegiac Stanzas.'" *Explicator* 23 (May 1965): number 71.

Berridge, Virginia, and Griffith Edwards. *Opium and the People: Opiate Use in Nineteenth-Century England.* 1981. New Haven: Yale University Press, 1987.

Brewer, John. *The Pleasures of the Imagination: English Culture in the Eighteenth Century.* New York: Farrar Straus Giroux, 1997.

Brooks, Cleanth. "Wordsworth and Human Suffering: Notes on Two Early Poems." In *From Sensibility to Romanticism: Essays Presented to Frederick A. Pottle*, edited by Frederick W. Hilles and Harold Bloom. New York: Oxford University Press, 1965.

Carey, W. H. *The Good Old Days of Honourable John Company, being curious reminiscences illustrating manners and customs of the British in India during the rule of the East India Company from 1600–1858.* Calcutta: R. Cambray, 1906.

Chandler, James K. *Wordsworth's Second Nature: A Study of the Poetry and Politics.* Chicago: University of Chicago Press, 1984.

Collings, David. *Wordsworthian Errancies: The Poetics of Cultural Dismemberment.* Baltimore: Johns Hopkins University Press, 1994.

Cronin, Richard. "Wordsworth's Poems of 1807 and the War Against Napoleon." *Review of English Studies*, n.s. 48 (1997): 33–50.

Curwen, John F. Art. xii. "Piel Castle, Lancashire." Read at the site, 9 September 1909. *Transactions of the Cumberland & Westmorland Antiquarian & Archaeological Society.* X. New Series. Edited by W. G. Collingwood. Kendal, 1910. 271–87.

Davis, Norma. "William Wordsworth, Haydon, and Beaumont: A Change in the Role of Artist Patronage." *Charles Lamb Bulletin* 55 (1986): 210–24.

Dermigny, Louis. *La Chine et L'Occident: Le Commerce à Canton Au XVIII Siecle 1719–1833. Album.* Paris: SEVPEN, 1964.

Douglas, Wallace W. "Wordsworth as Business Man." *PMLA* 63 (1948): 625–41.

Drew, Peter. *India and the Romantic Imagination*. New York: Oxford University Press, 1987.

Embree, Ainslee T. *Charles Grant and British Rule in India*. New York: Columbia University Press, 1962.

Fay, Peter Ward. *The Opium War, 1840–1842: Barbarians in the Celestial Empire in the Early Part of the Nineteenth Century and the War By Which They Forced Her Gates Ajar.* 1975; Chapel Hill: University of North Carolina Press, 1998.

Foster, W. *John Company*. London: 1926.

Franson, J. Karl. "The Fatal Voyage of Edward King, Milton's Lycidas." *Milton Studies* 25 (1989): 43–67.

Galperin, William. *Revision and Authority in Wordsworth: The Interpretation of a Career.* Philadelphia: University of Pennsylvania Press, 1989.

Gill, Stephen. *William Wordsworth: A Life*. Oxford: Clarendon, 1989.

Goldberg, Brian. "'Ministry More Palpable': William Wordsworth and the Making of Romantic Professionalism." *Studies in Romanticism* 36 (1997): 327–47.

Greaves, Margaret. *Regency Patron: Sir George Beaumont*. London: Methuen, 1966.

Greenberg, Michael. *British Trade and the Opening of China: 1800–42*. Cambridge: Cambridge University Press, 1951.

Greenhill, Basil. *The Life and Death of the Merchant Sailing Ship, 1815–1965*. London: Her Majesty's Stationary Office, 1980. Vol. 7 in the National Maritime Museum's *The Ship*.

Griffin, Robert. *Wordsworth's Pope: A Study in Literary Historiography*. Cambridge: Cambridge University Press, 1995.

Griggs, William. *Relics of the Honourable East India Company. A Series of Fifty Plates.* London: Bernard Quaritch, 1909.

Grocott, Terence. *Shipwrecks of the Revolutionary and Napoleonic Eras*. London: Chatham, 1997.

Harrison, William. Art XXV. "Piel Castle." Read at Piel Castle, 17 August 1877. *Transactions of the Cumberland and Westmoreland Antiquarian and Archaeological Society*. III. Edited by Richard S. Ferguson, 1876–77. Kendal, 1878: 232–40.

Hartman, Geoffrey. *Wordsworth's Poetry*. 1964. 2d ed. New Haven: Yale University Press, 1971.

Higginbotham, J. J. *Men Whom India Has Known: Biographies of Eminent Indian Characters*, 2d ed. Madras: Higginbotham, 1874.

Hirsch, E. D., Jr. *Validity in Interpretation*. New Haven: Yale University Press, 1967.

Horne, C. Silvester. *The Story of the L.M.S. 1795–1895*. London: London Missionary Society, 1894.

Hotchkiss, Wilhelmina L. "Coleridge, Beaumont, and the Wordsworthian Claims for Place." *The Wordsworth Circle* 21 (1990): 51–55.

Howse, Ernest Marshall. *Saints in Politics: The 'Clapham Sect' and the Growth of Freedom.* London: George Allen & Unwin, 1952.

Huntress, Keith, ed. *Narratives of Shipwrecks and Disasters, 1586–1860*. Ames: Iowa State University Press, 1974.

Johnston, Kenneth R. *The Hidden Wordsworth: Poet Lover Rebel Spy*. New York: Norton, 1998.

———. *The Hidden Wordsworth*. New York: Norton, 2002.

———. *Wordsworth and the Recluse*. New Haven: Yale University Press, 1984.

Johnston, Kenneth R., and Gene W. Ruoff, eds. *The Age of William Wordsworth: Critical Essays on the Romantic Tradition*. New Brunswick, N.J.: Rutgers University Press, 1987.

Jones, Alun R., ed. *Wordsworth: The 1807 Poems: A Casebook*. London: Macmillan, 1990.

Kaye, John William. *The Administration of the East India Company; A History of Indian Progress*. London: Richard Bentley, 1853.

Kelley, Theresa M. *Wordsworth's Revisionary Aesthetics*. Cambridge: Cambridge University Press, 1988.

King, David J. Cathcart. *Castellarium Anglicanum: An Index and Bibliography of the Castles in England, Wales, and the Islands*. 2 vols. London: Kraus International Publications, 1983.

Kishel, Joseph F. "The 'Analogy Passage' from Wordsworth's Five-Book *Prelude*." *Studies in Romanticism* 18 (Summer 1979): 271–85.

Klancher, Jon P. *The Making of English Reading Audiences, 1790–1832*. Madison: University of Wisconsin Press, 1987.

Kroeber, Karl. *Romantic Landscape Vision*. Madison: University of Wisconsin Press, 1975.

Lavery, Brian. *The Arming and Fitting of English Ships of War, 1600–1815*. London: Conway Maritime Press, 1987.

Leask, Nigel. *British Romantic Writers and the East: Anxieties of Empire*. Cambridge: Cambridge University Press, 1992.

Levinson, Marjorie. *Wordsworth's Great Period Poems*. Cambridge: Cambridge University Press, 1986.

Lovett, Richard. *The History of the London Missionary Society 1795–1895*. London: Frowde, 1899.

Mackenzie, James D. *The Castles of England, Their Story and Structure*. Vol. 2. London: Heinemann, 1897.

Mahoney, John L. *William Wordsworth: A Poetic Life*. New York: Fordham University Press, 1997.

Manning, Peter. *Reading Romantics: Texts and Contexts*. New York: Oxford University Press, 1990.

———. "Wordsworth at St. Bees: Scandals, Sisterhoods, and Wordsworth's Later Poetry." *ELH* 52 (1985): 33–58. Reprinted in *Reading Romantics: Text and Context* (New York: Oxford University Press, 1990).

Marshall, P. J. *Problems of Empire: Britain and India 1757–1834*. London, 1968.

Matlak, Richard E. "Captain John Wordsworth's Death at Sea." *The Wordsworth Circle* 31 (2000): 127–33.

———. "Hindoo/Yahoo: Charles Grant and the Christianizing of India." In *The Enigmatic Dean: Festschrift for Hermann Josef Real*. Edited by Rudolf Freiburg, Arno Loffler, and Wolfgang Zach. Tubingen: Stauffenburg Verlag, 1998: 113–25.

———. *The Poetry of Relationship: The Wordsworths and Coleridge, 1797–1800*. New York: St. Martin's Press, 1997.

McAdam, E. L. "Wordsworth's Shipwreck." *PMLA* 77 (1962): 240–47.

McFarland, Thomas. *Romanticism and the Forms of Ruin: Wordsworth, Coleridge, and Modalities of Fragmentation.* Princeton, N.J.: Princeton University Press, 1981.

———. *William Wordsworth: Intensity and Achievement.* Oxford: Clarendon, 1992.

McGowan, Alan. *The Ship: The Century Before Steam: The Development of the Sailing Ship, 1700–1820.* Vol. 6 in the National Maritime Museum series *The Ship.* London: Her Majesty's Stationery Office, 1980.

*Memorials of Old Lancashire.* Edited by Lieut.Colonel Fishwick and Rev. P. H. Ditchfield. Vol 2. London: Bemrose and Sons, 1909.

Miller, Russell. *The Seafarers: The East Indiamen.* Alexandria, Va.: Time-Life Books, 1980.

Milligan, Barry. *Pleasures and Pains: Opium and the Orient in 19th-century British Culture.* Charlottesville: University Press of Virginia, 1995.

Moorman, Mary. *William Wordsworth: the Later Years, 1803–1850.* Oxford: Clarendon, 1965.

Morris, Henry. *The Life of Charles Grant: Sometime Member of Parliament for Inverness-shire and Director of the East India Company.* London: John Murray, 1904.

Morse, Hosea Ballou. *The Chronicles of the East India Company, Trading to China 1635–1834.* Vols. 2–3. Oxford: Clarendon, 1936.

Murphy, Peter. *Poetry as an Occupation and an Art in Britain, 1760–1830.* Cambridge: Cambridge University Press, 1993.

O'Hara, J. D. "Ambiguity and Assertion in Wordsworth's 'Elegiac Stanzas.'" *Philological Quarterly* 47 (January 1968): 69–82. Rpt. in *Wordsworth: the 1807 Poems: A Casebook.* Edited by A. R. Jones. London: Macmillan, 1990.

Owen, David Edward. *British Opium Policy in China and India.* New Haven: Yale University Press, 1934.

Owen, Felicity, and David Blayney Brown. *Collector of Genius, A Life of Sir George Beaumont.* New Haven: Yale University Press, 1988.

Parkinson, C. Northcote, ed. *The Trade Winds: A Study of British Overseas Trade During the French Wars 1793–1815.* London: Allen and Unwin, 1948.

———. *Trade in the Eastern Seas.* Cambridge: Cambridge University Press, 1937.

Parrish, Stephen Maxfield. "*Michael* and the Pastoral Ballad." In *Bicentenary Wordsworth Studies in Memory of John* Alban Finch, edited by Jonathan Wordsworth. Ithaca: Cornell University Press, 1970.

Pearson, Thomas. "Coleorton's 'Classic Crowd': Wordsworth, the Beaumonts, and Politics of Place." *Charles Lamb Bulletin* 89 (1995): 9–14.

Pevsner, Nikolaus. *Lancashire: The Rural North.* Harmondsworth: Penguin Books, 1969.

Pfau, Thomas. *Wordsworth's Profession: Form, Class, and the Logic of Early Romantic Cultural Production.* Stanford: Stanford University Press, 1997.

Philips, C. H. *The East India Company, 1784–1834.* 1940; 2nd ed., Oxford: Oxford University Press, 1961.

Porter, A. N. *Atlas of British Overseas Expansion.* London: Routledge, 1991.

Rand, Frank P. *Wordsworth's Mariner Brother.* Amherst, Mass.: Jones Library, 1966.

Robertson, Eric. *Wordsworthshire: An Introduction to a Poet's Country.* London, 1911.

Ruoff, Gene W. *Wordsworth and Coleridge: The Making of the Major Lyrics, 1802–1804.* New Brunswick, N.J.: Rutgers University Press, 1989.

Rzepka, Charles J. "A Gift that Complicates Employ: Poetry and Poverty in 'Resolution and Independence.'" *Studies in Romanticism* 28 (1989): 225–47.

Sacks, Peter M. *The English Elegy: Studies in the Genre from Spenser to Yeats.* Baltimore: Johns Hopkins University Press, 1985.

Said, Edward W. *Culture and Imperialism.* London: Chatto and Windus, 1993.

———. *Orientalism.* London and Harmondsworth: Penguin Books, 1985.

Schoenfield, Mark. *The Professional Wordsworth: Law, Labor & the Poet's Contract.* Athens: University of Georgia Press, 1996.

*Sir George Beaumont and His Circle.* Leicester: Leicester Museum and Art Gallery, 1953.

*Sir George Beaumont of Coleorton, Leicestershire: A Catalogue of Works by Sir George Beaumont at Leicester Museum and Art Gallery.* Leicester: Leicester Museum and Art Gallery, n.d.

Simpson, David. *Wordsworth's Historical Imagination.* New York: Methuen, 1987.

Siskin, Clifford. *The Historicity of Romantic Discourse.* Oxford: Oxford University Press, 1988.

———. "Wordsworth's Prescriptions: Romanticism and Professional Power." In *The Romantics and Us: Essays on Literature and Culture,* edited by Gene W. Ruoff, 303–21. New Brunswick, N.J.: Rutgers University Press, 1990.

Slater, Philip E. *The Pursuit of Loneliness: American Culture at the Breaking Point.* Boston: Beacon Press, 1970.

Smyser, Jane Worthington. "Wordsworth's Dream of Poetry and Science." *PMLA* 71 (1956): 269–75.

Spiegelman, Willard. *Wordsworth's Heroes.* Berkeley: University of California Press, 1985.

Spurr, David. *The Rhetoric of Empire: Colonial Discourse in Journalism, Travel Writing, and Imperial Administration* Durham, N.C.: Duke University Press, 1993.

"The Story of Piel Island and Castle." Tourist Information Center, Barrow-in-Furness. Undated.

Tayler, Irene, "By Peculiar Grace: Wordsworth in 1802." In *The Evidence of Imagination: Studies of Interactions between Life and Art in English Romantic Literature,* edited by Donald H. Reiman, Michael C. Jaye, and Betty T. Bennett. 119–141. New York: New York University Press, 1978.

Townsend, R. C. "John Wordsworth and his Brother's Poetic Development." *PMLA* 81 (1966): 70–78.

Waldoff, Leon. *Wordsworth in His Major Lyrics:The Art and Psychology of Self-Representation.* Columbia: University of Missouri Press, 2001.

Williams, John. *William Wordsworth: A Literary Life.* New York: St Martin's Press, 1996.

———, ed. *Wordsworth.* New Casebooks series. London: Macmillan, 1993.

Wilson, Douglas B. *The Romantic Dream: Wordsworth and the Poetics of the Unconscious.* Lincoln: University of Nebraska Press, 1993.

Wilson, Edward. "An Echo of St. Paul and Words of Consolation in Wordsworth's 'Elegiac Stanzas.'" *Review of English Studies* 43 (February 1992): 74–80.

Wordsworth, Gordon Graham. *Some Notes on the Wordsworths of Peniston and their Aumbry.* St. Oswald's Press, 1929.

Wordsworth, Jonathan. *William Wordsworth: The Borders of Vision.* Oxford: Clarendon, 1982.

Wordsworth, Jonathan, Michael Jaye, and Robert Woof. *William Wordsworth and the Age of English Romanticism.* New Brunswick, N.J.: Rutgers University Press, 1987.

## National Maritime Library, Prints and Drawings

PAD 6362. *The Wreck of the Hindostan; East-Indiaman, on the Wedge Sand, Off Margate,* 11 Jan., 1803. John Fairburn (publisher), 31 Jan. 1803.

PAD 6368. *Earl of Abergavenny.* J. Stratford (publisher). 18 Feb. 1806.

PAD 6369. *Earl of Abergavenny.* Thomas Tegg (publisher), 24 Dec. 1808.

PAF 4756. *The Signal Defeat of the French Admiral Linois Squadron. By the Honorable East India Company Ships, commanded by Nathanial Dance, Esqr . . . on the 15th Feby 1804.* Laurie & White (publishers), 24 June 1805.

PAF 5799. *Straight of Malacca. Defeat of Admiral Linois Squadron.*

PAG 9019. *The China Fleet Heavily Laded Commanded by Commodore Sir Nathaniel Dance beating off Adml Linois and his Squadron the 15th of Feby 1804.* Edward Orme (publisher), 25 Nov. 1804.

PAH 0502. *The Loss of the* Halsewell. *East Indiaman, Capt Richard Pierce. This rich laden ship (outward bound) was wreck'd off Seacombe in the Isle of Purbeck in Dorsetshire, on the 6th Jan. 1786.*

PAH 0503. *To the Survivors and Relations . . . who* perish'd in the Halsewell.

PAH 0509. *The Essex . . . in a heavy Gale of Wind.* 23 Apr. 1781

PAH 7421. *To the Directors of the Hon'ble East India Company this Print representing the Loss of their ship* Halsewell *in the Night between the 5th & 6th of January 1786 with precarious situation of the Survivors in a cavern of the Rock.* Robert Dodd, artist and engraver.

PAH 8006. *Repulse of Linois by the China Fleet . . . Ships in the Fleet making Sail in pursuit of the retreating enemy, 15th Feby 1804.* Robert Dodd (publisher) Jan 1805.

PAH 8009: *Sir Nathaniel Dance, Captain of the* Lord Camden

PAI 5923. *The Loss of the* Abergavenny *East-Indiaman off the Isle of Portland.* J. Stratford (publisher). 28. Feb 1806.

PAI 6126. *The Homeward Bound Fleet of Indiamen from China under the command of Captain Dance engaging and repulsing a squadron of French Men of War near the Straits of Malacca Feby 15th, 1804.* William Daniell (artist, engraver, and publisher). 10 Dec. 1804.

PAI 8080. *The Diving Machine & Apparatus used in recovering the property lost in the* Abergavenny.

PAI 9482. *The Gallant Commodore Dance beating off Admiral Linois' Squadron.*

# Index